How Voters Feel

This book sets out to unearth the hidden genealogies of democracy, particularly its most widely recognized, commonly discussed and deeply symbolic act – voting. By exploring the gaps between voting and recognition, being counted and feeling counted, having a vote and having a voice and the languor of count taking and the animation of account giving, there emerges a unique insight into how it feels to be a democratic citizen. Based on a series of interviews with a variety of voters and non-voters, this book attempts to understand what people think they are doing when they vote; how they feel before, during and after the act of voting; how performances of voting are framed by memories, narratives and dreams; and what it means to think of oneself as a person who does (or does not) vote. Rich in theory, this is a contribution to election studies that takes culture seriously.

Stephen Coleman is Professor of Political Communication and co-director of the Centre for Digital Citizenship at the Institute of Communications Studies at the University of Leeds. He is also an honorary professor of political science at the University of Copenhagen and a research associate at the Oxford Internet Institute, University of Oxford. Coleman's most recent publications include *Connecting Democracy: Online Consultation and the Flow of Political Communication* (with Peter M. Shane, 2011); *The Media and the Public: 'Them' and 'Us' in Media Discourse* (with Karen Ross, 2009) and *The Internet and Democratic Citizenship: Theory, Practice and Policy* (with Jay G. Blumler, 2009) – winner of the American Political Science Association award for best book of the year on politics and information technology. He has served as a specialist adviser to the House of Commons Information Select Committee inquiry on ICT and public participation in Parliament, as a member of the Puttnam Commission on parliamentary communication with the public and as chair of the Electoral Reform Society's Independent Commission on Alternative Voting Methods.

How Voters Feel

STEPHEN COLEMAN
University of Leeds

CAMBRIDGE
UNIVERSITY PRESS

CAMBRIDGE
UNIVERSITY PRESS

32 Avenue of the Americas, New York NY 10013-2473, USA

Cambridge University Press is part of the University of Cambridge.

It furthers the University's mission by disseminating knowledge in the pursuit of education, learning, and research at the highest international levels of excellence.

www.cambridge.org
Information on this title: www.cambridge.org/9781107014602

First published 2013
Reprinted 2014

A catalog record for this publication is available from the British Library.

Library of Congress Cataloging in Publication data
Coleman, Stephen, 1957–
   How voters feel / Stephen Coleman, University of Leeds.
      pages   cm
   Includes bibliographical references and index.
   ISBN 978-1-107-01460-2
   1. Voting.   2. Political participation.   3. Democracy.   I. Title.
   JF1001.C56   2012
   324.9–dc23   2012033601
ISBN 978-1-107-01460-2 Hardback

Contents

Preface		*page* vii
1.	What Voting Means	1
2.	Narratives of Voting	34
3.	Memories of the Ballot Box	76
4.	Acquiring the Habit	107
5.	The Burdens of Being Represented	129
6.	Spaces of Disappearance	149
7.	Becoming Us	169
8.	Who Feels What, When and How	191
References		237
Index		263

Preface

A persistent imbalance between attention to macro-level trends and forces and micro-level situations and experiences characterises much social science scholarship. Randall Collins's important observation that 'sociological concepts can be made fully empirical only by grounding them in a sample of the typical micro-events that make them up'[1] too often goes unheeded, as sweeping currents of systemic and structural effects are meticulously chronicled to the exclusion of situated phenomonologies of sensation and affect. Rarely has this been more evident than in the study of elections, which have tended to focus upon vast quantifiable entities, such as electorates, majorities, constituencies and swings, rather than the lived and felt experiences of voters. This is understandable: political science, and its strange subculture, psephology, have been mainly preoccupied by instrumental questions: Who wins and loses? How do campaigns succeed or fail? How do the numbers stack up? Whether or not one agrees with Larry Bartels's disparaging reflection that 'it would be fruitless to deny that a good deal of voting research consists of dreary minutiae utterly devoid of any broader political significance',[2]

---

[1] Collins, R. (1981) 'On the Microfoundations of Macrosociology', *American Journal of Sociology*, 86:984–1014.

[2] Bartels, L. (2001) 'An Agenda for Voting Research' in Katz, E. and Warshel. Y. (eds), *Election Studies: What's Their Use?* Boulder, CO: Westview Press, pp. 59–82.

there surely is a sense in which the act of voting as described in most election studies is stripped of its cultural vitality, leaving the individual voter as a disembodied cog in a vast political counting machine. This book sets out to encounter voters on new terms; to explore their memories, practices, anxieties, hopes, uncertainties and embarrassments as if these really mattered.

A study of how voters feel must address the two-sidedness of feeling. We are made to feel certain ways by situations in which we find ourselves. We feel our way through situations, reshaping them by our touch. How voters are made to feel and how they feel their way are matters of democratic sensibility. Making sense of such sensibility entails disacknowledging the taken-for-granted routines that surround the ballot box and observing the performance of voting as if it were a strange and exotic ritual. Only through the blur of unfamiliarity can the unexpected contours of the seemingly self-evident become truly vivid.

At the normative core of the analysis set out in the following pages is the assumption that, like any other complex communicative act, the expression of preferences calls for affective investment. The act of voting is not simply a statement of what people want, but a performance of who *the people* are. Before 'we want' there must be a plausible 'we' capable of exerting democratic autonomy. Democracy in this sense is an inherently creative project, the success of which depends upon a certain mode of sensibility. I suggest in the following pages that at its best such democratic sensibility is interruptive and improvisational rather than citational and repetitive. As Melanie White has put it, thinking about citizenship in terms of creative acts 'forces us to consider those "openings" where citizens break or destabilize the bonds of habitual activity, and in so doing unleash a creative energy'.[3] Such 'openings' have been conspicuously visible in historical situations – some very recent – where hitherto disenfranchised people have asserted their right to hold social powers to account. These moments of political interruption constitute what

[3] White, M. (2008) 'Can Acts of Citizenship Be Creative?' in Isin, E. and Nielsen, G. (eds), *Acts of Citizenship*. New York: Zed Books, pp. 44–56.

Engin Isin calls 'ruptures in the given'.[4] In contrast, the experience of electoral democracy as a citational routine, embedded deeply in the given, is the main empirical focus of this study.

The research upon which this book is based emerged from the Road to Voting project, funded by the UK Arts and Humanities Research Council. My partners in this project – Vanalyne Green, Steve Bottoms, Bryan Davies, Brenda Hollweg and Irena Bauman – were a source of support and inspiration. Valentina Cardo, who was my research assistant during the first phase of the study, played a key role not only in setting up the interviews reported in Chapters 4 to 7, but also in sustaining my confidence in the idea of thinking about voters as people with stories to tell. I am grateful to Kate Percival for transcribing the interviews. Ben and Mimi and the LookleftLookright theatre company, who produced the play *Counted* based on the interviews I conducted, provided me with some fascinating insights into the ambiguities of the text. Above all, I am grateful to the sixty interviewees who contributed their time and thought to this research. In Chapter 3 I reflect upon the problematics of the interview as a technique for extracting raw experience. But here I want to acknowledge the generosity of the people who agreed to speak with me and express my sincere hope that this book will not in any way add to injuries of misrepresentation they might feel.

Every book is founded upon cumulative intellectual debt. Much of this is acknowledged implicitly by the many references to works of great scholars within this text. Other debts arise from the pleasure of direct conversation with friends and colleagues over the years. Richard Allan, Henrik Bang, Jay Blumler, David Butler, John Corner, Shelagh Diplock, Irving Rappaport and Mathew Taylor have all helped me to think differently about democracy; my colleagues and students at the Institute of Communications Studies at the University of Leeds have offered me an environment in which creative thought is the norm; Lew Bateman and his colleagues at Cambridge University Press have

[4] Isin, E. (2008) 'Theorising Acts of Citizenship' in Isin, E. and Nielsen, G. (eds), *Acts of Citizenship*, New York: Zed Books, pp. 15–43.

impressed me with their commitment to the publication of books containing ideas rather than bullet points; and Bernadette Coleman has shared with me a depth of insight and intuition that never ceases to amaze me. I am full of appreciation to all of these people, but they are not responsible for my worst arguments or least comprehensible phrases in the pages that follow.

What Voting Means

Neutral dictionary definitions of the words of a language ensure their common features and guarantee that all speakers of a given language will understand one another, but the use of words in live speech communication is always individual and contextual in nature. Therefore, one can say that any word exists for the speaker in three aspects: as a neutral word of a language belonging to nobody; as an *other*'s word, which belongs to another person and is filled with echoes of the other's utterance; and finally, as *my* word, for, since I am dealing with it in a particular situation, with a particular speech plan, it is already imbued with my expression. In both the latter aspects, the word is expressive, but ... this expression does not inhere in the word itself. It originates at the point of contact between the word and actual reality, under the conditions of that real situation articulated by the individual utterance. In this case the word appears as an expression of some evaluative position of an individual person.

(Bakhtin, *Speech genres and other late essays*, 1986)

What does it mean to think of oneself as a voter? What does the act of voting involve, physically, intellectually and emotionally? What sort of memories, allusions and anxieties are evoked by the phrase, 'It's time to vote'? How do meanings of voting flutter between the seemingly neutral process-focus of officialdom, the tainted manipulations of campaign strategists and the situated contingency of everyday life, in which the vote is one of many communicative encounters likely to end badly? How does it feel to be addressed as a voter upon whom the heavy burdens of duty, choice and worldliness are so frequently reducible to confusion, stealth and shame? This book is about the feeling of voting – a feeling so rarely probed that the act of voting seems smothered by the neutralizing anaesthetic of unreflective routine.

Few subjects arouse more radically conflicting associations than voting. It is the symbol of freedom; it is a futile gesture. It holds the powerful to account; whoever you vote for, the government always wins. It confers the dignity of citizenship; it affirms the gullibility of the led. It is the people's chance to be heard; it is a tedious period to be endured. It is hard to think of any other social practice that bears such a great weight of instrumental and affective signification. The political obsession of modernity has been the making of voters. Media images of people, long denied the vote, forming winding queues to assert their entry into the enfranchised world stand as semiotic markers of political progress. 'I'm about to tick a box', explained Marwa Gamil who was voting for the first time ever in the Egyptian election of November 2011, 'and someone far away is going to count it and in that way I'm going to make a difference'.[1] The alchemistic transmutation from a small 'tick' into a big 'difference' hovers somewhere between ritual fantasy and rational expectation. And yet, the intensity of attachments to voting as a right contrasts sharply with popular disappointments surrounding voting as a practice. Conceived generally as a sort of civic chore, both the act of voting and its outcomes seem over-determined and lifeless. In Russia's deeply flawed presidential election of March 2012, Vladimir Putin ordered that webcams be installed in 91,000 of the 96,000 polling stations across that vast polity in the hope that this would allay fears about the fraudulence that had previously led to mass demonstrations. Watching the archive of these long hours of plebiscitary tedium, there is scant evidence of the vibrant jubilation that had so movingly marked the fall of the

---

[1] 'Egypt elections: "my vote will make a difference"', *The Guardian*, 29 November, 2011.

Berlin Wall and the first multi-party elections in countries long under the yoke of dictatorships. Voters shuffled in and out, rarely pausing to speak. They might have been collecting their pensions or registering a death. There seemed to be a lot of sighing in the air. This was not just a manifestation of Russian lugubriousness. When people, from London and Los Angeles to Nairobi and Mumbai, are called upon to act as voters, they seem to adopt a posture of stolid resignation. As they perform from a democratic script, their postures and dispositions are inflected by the weight of thwarted experience.

In the course of my study of voting and voters within contemporary political culture, I observed a wide range of people casting votes in a number of different contexts, from parish and general elections to corporate and supranational plebiscites. My custom was usually to stand or sit inconspicuously at the back of a voting area for up to an hour, observing comings and goings, public interactions and secret scribblings. My observations, which were confined to Britain, were certainly not systematic, but they left me with three strong impressions. First, moments of voting are remarkably fleeting. Most voters entered, did their business and left within three to seven minutes; about as long as most people spend buying fast food or using a public convenience. Second, the event of voting seems curiously socially disconnected, giving it the appearance of something lodged between the scenes of a bigger social drama rather than an integral part of it. Voters would enter from and return to lives filled with personal hopes, frustrations, stories, characters and familiar settings, but the impersonal spaces of voting were devoid of these registers of intimacy. Third, acts of voting are surrounded by an eerie silence. There would be occasional interruptions of whispered uncertainty about procedural propriety and rare moments of cordial interaction between officials and voters, but the scarcity of these outbreaks only served to amplify the pervasive hush. As an observer, I was left with a strong sense that voters had more to say than they were ever encouraged to make known within the official places of voting. There were feelings to be explored that could not be articulated through a marked X on a ballot paper.

(The results of this exploration can be found in the interviews reported in Chapters 4 to 7).

Political scientists have paid scant attention to whether the experience of democracy is joyful or sombre, satisfying or frustrating, dignifying or shaming, or simply emotionally numbing. Such questions, they would say, are hardly matters of concern in evaluating the instrumental effectiveness of democracy. If elections are conducted fairly, governing institutions are sufficiently transparent, majorities are plausibly represented and minorities not unduly excluded; effective democracy can live with a range of affective deficits and failures.

To be interested in the affective character of voting is not to suggest that it should be thought of as primarily an affair of the passions, severed from its more common cognitive and instrumental connotations. Rather than seeking to sensationalise experiences of democratic engagement, the more modest aim of this book is to acknowledge that the sustainability of any cultural practice depends to a large measure on how it feels to participate in it. Democracy is experienced through a series of taken-for-granted and taken-by-surprise encounters, some direct and others mediated through vast institutions. These encounters leave impressions upon people's senses that cannot be expressed or explained in the clinical language of rationality. But neither are they irrational. As Sayer (2005:950) puts it:

> When someone says that they 'have good reason to be angry', they imply that, for example, someone has done something that objectively harms them, such as injuring them or slandering them. Likewise, feelings ... such as envy, resentment, compassion, contempt, shame, pride, deference, and condescension are evaluative responses to particular properties of ... inequalities and relations. They are influenced but not predetermined by positions within the social field.

To speak of responses to contemporary political democracy as being affective is not, therefore, to dismiss their evaluative nature, but to recognise that these are performative rather than objective appraisals of instrumental phenomena. Affects are best understood at the level of subjective experience; the impressions that surround them have more to do with sentient expectations than pragmatic accomplishments. The acknowledgement of an affective deficit in contemporary democracy is based on an assumption that the way in which politics in general, and voting in particular, are conducted is incongruent with the sensibilities of citizens as rational and emotional makers of meaning.

Democracy, if it is to achieve shared and credible meaning, depends on commonly recognisable social performance. That is to say, there must be a widely understood relationship between how people act and what their actions are assumed to mean. As Alexander (2006:32) has pointed out, in simple, pre-modern societies, symbolic action and cultural meaning were fused through rituals based on shared beliefs and direct interactions within physical space. In complex, modern society, populations are more fragmented, beliefs less commonly shared and communicative interaction less immediate. The greatest risks facing late-modern culture emanate from cultural defusion: breakdowns in shared understandings of what it means to be and act together in the world. For Alexander (2006:55), 'The challenge confronting individual and collective symbolic action in complex contemporary societies ... is to infuse meaning by re-fusing performance'. In other words, when voters are told that real power resides in their expressed preferences or that the noise emanating from parliaments and congresses is the sound of democratic representation, or that laws are the culmination of a process beginning at the ballot box, great cultural effort must be invested in ensuring that such messages have about them a ring of experiential credibility.

The risk of socially binding meanings of institutionalised acts such as voting being ignored, misunderstood or rejected is an abiding feature of late modernity. Traditional voices of authority can no longer rely on the attention of deferential listeners. Public trust in political institutions and processes has been slowly atrophying over a period of decades. The rules of the political game seem too much like imposed rules and someone else's game. These misalignments between official meaning and popular belief can be read as a direct response to the performative deficit of political elites. For, while there is a widespread public belief that civic participation is important in principle, the feeling that there is a seamless connection between personal input (such as voting) and social outcome (the political order) is weak.

Whereas in the past (and still today for a dwindling minority of citizens), voting was a task to be performed as an act of solemn duty, it must now compete with a range of other public acts (including other, non-political forms of voting as entertainment) in which people might be enticed to engage. Post-ritualistic cultures must invent new ways of promulgating the joys of doing what their predecessors did without any hope of pleasure. Consider, for example, what was perhaps the most implausible political advertisement ever made, produced in November 2010 by the youth wing of the Socialist Party of Catalonia as part of its campaign to elect José Montilla as President of the Generalitat de Catalunya. The 90-second ad features an attractive young woman who is shown entering a polling station with a view to casting her vote. Exhibiting signs of uncontrollable excitement, she fills in her ballot paper and inserts it into the slit of the ballot box, not once, but several times, becoming visibly aroused with each repeated act of penetration. Then, observed by dull and disapproving polling officials, she reaches orgasm. The ad ends with the appearance of the words 'VOTAR ÉS UN PLAER' (voting is a pleasure) across the face of the screen.

What is it about this depiction of voting as an exciting – indeed, erotic – act that is both ridiculous and unsettling? Why is this image of democratic participation as a scene of impassioned exuberance most likely to make us think about everything that democratic participation is not? What is it about the social performance of voting that leads us to speak of it as a highly important and consequential act, but experience it as a cursory and nondescript chore? As the Catalan campaigners were to discover (their ad became a huge object of ridicule on YouTube), it is much easier to persuade people that something not in their interest is than to lead them to believe that something that feels tedious is exciting.

Consider another example of the radical misalignment between the act and meaning of voting. Until 2008, the UK

Channel island of Sark was regarded as the last feudal polity in Europe. It was governed by a *Seigneur*, who, holding his position as a fief from the Crown, was empowered to appoint the members of the island's governing council. Much of the island's economy (mainly comprising hotels and shops) was owned by two men: Sir David and Sir Frederick Barclay, proprietors of the *Daily Telegraph* and the Ritz Hotel, who live on the neighbouring island of Brecqhou. As political 'modernisers', the Barclay brothers called for the island council to be democratically elected rather than appointed. In the island's first-ever election, which took place on 10 December 2008, the Barclays championed their own slate of anti-feudal candidates. Ninety per cent of the population of Sark voted, but not for candidates favoured by the Barclay brothers. They seemingly preferred the continued rule of the island's pre-democratic political elite. The immediate response of the Barclay brothers was to withdraw their investments from the island, thereby punishing voters for their recalcitrant stance. Two days after the election, the *Daily Mail* reported that 'the outcome of the election has upset the billionaire Barclay brothers who yesterday closed several hotels and shops that they own on the island.' Gordon Dawes, the twins' Guernsey-based lawyer, said: 'You can't expect people to continue throwing a lot of money into a community that doesn't want them.'

The story of this provincial spat between the politics of the ballot box and the economics of unaccountable investment is not peculiar to Sark. If, in all sorts of contexts, voters have come to believe that their decisions are only ever final if they are consistent with the intentions of other, rather less transparent sources of social power, how are they supposed to feel when they are told that they are the sovereign *demos* whose will is more important than that of anyone else? When, in reality, voters do not inscribe their wishes onto a fresh canvass, but must join dots put in place long before they were invited to form an opinion, the gap between voting and recognition comes to feel like an unyielding chasm. The consequential meaning of voting undermines the surrounding rhetoric of the act.

Political science textbooks and scholarly journals, dominated by discourses of rational choice, tend to describe the act of voting as if it were an affect-free operation. Psephologists have endeavoured to find out how voters make choices, the time of day they vote, the consequences of weather conditions on the turnout, the effects of ballot paper design and ordering of candidates' names on voting preferences, the influence of local votes on national ones and vice versa and the extent to which voters tell the truth about how or whether they voted. But not a single study (before this one) has ever asked people how it feels to vote; what it is like to walk to a polling station in the knowledge that one is about to exercise a democratic right (and perhaps perform a democratic rite); whether the experience of having voted leaves people feeling that they – or the world around them – is somehow different; or, indeed, why some people seem to like voting, on all sorts of issues in all kinds of social contexts, whereas for others the act of casting a vote possesses all the charm and potency of boiling a kettle. It is as if pursuing such visceral inquiries might taint the pristine scientificity that legitimates the traditional study of politics, as if the fullness of the democratic process is best captured through the cold measurement of numbers rather than the torrid excavation of messy affects.

This book sets out to challenge accounts of democracy that undervalue the vitality of affect. In exploring the gap between being counted and feeling counted, having a vote and having a voice, the languor of count-taking and the animation of account-giving, the aim of this study is to unearth the hidden genealogies of democracy, and particularly its most widely recognised, commonly discussed and deeply symbolic act – voting. As in all genealogical accounts, what has been lost is not immediately apparent; what is at stake is revealed through a slow process of questioning the taken-for-granted, engaging creatively with the fragmented and seemingly unrelated survivals of intellectual history and insisting on the non-essentiality of the subject. The aim here is to speak about voting as if there is nothing well-understood, obvious and ingrained about the concept. In doing so, I draw upon theoretical insights from thinkers who have been eager to 'make visible the process by which what looks like homogeneity was written into modern mass culture' (Poovey, 1995:3). I propose to approach the idea of voting in the manner of Rorty's (1989:75) archetypal ironist who

> spends her time worrying about the possibility that she has been initiated into the wrong tribe, taught to play the wrong language game. She worries that the process of socialization which turned her into a human being by giving her a language may have given her the wrong language, and so turned her into the wrong kind of human being.

The account of voting presented here distances itself from the political scientist's assurance that 'voting is voting; you know it when you see it.' Like Rorty's anxious ironist, my interest is in thinking of voting as an exotic, unsettled and problematic act that is most effectively apprehended through repeated redescription rather than semantic certitude. Language is not a self-contained system, but a process of intersubjective exchanges in which the production of meanings often exceeds the formal definition of terms. Terms like voting only acquire meaning when they are addressed to people who can be expected to make some kind of sense of them. But words do not come at us fresh: each time a word is uttered in speech or writing, it carries with it a history of authority or frivolity or intimacy or publicness. In short, language is experienced discursively and negotiated contingently. This point underlies the enormously important theoretical work of the Russian literary philosopher, Mikhail Bakhtin, who argued:

> For the consciousness living in it, language is not an abstract system of normative forms, but a concrete heteroglot opinion on the world. All words taste of a profession, a *genre*, a movement, a party, a particular work, a particular person, a generation, an age group, a day and an hour.

It is upon 'the consciousness living in' accounts and acts of voting and the 'taste' they convey and leave behind that this chapter is focussed. The aim here is to show how voting is constructed as a meaningful social performance. Fusion between act and meaning is realised in many ways. The three outlined here – voting as metaphor, affirmation and quantification – certainly do not exhaust the repertoire of cultural perspectives, but are intended to cast light upon the constructed nature of conventional meaning.

Metaphors

A perusal of the extensive collection of Anglo-American political science textbooks would lead one to the conclusion that voting is a wholly disembodied experience. Votes are cast and counted, but by whom and how? There are swings and fluctuations, peaks and troughs, abstentions and miscounts, pounding and slender majorities, but these seem to be played out within a system of abstract dynamics, separated in every way from the fleshy, visceral world of the human body. It is as if votes have a life of their own: 'the vote determined that the airport will be built' or 'the Opposition benefited from the urban vote.' Pope's account of a man 'bled and purged ... to a simple vote' well describes the discarnate electorate as conceived by political science. And yet everyday language tells a different story. In popular parlance, 'where the knots of narrative are tied and untied' (Bakhtin, 1981:25), the body is returned to the voter. Hands are raised, heads are counted, thumbprints are stamped, the indifferent vote with their feet and, above all, there is the vote as voice, connecting brain and lungs to make sounds that give meaning to the world.

In traditional societies, to vote was literally to give voice. Before votes were ever cast or counted, people spoke to one another: they shared stories, argued the toss, presented evidence, told jokes, recited ballads, circulated rumours and orated poetically. Until the establishment of the Spartan *gerousia* (senate) in the seventh century BCE, support for proposals in the Homeric councils and assemblies was never counted, but shown by vocal acclamation.

Voices and votes are both historically and semantically intertwined: *vox* and *votum* in Latin, *voz* and *voto* in Spanish, *voix* and *vote* in French, *voce* and *voto* in Italian, *stem* and *stemming* in Dutch, *Stimme* and *Stimme* in German and *golos* and *goloso-vanie* in Russian. This affinity between the voice and the vote emanates from a metaphorical way of mapping the world in which ideas, judgements, aspirations and motives reside *within* the body (sometimes thought of as mind or soul) and have to be somehow discharged in order to act upon the external world. From this Cartesian perspective, the voice is regarded as an entry point to the inner life of the individual. According to Hegel, 'It is primarily through the voice that people make known their inwardness, for they put into it what they are'. But the voice is unreliable in at least two ways: it can be manipulated by speakers seeking to convey what they do not mean and it can be interpreted by hearers who do not read utterances as they were intended. In short, the voice has a social life of its own. This is a point that has been powerfully expressed by Jonathan Ree (1999:375) in his magisterial philosophical history of the voice:

> We are none of us linguistic islands, after all; more like lost swimmers out at sea, buffeted by waves and dragged by currents that have no regard for our carefully groomed individualities. And our interpretations of ourselves will never become the serene sky-borne perspectives we might like them to be. They are just our wary thoughts about the changeable weather of our existence: not objective sciences gone wrong, but anxious glances at the fragile techniques with which we try to keep ourselves and our objectivities afloat. Strictly speaking, we have no such thing as a voice of our own.

Voice always entails a compromise between the individual interests, values, self-perception and intended self-projection of speakers and the rhythms, norms, taboos and contingent expectations of the cultures in which they speak. When only a few voices really mattered politically – the king in his court, the bishop in his church, the landlord in his domain – the work of interpreting what was being said remained feasible. But this changed as society became more complex, with mass populations possessing diverse interests, experiences and modes of expression entering the sphere of political communication. Voting is a way of making sense of input to decision making in situations where interpersonal discussion with a view to reaching agreement is not possible. Instead of asking each person to voice their thoughts on a particular issue, and then having to infer what they said and meant, voting is a technology (in the broad sense of being a means of making something happen) for making preferences countable. Substituting votes for voices is a means of compressing multivocality into a single communicative act, designed to exclude qualification or nuance from the expression of preferences.

As a response to the intractable vastness of sociality, which throws together as strangers people whose fortunes cannot be separated, voting serves to make discrete and private preferences composite and public, thereby bridging the chasm between the interiority and sociality of Cartesian communication. Because the voter is always one of many – an agent whose autonomy is constrained by the structural logic of collective action – voting is a means of aggregating voices so that they possess a collective social meaning. Another way of putting this is to see voting as a process of social embodiment. Voice emanates from the body – from a particular body, with its own brain to think of what to say and its own mouth with which to say it. Voice is perhaps the most distinguishing of all the bodily characteristics, incarnating the most unique quality of being human. For Herder, 'speech alone has rendered man human'. Voting shifts the point of reference from the *particular* body to the *social* body: the collectivity, electorate or amorphous public. Individual bodies are counted, but only in order to be dissolved into the body politic. The composite body which emerges from the process of aggregation no longer has a voice, but *is* a voice, destined to repeat over and again the paltry script of its mandate. Its strength lies in the weight of its support; its weakness lies in the narrowness of its discursive range.

In tracing the figurative tributaries from which meanings of the vote and voting have emerged, it becomes clear how the everyday poetics of idiom and analogy translate the apparent obviousness of official meaning into the absorbed sensation of life as it is experienced. Words arrive in dictionaries with flavours formed by history, and sometimes shorn of qualities that leave them bearing scarcely perceptible stumps of truncated meaning. Lakoff refers to metaphors as 'mappings across conceptual domains' which 'conceptualize one mental domain in terms of another' (Lakoff, 1992:203). For example, while voting seems on the surface to strip the body of any creative role, popular language still holds fast to the ideal of the vote as an embodiment of distinct voices. For example, the U.S. National Rifle Association's Web site, urging its members to vote in the 2008 presidential election, declared that 'YOUR VOTE IS YOUR VOICE.'[2] Matt Pitcher, the Electoral Services Officer for the British seaside town of Bournemouth, is quoted as saying: 'We would encourage everyone to make the most of their democratic right – your vote is your voice.'[3] West Lancashire District Council's Web site makes the point with even greater force: 'DON'T LOSE YOUR VOICE – IT'S YOUR VOTE!'[4] An MTV 'citizen journalist' urges his blog readers to vote: 'DON'T LET ANYONE TAKE AWAY YOUR VOICE.'[5] Seth Buchsbaum, writing in *The Michigan Daily*, advises readers to 'FIND YOUR VOICE' by voting in the presidential election, 'because even when you feel like you don't have a voice in this country, you still do.'[6] What do these semantic conflations mean? In what symbolic sense can one's vote be seen as the same as a voice? After all, the act of voting in most regulated political elections is anything but a vocal event. It is forbidden to voice one's opinions or speak to others during the act of casting a vote. Why refer to such a manifestly muted event as having a voice?

A related metaphor in the everyday language of voting is the image of counting: Your Vote Counts. For example, the European Confederation of Young Entrepreneurs (YES) declares

[2] http://www.nraila.org/Issues/Articles/Read.aspx?id=276&issue=047
[3] http://www.bournemouth.gov.uk/News/press_office/Press_Releases/April_2008/election.asp
[4] http://www.westlancsdc.gov.uk/council__democracy/news_and_publications/september_2008_news/dont_lose_your_voice.aspx
[5] http://think.mtv.com/044FDFFFF00989E50000800994B63/User/Blog/BlogPostDetail.aspx
[6] http://www.michigandaily.com/content/na/voice-your-vote-viewpoint

on its Web site: 'The motto VOTE! YOUR VOTE COUNTS! is
what YES wishes to emphasise. According to the statistics, the
participation rate among the European citizens has been quite
low. Partially being uninformed on the European electoral process and partially due to lack of confidence on the power of
their vote.'[7] The official Web site of Leeds United football club
urges supporters to vote for the team's player of the year with
the slogan 'YOUR VOTE COUNTS'.[8] Alex Massie, writing in
The Spectator magazine, reminds his readers that it's 'NOT TOO
LATE TO MAKE YOUR VOTE COUNT'.[9] And the iVillage
Web site warns viewers of *American Idol* that 'If your favorite
was booted off tonight and you didn't vote, it's your fault ...
EVERY VOTE COUNTS!'[10] In its most obvious sense, these are
little more than statements of confidence that votes cast will be
tallied; by casting them one has a chance of making a difference
that a non-voter cannot expect to enjoy. But something more is
being said about the status of the voter: not only will her vote be
counted, but, by the very act of casting it, she has affirmed and
perhaps even enhanced her value as a citizen who is entitled to
contribute to making a difference. Even if one's vote is unlikely
to sway the aggregate outcome, the act of casting it attests to
one's claim to be taken into account. Conversely, those who do
not vote – particularly those who are denied the right to vote –
are deemed to count less precisely because they cannot expect
to generate such effects. Voice as metaphor constructs a similar
meaning: to have a voice is to be counted as a participant in
decision making, whose views cannot be ignored. The voiceless
do not count; those whose voices count possess votes that must
be counted. And unless your vote is counted, your voice will not
count subsequently in criticising the consequences of decisions

---

[7] http://www.yes.be/index.php/vote
[8] http://www.leedsunited.com/page/LatestNewsDetail/0,,10273~1609511,00.
html
[9] http://www.spectator.co.uk/alexmassie/3250231/not-too-late-to-make-your-
vote-count.thtml
[10] http://tvcocktail.ivillage.com/entertainment/archives/2008/03/american-idol-
results-every-vo.html

made by those whose votes were counted. The ethical right to a voice, in this sense, is dependent on having contributed to bringing about a state of affairs, even if by voting against it.

These metaphors reinforce the idea of voting as a performative act – as something more than a mere register of preferences; as a means of saying something with a view to making things happen. Having a voice as a means of being heard and being counted and as a means of making a difference point to the performative character of voting. Beyond its instrumental rationale, voting is an affective social performance which links action to meaning by investing personal feeling in social consequence. Schechner (1988: 156) quite cannily captures the nuanced aesthetics of such social performance when he states:

> Performance originates in impulses to make things happen and to entertain; to get results and to fool around; to collect meanings and to pass the time; to be transformed into another and to celebrate being oneself; to disappear and to show off; to bring into a special place a transcendent Other who exists then-and-now and later-and-now; to be in a trance and to be conscious; to focus on a select group sharing a secret language and to broadcast to the largest possible audience of strangers; to play in order to satisfy a felt obligation and to play only under an Equity contract for cash.

As in Lauren Berlant's (1993:395) astute account of American citizens' pilgrimages to witness their own representation in Washington, in which civic pegagogy is manifested as 'a patriotic performance', voting can be understood as engagement in a pageant of political identification in which what it means to be a democratic citizen is acted out. As we shall see in the next chapter and throughout this book, the narratives, tropes and gestures that give specificity to particular voting performances are diverse, but that does not mean that they are without unifying characteristics. Performing the part of a democratic citizen entails a number of routine tensions. First, voting performances involve both the bodily presence and disembodied aggregation of the individual citizen. The social performance of voting is both profoundly private and inescapably public. There is something quite

unique about this performative characteristic. Great efforts are
made to make bodies present so that they can be authenticated as
real, only in order to transcend their singularity by adding them
to the compound, anonymised body politic. For the voter, this
experience of autonomous expression of will and public incorporation within a mass collectivity underscores what it means
to be a social animal, individuated and belonging at the same
time. As a 'free individual', whose vote-casting power represents
a secret asylum from peer judgement and civilised appearance,
one cannot escape the magnetic pull of the body politic. This is
the affective fissure of democratic citizenship: the private per-
sona is always under the shadow of a greater good to which it
must sacrifice a part of itself.

Second, the social performance of voting entails submission
to foundational rules. One does not set up one's own polling
station, design one's own ballot paper or insist on one's own procedure for counting votes. To vote is to collude with an existing
technology of reckoning. Technically, voting is an easier act to
perform than, say, deliberating in public or advocating a cause,
but for many it is a daunting challenge, entailing a search for
ambiguous information and entry into strange spaces. While
all votes are supposed to be equal, personal experiences of voting are marked by ineluctable inequalities between voters who
understand how it all works and the ones who feel trapped in a
political maze; voters who can afford to escape the consequences
of decisions made and the ones who are dependent on what is
decided; voters who think they can back the winner and the
ones who feel destined to lose; voters for whom the vote is one
resource amongst many and others with only a single chip on the
table. Voters are encouraged to behave during the few moments
of this social performance as if all other inequalities in their lives
are incidental externalities. For some of them, as we shall see,
feelings of political equality are readily countenanced, whereas
for others such pretence evokes a sense of shame, embarrassment, resentment and recoil. By focusing some people's minds
on the failures of democratic citizenship to engender in practice
what it offers in principle, the social performance of voting can

serve, paradoxically, to cast doubt on the rhetorical claims of the constitutional state.

Third, voting performances are linked intimately to experiences of being represented, misrepresented, acknowledged, ignored, spoken for and spoken to. To represent is to ventriloquise. It is to *re-present* the absent as if they were present. It is to give voice to the silent. It is to conjure into being an aggregation of public interests, preferences and values; to afford univocality to the circulating noise of public aspiration, fear and confusion. So defined, political representation is never a simple task and is always doomed to fail if it is conceived as an act of communicative correspondence. That is to say, if voters imagine that the task of political representation is to reproduce mimetically that which is being represented, they shall always be frustrated by the failure of representatives. As Ernesto Laclau (1996:87) has rightly observed, 'it is the essence of the process of representation that the representative contributes to the identity of what is represented.' In this sense, the voter, rather than being replicated and 'spoken as', is invented and spoken for. Claude Lefort (1986:110) has put this very well when he stated: '[P]ower belongs to the individual or individuals who ... speak in the name of the people and give them their name'. For Lefort, democracy is famously an empty space, to be filled in – and then revised, erased and revised again – by countless acts of representative creativity. Representation, in this sense, is inherently an act of mediation. Only through mediation can representatives circulate their claims to speak for the public – and only through mediation can the public determine whether such claims are justified. To represent is to mediate between the absent and the present, between the spaces in which decisions have to be made and the spaces in which they cannot be made.

Each of these knotty tensions – between bodily presence and aggregated disembodiment; civic equality and social difference; being made present and being made up– call for performative energy and inventiveness with a view to constructing a balance between official and quotidian understandings of voting. To speak of voting as a performative act is not to trivialise it by implying that it is inauthentic or theatrical, but to distinguish it as a complex combination of 'public dreaming' and 'interior drama' (Schechner, 1988: 265) through which societies represent to themselves the most significant and challenging ideals of their cultural order. Social performance registers the ambiguity of cultural practices. In exploring voting as a performative act, one is seeking to access the gap that exists between institutional norms and everyday experiences. There is now an extensive literature on the theory of performativity, applied to subjects as diverse as the economy (Callon, 2006; Kessler, 2007; Mackenzie et al., 2007), civic belonging (Bell, 1999; Joseph, 1999; Caunce et al., 2004; Tucker, 2005; Negra, 2007), sport (Blackshaw and Crabbe, 2005; Tzanelli, 2008), dieting (Jagodzinski, 2003; Heyes, 2009; Cooks, 2009), and education (Avis, 2003; Ball, 2003; Troman et al., 2007; Rich and Evans, 2009). In all of these cases, performative explanations differ from descriptive accounts of structures, processes and effects in two principal ways. First, they draw attention to the power of utterances to make things happen. Writers as diverse as Austin (1962), Berger and Luckman (1967), Searle (1995) and Butler (1997) reject the idea that social reality possesses a pre-discursive essence which is then mediated by language, arguing instead that words, texts and images, when employed felicitously, serve to constitute the experience of reality. For example, the injunction 'Put this to the vote' does more than set in motion a conventional constitutional process; it invokes ideals of moral authority, contained contestation and predictable consequences that are performed as the injunction is acted out.

A second feature of performative theory is its acknowledgement of the need for people to improvise creatively as they negotiate the unstable relationship between structure and agency. Writing from the perspective of legal anthropology, Moore (1978:39) puts this very well:

> Established rules, customs and symbolic frameworks exist, but they operate in the presence of areas of indeterminacy, of ambiguity, of uncertainty, and manipulability. Order never fully takes over, nor could it. The cultural, contractual and technical imperatives always leave gaps, require adjustments and interpretations

to be applicable to particular situations, and are themselves full of ambiguities, inconsistencies, and often contradictions.

In the context of such indeterminacy, it is important to pay attention to the contingent ways in which people make sense of the world through performances that are neither structurally circumscribed nor fully autonomous. Voting is a striking illustration of this kind of performative negotiation, and, as I hope to show in Chapters 4 to 7, the most useful approach to understanding the act of voting is to explore what people think they are doing rather than what they think they are supposed to be doing.

It is here that metaphors of voice and counting have real force. The voter's voice may or may not be in the vote that he casts in the silence of the polling booth, but it is manifestly present in the overall performance that begins long before the walk to the ballot box and often continues long afterwards. Voice gives the democratic citizen a speaking part in the social drama of democracy. *Being* counted is only a small part of the experience of casting a vote. Far more important is the sense of *feeling* counted (or otherwise). When people are addressed through the television screen as if they were king-makers, respected by neighbours, employers and officials as citizens with a vote to cast that is no less valuable than their own, and invited to witness the verdict of the electorate, of which they feel themselves to be a part, they feel present and counted in ways that contrast sharply with the feelings of exclusion borne by the disenfranchised.

Rules

To speak of voting as a social performance is not to say that anyone can play the role of a voter. Dahl's (1989:233) glib assertion that 'practically all adults have the right to vote' is in danger of collapsing under the weight of its casually placed adjective. 'Practically' all may vote – and therefore some may not. Who are they? Who decided that this social performance was not for them? What are the consequences of these exclusions for affective democracy?

Historically, the right to vote has been denied to people for many reasons; age, gender, skin colour, ethnicity, poverty, illiteracy and place of residence are perhaps the most common. Katz (1997:216–33) has pointed to three categories of people who have been denied the right to vote in political elections: those who are not regarded as full members of a community or affected by what happens in a community; those regarded as lacking the competence to make a political judgement; and those regarded as lacking the autonomy to make an independent judgement. Some categories of people are excluded on all three grounds. For example, children are deemed to have too little direct interest (through property ownership or tax-paying) to be classed as full members of a community, to have insufficient experience or knowledge to act as competent voters, and to be too dependent on adults to exercise their own judgements. The same grounds for exclusion were formerly applied to slaves and women. Other categories of people have been disenfranchised on only one of these grounds: for example, expatriates have been denied the right to vote in certain territories because they no longer physically live there, even though they might continue to own property or have business interests in the area. Or members of monastic orders are denied voting rights in some countries on the grounds that they are forbidden to exercise autonomous personal judgement. Rather than considering disenfranchisement in isolation from its cultural sources, two specific modes of exclusion – that of the 'mentally incompetent' and the 'criminally incarcerated' – might help to illuminate the subtle ways by which citizenship has been constructed through the elimination of difference.

Most countries in the world regard some of their citizens as lacking the mental competence to vote.[11] Those excluded on these grounds are variously referred to in existing legislation as 'idiots', 'lunatics', 'persons of unsound mind', 'the mentally deficient' and 'the insane.' The first U.S. state to ban such people from voting was Maine in 1819 and today legislatively determined disenfranchisement prevails in all but six states of the United States (Schriner, 2002). This begs three critical questions:

---

[11] Canada, Italy, Sweden and Ireland are rare exceptions.

What constitutes incompetence in the context of democratic citizenship? How is such incompetence tested? How does 'mental incompetence' compare with the empirically observable levels of competence possessed by those who are eligible to vote?

Telling people that they are incompetent to exercise the rights that are generally accorded to citizens is a sensitive matter, but not one that is unique to voting. Determining people's mental capacity to make binding decisions is a problem that was first addressed officially in the thirteenth century when the English Crown produced a document, *Perogitiva Regis*, the eleventh and twelfth chapters of which were devoted to the king's duties in relation to 'natural fools' and persons labelled as being '*non compos mentis*'. The former were congenitally retarded, whereas the latter included anyone suffering from mental illness or disability that developed after they were born, even if such symptoms were not permanent. The legal position of those deemed mentally incompetent was as charges of the king. This meant that the Crown would have custody over any land owned by people deemed to be mentally incapable of making judgements on their own behalf. The medieval idea of guardianship still operates, but now through the courts which are empowered to appoint family members or trained carers to represent those whose reasoning is deemed so impaired as to prevent them from acting in their own interests. Guardianship denies citizens characterised as 'mentally incompetent' the right to make their own decisions about spending, investing or bequeathing money, entering into marriage, driving a car, giving evidence in court and travelling freely. The function of legal guardianship is to represent the best interest of the ward: to act for them as they might act themselves if they possessed sufficient reason (McLaughlin, 1979; Carney and Tait, 1998). In the case of voting, however, this does not happen: guardians are not allowed to vote on behalf of what they understand to be the best interests of the mentally incompetent. Once a person is classified as mentally incompetent, they are effectively disenfranchised.

The grounds on which someone can be classified as mentally incompetent to vote are not obvious. Only four American states have attempted to define a standard. Three of these (Iowa, Delaware and Washington) have circular definitions: one is not allowed to vote if one lacks the cognitive capacity to do so. The law of the state of Wisconsin denies the right to vote to those who are 'incapable of understanding the objective of the elective process' (Hurme and Appelbaum, 2007:961). How is such incompetence tested? In the thirteenth century, establishing whether someone was a 'natural fool' or '*non compos mentis*' was determined by a jury (referred to as an inquisition) of twelve or more laymen which would test allegedly mentally incompetents' ability to count money or state the name of the town they were in. Inquisitions were charged with determining 'whether the said be foolish and an idiot ... or not: and if he be then whether from his nativity, or from any other time, and if from any other time, then from what time, and how and in what manner, and if he enjoys lucid intervals' (Neugebauer, 1978:161).

The question of 'lucid intervals' raises particular problems. Can a person who is sometimes incapable of voting, according to the rather vague standards that have been established, at other times exhibit sufficient reason to constitute mental competence? Might voting be an activity that should only be performed under specific psychological circumstances – such as not having been intoxicated recently or not having shown signs of unreasonable behaviour for a specific period of time – and, if this is so, might this lead to considerable uncertainty as to who is competent to vote at any particular moment? In response to these questions, Appelbaum et al. (2005) have invented what they call the Competence Assessment Tool for Voting (CAT-V) which has now been tested on a number of cognitively impaired potential U.S. voters. The terms of the test cast light upon what exactly might be required of 'competent citizens' in the social performance of voting. Subjects are first asked to imagine that two candidates are running for the governorship of a U.S. state and today is election day. They are then asked to state what the people of this state will do in order to pick the next governor: 'How would you actually indicate your choice?' The test script suggests that a 'completely correct response' would be

'They will go to the polls and vote for one or the other.' An 'incorrect' response indicated by the script would be 'There's nothing you can do; the TV guy decides.' Subjects are then asked about the effect of voting: 'When the election for governor is over, how will it be decided who the winner is?' The 'completely correct response' here is 'The votes will be counted and the person with more votes will be the winner.' Subjects are then given a card setting out the views of the two imaginary candidates, one favouring higher taxes and the other lower taxes, and then asked, 'which candidate do you think you are most likely to vote for: A or B?' If subjects do not answer, they are then asked to consider how they would vote if they were required to make a choice between the two candidates. The proposed scoring here is as follows:

> Score of 2: Clearly indicates choice. Score of 1: Choice is ambiguous or vacillating, e.g. 'I think I might go for the guy who doesn't like taxes, but I'm not sure because schools are important too.' Score of 0: No choice is stated, e.g. 'I don't know. I can never make up my mind'. (Hurme and Appelbaum, 2007:967–9)

Formulaic trials of this kind no doubt help to distinguish between people who know 'the rules of the game' and those who, for whatever reason, are hesitant, leery or confused about the practices and purposes of voting. In experiments, the CAT-V test has been used to determine whether sufferers from senile dementia can recall enough to play their part in an election (Appelbaum et al., 2005). But this catechistic mode of examination only serves to reinforce a ritualistic conception of the voting performance that combines reinforcement of the routine of established convention with a prescriptively rationalist notion of practical intelligence. While this test does measure capacity to engage in a certain kind of social performance, can it be said to establish a person's capacity to register civic presence and contribute meaningfully to the body politic? That depends on whether we believe that most voters, who are not deemed to be 'mentally incompetent', are universally and distinctively capable of acting in accordance with such norms. The evidence from most political scientists who have considered the competence of average voters is not encouraging on this point.

Political scientists have long argued that most voters face information challenges that are simply too great for them to overcome; they are doomed to vote for leaders whose visions and promises they cannot comprehend and rely upon the most elementary heuristic strategies as cognitive shortcuts to achieving 'low-information rationality' (Lippmann, 1922; Popkin, 1991; Lau and Redlawsk, 1997; Boudreau, 2006). The claim that around a third of the electorate are 'know nothings' (Hyman and Sheatsley, 1947; Bennett, 1988, 2003; Althaus, 1998; Somin, 1998, 2004; Weinshall, 2003; Deneen, 2008) has been criticised by Lupia (2006:3) as symptomatic of an elitist 'worldview that is shared by a select set of academics, journalists and politicos, but few others.' Lupia and other scholars argue that just because voters do not base their judgements on the agendas and pre-occupations of political elites is not in itself a reason to brand them as incompetent. Indeed, some optimism about the democratic capacity of voters emerges from research on the stability and cohesion of citizens' judgements over time. According to Page and Shapiro's (1993:40) analysis of more than a thousand repeated survey questions asked of U.S. voters between the 1930s and 1990s, 'Collective opinion forms coherent patterns that differentiate among alternative policies in reasonable ways' and indeed the 'public reacts in sensible ways to the information that is made available to it'. Though critical of Page and Shapiro's empirical methodology, their conclusions are endorsed firmly by Barber who claims that the electorate is basically 'competent and rational'. Despite their differences, both groups of political scientists – those who affirm and those who deny the rational competence of most voters – are in favour of universal suffrage. The 'elitists' (as Lupia refers to them) do not argue that the huge gap between actual and desirable voter knowledge should be a basis for disenfranchising the incompetent – and the anti-elitists, in dismissing the empirical claims about widespread voter ignorance, while accepting that there are deep inequalities in voter knowledge, are convinced that all votes should count equally. That being the consensus, the argument for barring some people from voting for alleged 'incompetence' seems to be somewhat unfair.

Unease about ways of identifying and then politically excluding 'incompetent' citizens are reinforced by an extensive literature questioning the ideological foundations of psychological stigmatisation (Szasz, 1970; Foucault, 1973; Conrad and Schneider, 1992; Wakefield, 1992; Horwitz, 2002; Maddux and Winstead, 2007). The nub of this critique is that social authorities have been too prone to categorise in pathological terms cultural traits that they either fear or do not understand. The disproportionate ascription of mentally stigmatising classifications to certain ethnic groups is cited as evidence that people whose behaviour and values are simply different from those promoted by the state run the risk of being negatively labelled and excluded (Gaw, 1993; Fernando and Campling, 2002). Competence comes to be seen as less a functional account of capacity than a judgement about moral worth, leading to fears that attitudinal oddity might be used to justify civic exclusion. A second rationale for disenfranchisement adds to these anxieties, for this relates explicitly to the notion of moral incompetence.

In medieval Europe, wrongdoers were subjected to the grotesque fate of 'civil death'. This meant that they were stripped of all rights of citizenship and left to subsist without the protection of the state. In some cases, this meant that they were murdered with impunity, the state having no obligation towards those who defy its laws. The same principle persists in those countries that deny convicted felons the right to vote. This is a contemporary form of civil death for the morally deviant. Whether or not one meets this fate depends on where in the world one commits a crime. In countries such as Bosnia, Albania, Iran, South Africa, Pakistan and Canada,[12] those who are sent to prison retain the right to vote. In

[12] The full list includes Albania, Bangladesh, Bosnia, Canada, Croatia, the Czech Republic, Denmark, Finland, France, Greece, Iceland, Iran, Ireland, Israel, Kenya, Latvia, Lithuania, Macedonia, Montenegro, Norway, Pakistan, Peru, Poland, Puerto Rico, Serbia, Slovenia, South Africa, Sweden, Switzerland and Ukraine (Rottinghaus, 2005:22).

others it depends on the length of the prison sentence (Austria, Jamaica, the Netherlands, Zimbabwe), whether one faces execution (China) or the nature of the offence committed (Spain). In some countries, such as Brazil, India, Russia, Nigeria, Argentina and the United Kingdom, all convicts are disenfranchised while they are in prison.[13] In other countries, such as Finland, Chile and Cameroon, prisoners are prevented from voting for a certain number of years after they have served their time. And in one country, the United States, some states have laws permanently disenfranchising all convicted felons, even after their release. With the second-largest prison population in the world after Russia, one in fifty adults in the United States (4 million people) are denied the vote on these grounds. More than 25 per cent of these are black men, comprising 13 per cent of the country's black male population. In some states this proportion is much higher: one in every three black men are permanently disenfranchised in Florida and Alabama and one in every four in Mississippi, New Mexico, Virginia, Washington and Wyoming (Rottinghaus, 2005). A majority of disenfranchised criminals are not in prison and one in four of them have completed their sentences.

These decisions to exclude the morally deviant from the voting process have been defended by governments on the grounds that they have 'breached the social contract' (*Hirst v. UK*, 2005:para 50) and 'lost the moral authority to vote' (Home Office, 1999:para 2.3.8). In accordance with the rationale for civil death, disenfranchised wrongdoers are considered unworthy of being counted. As one U.S. judge has put it, 'When brought beneath its axe, the disenfranchised is severed from the body politic and condemned to the lowest form of citizenship, where voiceless at the ballot box ... the disinherited must sit idly by while others elect his

---

[13] The full list includes Azerbaijan, Angola, Argentina, Bahamas, Barbados, Belarus, Botswana, Brazil, Bulgaria, Cape Verde, Comoros, Cyprus, Egypt, Equatorial Guinea, Estonia, Georgia, Guatemala, Haiti, Honduras, Hungary, India, Kazakhstan, Kenya, Kyrgyzstan, Latvia, Lithuania, Luxembourg, Madagascar, Malaysia, Moldova, Mongolia, Mozambique, Nigeria, Palestinian Territories, Panama, Peru, Poland, Portugal, Romania, Russia, Sao Tome, Senegal, Sierra Leone, St Lucia, St Vincent, Vietnam, Uganda, United Kingdom, Uruguay and Venezuela (Rottinghaus, 2005:24).

civic leaders and while others choose the fiscal and governmental policies that will govern him and his family' (*McLaughlin v. City of Canton*, 1995). It is as if the presence of the morally deviant within the body politic would somehow contaminate what one American court referred to as 'the purity of the ballot box' (cited in Keyssar, 2000:305), in much the same way as the mentally incompetent might adulterate its aggregate intelligence.

Our interest here is not so much in the explicit justifications of voter exclusion advanced by its advocates as in the tacit norms of democratic citizenship that such perspectives take for granted. As Isin (2002:275) has compellingly argued, 'When social groups succeed in inculcating their own virtues as dominant, citizenship is constituted as an expression and embodiment of those virtues against others who lack them'. The purgation of the mentally incompetent and morally deviant from rights of citizenship is a way of making identity in contrast to alterity. Isin argues that in order for any group to construct its own civic identity it must 'confer rights on and impose obligations on each other, institute rituals of belonging and rites of passage and, *above all, differentiate themselves from others, constructing an identity and an alterity simultaneously*' (Isin, 2002:2, my emphasis). The more that the excluded can be differentiated (and the differentiated excluded), the more plausible claims to a distinctive civic identity become. The exclusions we have considered serve to uphold a conception of voting as a social performance that rests on two delicately aligned balancing acts: first, eligible voters are seen as those who possess the capacity to engage reflexively in the process of public judgement, while needing to adhere only minimally to conditions of political intelligence and civic commitment; and second, eligible voters are those fit to be valued by their peers as autonomous beings, worthy of being counted as one, while consenting to being disembodied through incorporation into the body politic.

Voters are expected to be reflexive, in the sense that they are called upon to acknowledge the significance of the performance in which they partake. Stumbling into a polling station by accident and putting a cross next to the first name on the ballot paper is not forbidden, but seems to be at odds with implicit beliefs about how voters are supposed to act. The voter might think that the election is a waste of time, but must at least know that it is not meant to be a casual or pointless act. She might pick her chosen candidate randomly, but is expected to realise that this is not how the game is supposed to be played. She might have total contempt for her fellow voters, but should know that in casting a vote she is engaging with them in an act of equal collaboration, the end result of which will be a composite judgement that will not distinguish between her and them. Voters are not expected to be constitutionalists or political pundits, any more than law-abiding citizens are expected to be lawyers or judges, but, just as jurors are expected to act as if the defence of the law matters to them, so voters are called upon to perform as if they are directed by at least some awareness of what they are doing and why, rather than entering into a mysterious ritual.

At the same time, voters must appear to possess the mental and moral competence that allows them to be counted as equals within the demos. The cognitively impaired appear to lack this because they cannot convince society of their reasonableness. The criminally convicted appear to lack this because they have disrespected social norms in unforgivable ways. The mentally and morally competent voters are those who lack these differences and deficiencies; their fitness as citizens is contingent upon the existence of others whose unfitness defines them.

What exactly are they fit for? They are fit to be counted. Saved from the awful destiny of civil death, they constitute one rather than zero in the binary order of political representation. The opaque terms of aggregation may well be beyond them; how they are counted and how they make what little voice they have count may be more than most voters know, but it is as numbers, counted one by one, that they both qualify and are quantified as democratic citizens.

Numbers

It is through quantification that voting is most commonly explained and apprehended. Despite the complexities, nuances

and intensities of voters' preferences and commitments, aggregation degrades mass judgement to the counting of heads. As Peters
(2001:435) has ably put it:

> Numbers can model a serene indifference to the world of human
> things. There is something inhuman, even cruel about their indif-
> ference to our projects. Numbers have a rigor and logic that is
> fully independent of the human will. ... Although they may model
> ideals of democratic citizenship, especially impartiality and self-
> sacrifice, they also evoke the fears of a mass society where no one
> has a name, only a number.

The work of counting people, things, time and money has preoccupied society from the eve of modernity. According to Crosby
(1997:19), the half-century between 1275 and 1325 witnessed

> Europe's first mechanical clock and cannon, devices that obliged
> Europeans to think in terms of quantified time and space.
> *Portolano* marine charts, perspective painting, and double-entry
> bookkeeping cannot be precisely dated because they were emerg-
> ing techniques, not specific inventions, but we can say that the
> earliest surviving examples of all three date from that half century
> or immediately after.

In the same period, the angle of the rainbow was measured, the
cash economy expanded dramatically and universities emerged
as newly institutionalised centres dedicated to the dissemination of metrological assurance. In time, compilation, classification and quantification came to be equated with objectivity:
truth untainted by personal feeling. The allure of counting to
the modernist (capitalist) social order derives from three sources
which, between them, summon up a seemingly unassailable aura
of scientificity.

The first of these is *detachment*. Quantification depends
on methods of measurement that stand outside what is being
counted. Counting votes in an election, for example, cannot be
influenced by the character of those who cast them, the topic of a
particular plebiscite or the historical significance of the outcome.
Quantitative counting squeezes out cultural meaning in its ambi-
tion to express incremental value in terms that are not determined
by the nature of what is being counted. This celebrated scientific

detachment entails a dispassionate perspective: one that does not succumb to the recognition of feelings, which destabilise quanta, just as the latter standardise feelings.

Second, counting aims to generate *commensurability*: the transformation of diverse qualities into an equivalent metric. This reductive strategy truncates information processing and conjures into being notions of universality where sameness or even similarity is far from obvious. In the social performance of voting, many and diverse interests, preferences and values are aggregated into a commensurable 'result', regardless of the varying and inconsistent motives, rationales, misunderstandings and intensities of commitment of individual voters. In order to make votes seem like a commensurable expression of desire, the nuance, texture and history of desire must be substituted by whatever can be enunciated through numbers. As Peters (2001:434) puts it, 'Democracy establishes justice and legitimacy through a social force, the majority, which exists only by way of math'.

A third source of quantification's seductive alchemy is its capacity to make abstractions *visible*. Counting gives life to categories; it embodies the disembodied. As a social entity, the public is frequently spoken for and sometimes to, but what exactly is it and what might it have to say for itself? Numbers seem to answer those questions. Opinion pollsters claim to identify views that can be attributed to the public through a process of quantification that makes the public speak as if it had a single voice. Elections take this further: you only count if you are counted, and you will only be counted if you count. Acts of quantification are always constitutive, inscribing realities rather than simply recording them. Those who do the counting are rarely mere slaves of the abacus; in Hacking's (1999) evocative phrase, they are in the business of 'making up people'. For all the talk of dispassionate scientificity, acts of quantification can be creatively ingenious or ruthlessly destructive in their inflexible commitment to certain units of value and not others; their claims to generate commensurability rely on beguiling rhetoric trickery that rides roughshod over popular understandings of what is precious beyond exchange; and their illumination of the hitherto invisible all too often renders classes and categories vulnerable to strategies of intrusive control. In short, counting people constitutes a political act. And, as in all exercises of power, it is the subjects of such acts who are least likely to be in control.

Much as quantification has its place (where would cricket scores and cake recipes be without it?), it can never tell the full story. Just as the cricket match is always more than the scoreboard and the cake more than the ratio between eggs, flour and sugar, political arrangements such as democracies, which are both complex and fragile, emotionally laden and symbolically charged, can never be adequately understood in terms of head counts and paper audits. As a mode of representing the complex aggregations of voting, numbers have their place, but, in reducing voters to mere quanta, rendering them commensurable with one another and explicable in terms of cold calculation, something important is lost. Consider, for example, the following account of the 1997 British general election.

At forty-two days, the period of the 1997 election campaign was longer than usual. Labour and the Liberal Democrats put up 639 candidates each. The Conservatives put up 648. On election day, 31,286,284 million votes were cast. The Conservative share of the vote fell from 49.9 per cent to 30.7 per cent, whereas Labour's increased from 34.5 per cent to 43.2 per cent, giving them a parliamentary majority of 179, with 418 seats – a vote-to-seat ratio of 0.81. (In 1970, Labour had won almost the same percentage of the national vote and lost to the Conservatives.) The swing from Conservative to Labour was 10.5 per cent on a turnout of 71.3 per cent. On average, it took 113,987 votes to elect each Liberal Democrat MP, 58,127 to elect every Conservative MP, and 32,318 to elect every Labour MP. Two hundred fifty-nine new MPs entered parliament after this election, 120 of whom were women.

Many more numbers could be added to this account: the percentage of vote-switchers, ticket-splitters between the local and general elections, regional swings, the demographic breakdown of voters for each of the parties, and the precise variations between how people reported voting in exit polls and the results as counted. What such numerical representations cannot begin to tell us is what it felt like to be immersed in a national drama of removing a government after eighteen years of unbroken political ascendancy. Nor can they tell us what it felt like for 'old Labour' voters to find themselves caught up in the electoral victory of leaders committed to the eradication of some of their core principles; or of the unprecedented number who stayed at home rather than casting a vote for anyone; or of those whose walk to the polling station involved an inner battle with the echoes of advice given to them as they were growing up; or those for whom the walk home after voting was filled with pride or shame or frustration. Numbers do not tell us about the viewers for whom the televised election results programme took the form of a cathartic carnival in which the once-mighty faced live public humiliation. Brian Cathcart's (1997) book, *Were You Still Up for Portillo?*, captures the theatricality of the occasion: its title refers to the symbolic moment which in numerical terms conveys little (the loss of a seat by one of 178 Conservative MPs), but in terms familiar to any audience of Greek drama or TV soap opera was loaded with symbolic affect.

Numbers are good for plotting chains of effect, but they do not – and cannot – explain how social practices are created, sustained, misunderstood, rearticulated and related to other practices, often in ways that defy rationalist sense-making. Bevir and Rhodes (2006:170) develop this point in relation to studies of voting:

> When other political scientists study voting behaviour using attitude surveys or models of rational action, they separate beliefs from actions to find a correlation or deductive link between the two. In contrast, an interpretive approach suggests that such surveys and models cannot tell us why, say, raising one's hand should amount to voting, or why there would be uproar if someone forced someone else to raise their hand against their will. We can explain such behaviour only if we appeal to the intersubjective beliefs that underpin the practice. We need to know that voting is associated with free choice and so with a particular concept of the self. Practices could not exist if people did not have the appropriate beliefs. Beliefs or meanings would not make sense without the practices to which they refer.

Pursuing this interpretivist perspective, we might say that the fact that the 1997 general election campaign was unusually long means very little unless we have a picture in our head of what an election campaign is supposed to look, feel and be like. To say that 31,286,284 million votes were cast but turnout was down does not tell us much about how people connect the casting of votes (or abstention) to their broader sense of selfhood and civic identity. To report that Labour won 418 seats does not begin to describe the drama of the unseated representative, the spontaneous and stage-managed jubilation of being part of a political landslide or the memories that would have connected this moment to others in 1945 or 1979. But these less tangible, quantifiable or even rationally explicable flows of affect are no less characteristic of democracy as it is experienced than exit polls, swings and vote-seat ratios. For, some things cannot be measured, but they can be told. It is to these narratives of tacit and explicit telling that we now turn.

2

Narratives of Voting

The narrow high street was thronged with voters. Tall policemen stationed there had nothing to do. The certainty of all that they were going to win seemed to keep everyone in good humour. ... It was evidently a religious ceremony, summing up most high feelings; and this seemed to one who was himself a man of action, natural, perhaps pathetic, but certainly no matter for scorn.

(John Galsworthy, *The Patrician*, 1911)

Standard stories ... pop up everywhere. They lend themselves to vivid, compelling accounts of what has happened, what will happen, and what should happen. They do essential work in social life, cementing people's commitments to common projects, helping people make sense of what is going on, channeling collective decisions and judgments, spurring people to action they would otherwise be reluctant to pursue.

(Charles Tilly, *Stories, Identities and Political Change*, 2002)

How is it that social performances such as voting arrive in our lives as seemingly natural occurrences? Emerging from a deep well of tradition, coated in pre-existing meanings and enmeshed in 'webs of interlocution' (Taylor, 1989:36), we are led to speak about them in certain ways – and never in others. They seem to be endowed with distinctive flavours that we imagine we have tasted before; governed by tacit norms and rules to which we can never quite remember subscribing, but which we rarely question.

We come to understand the world through narratives which give meaning to lived experience. Narratives set the scene for ordinary and extraordinary events, relate them to one another through emplotment and locate subjective experience within them. The narratives we live by are largely inherited rather than invented for ourselves; as Jameson (1981:9) puts it, 'texts come before us as the always-already-read; we apprehend them through sedimented layers of previous interpretations'. Through these pluralistic, cross-cutting and sometimes competing storylines, symbolic interactions, institutional processes, mundane rituals and grand events are made comprehensible, shareable and familiar.

Narratives of voting serve as civic heuristics, containing popular memories and shaping public expectations, allowing people to engage as voters as if they were reproducing a natural act. Writing of the function of myth in 'giving an historical intention a natural justification', Barthes (1957/2000:142–3) observes that 'A conjuring trick has taken place; it has turned reality inside out, it has emptied it of history and filled it with nature, it has removed from things their human meaning so as to make them signify a human insignificance'. Narratives of the voting performance realise these effects by normalising what should be an incomplete drama; by turning indeterminacy into cliché. Of course, there is not just one narrative of voting. There is a repertoire, but one which is limited by the impediments of the empirically known and the counterfactually imaginable. In the narrative typology that follows, we are concerned to identify the frames and tropes that constitute and delineate affective impressions of voting, and also to acknowledge the absences, undertones and hesitations which so often reveal what is being said much more than what is actually said.

The four narrative themes outlined in the chapter have been selected from a range of texts, images, anecdotes and allusions that suggest a cumulative representation of voting as a social performance. Weaving between historical and literary narratives, the accounts that follow endeavour to relate the experiential to the mythical, the half-forgotten to the almost-imagined. Sometimes

a novel or a play can capture a perspective in ways that no histo-
rian or social scientist can hope to achieve. Of course, these narratives cannot possibly account exhaustively for every story that
has ever been employed to frame the experience and meaning of
voting, but, as we shall see in Chapters 4 to 7, the themes identified here recur repeatedly when people come to reflect upon their
own experiences of being voters.

Ideal

Overshadowing every contemporary act of voting is the image
of the Greek *agora:* the democratic ideal to which representative
democracy is often contrasted as the diminished and impoverished degraded version. Conjuring up notions of popular rule,
direct plebiscites and collective deliberation, the narrative of
Athenian (or classical) democracy stands as a model of decision
making against which contemporary, plebiscitary practices seem
feeble and cadaverous. The uncertain shuffle of atomised voters
to the polling station to put an anonymous cross on a flimsy ballot paper is embarrassingly parsimonious in comparison with the
rich, embodied drama of the public assembly. In their lament for
the loss of civic enchantment, contemporary theorists call for the
rebuilding of the *agora* as a first step towards making 'individual autonomy both feasible and worth struggling for.' (Bauman,
1999:107) What was it about this millennia-old political experiment that inspires such high hopes and harsh comparisons?

The Athenian city state, like the hundreds of others centred
on the Mediterranean and Black Sea, was originally ruled by an
aristocratic oligarchy. Homer's account of Odysseus' address to
the Athenian military rank-and-file captures the spirit of pre-
democratic governance:

> Thou shalt neither be counted in war nor in counsel, for no good
> thing is a multitude of lords. Let there be one lord and one king, to
> whom Chronos has vouchsafed the sceptre and the judgments.

It was precisely to guard against such oligarchical tendencies
that Solon introduced his constitutional reforms in the early

sixth century BCE, abolishing the enslavement of Athenians by Athenians and awarding political rights on the basis of productive landownership rather than noble birth. The Solonian constitution introduced the appointment of magistrates by lot, but did not change the fundamentally aristocratic character of tribal representation. It was supplanted in 546 BCE by the tyranny of Peisistratus, after which came the rule of Cleisthenes beginning in 508 BCE. It was Cleisthenes who reorganised the Athenian population in a way that broke the control of the aristocratic tribal chieftains, introduced rotation of office and appointment by lot to most governmental functions and enhanced the powers of the Assembly of which all adult male citizens were members. Athens was not unique in its democratic experimentation (Robinson, 1997; 2008), but existed on a larger scale than any other and has given rise to a singularly enduring and influential legacy.

Three characteristics of the Athenian polity are generally cited as evidence of its democratic purity. First is its dependence on the physical ubiety of the citizenry. Unlike representative democracy, which is founded upon the aggregation of disembodied individuals into an imagined sovereign body, the strength of direct democracy resides in the embodied presence of the public. The conviction that representation can never authentically reproduce the voices and values of the absent-represented is often coupled with a sigh for the passing of a space of physical solidarity in which, thrown together, the public must arrive at collective judgments. Bauman (1999:87) argues that without the autonomy of the *agora*, 'neither the *polis* nor its members could gain, let alone retain, their freedom to decide the meaning of their common good and what was to be done to attain it'. At the heart of this desire for a reinvigorated public forum is a theory about the need for representation to escape from the usurping interventions of intermediaries. All mediating devices (from the ballot box to the television camera) are regarded as substitutes for embodied presence. Seduced by an aura of unqualified presentness, the narrative of the *agora* symbolises the antithesis of vitiating mediation. But can representation ever be truly free of mediation, in the sense of being able to transcend any distinction between representations and the represented? Is it the case that mediation always fails to register and transmit the authentic voice of the public – or might it be that the public can never have a single, replicable voice that articulates the full range of its affective dispositions? Fundamental to the argument of the current chapter are two claims: that representation (however democratic) is always an act of mediation that both reflects and creates the represented; and that voting as a technology of representation can never capture, contain or coordinate the multifarious affects that underlie public judgement. The return of mass embodied presence (or even virtual presence) in a revived *agora* may indeed provide a much-needed political space for opinions to be aired, policies scrutinised and preferences and values contested (Coleman and Blumler, 2009), but it would be to set up such a project for failure to expect it to operate according to a fantasy of unmediated communication.

This ties in with a second attractive feature of the narrative of Athenian democracy. As a narrative of inclusive decision-making, Athenian democracy combines both popular participation and extensive deliberation. Elitist political theorists have tended to regard these as mutually exclusive: either citizens are invited to participate, in which case the terms of engagement are set low (as when the mass media serve as a quasi-public sphere), or decision making on the basis of well-informed and reasoned discussion is promoted (as when legislators are elected to deliberate in exclusive chambers). The Athenian model of mass participation in public deliberation seems closer to the norms of democracy than the rather silent, languid system of electoral representation to which we have become accustomed. But perhaps this is more appearance than reality; a virtue of political narrative rather than historical reality. Indeed, Athenian deliberation was marked by two defects: the exclusion of the majority of the population from the citizenry and the non-participation of the majority of the citizenry in actual deliberation.

The exclusionary nature of Athenian citizenship is well known and need not be rehearsed at any length here. Women, slaves, foreigners and people who were in debt to the state, constituting a substantial majority of the Athenian population (approximately 160,000 out of 200,000), did not count as citizens. Although the Athenian political experiment was remarkable for its time in not distinguishing between the formal rights of rich property owners and poor citizens, it was nonetheless the case that

> a citizen of democratic Athens lived both in a constitutional realm where political equality was the norm and in a social matrix where inequality predominated. The voters in Assembly, lawcourt and Council were institutionally equal but socially unequal; the dissonance between the two spheres significantly influenced decision-making. (Ober, 1989:326)

Both sides of this paradox have contributed to an enduring narrative of Athenian democracy, one which refers to an ideal of egalitarian citizenship in which the Athenian Assembly serves as a model for the performance of civic belonging. The requisite condition for this performance is a willingness to disregard the dissonance between the right to be counted as a political equal and the awareness that social inequalities persistently mitigate the efficacy of poorer and weaker citizens. The implicit narrative entails a suspension of disbelief; a repression of the material metrics by which worth is counted beyond the political forum. When contemporary political theorists invoke the Athenian narrative as a democratic ideal, against which mediated, atomised representation stands as an adulterated compromise, they fail to acknowledge that Athenian democracy was itself a fragile accommodation between the effective equality of citizens qua citizens and the affective imbalance between economic elites, who experienced political power as a supplement to other social powers, and the mass of the citizenry for whom moments of plebiscitary authority contrasted sharply with the inefficacy of everyday life. The frustrations and resentments incurred by both Athenian and contemporary citizens in the performance this balancing act should not be understated.

These were exacerbated in the Athenian democracy by the reality that, although all citizens had a right to speak in the Assembly, most did not. The Periclean reforms, which paid poorer citizens to attend the Assembly, ensured their physical presence but not their vocal participation. Hansen (1991:268) writes of three kinds of Athenian citizen: the 'passive ones' who never attended the Assembly, even though they were eligible to do so; the 'standing participants' who attended the Assembly and voted, but 'did not raise their voice in discussion' and a minority of 'wholly active citizens' who spoke and proposed motions. As only 6,000 citizens could fit into the Pnyx, where the Assembly was held, and as meetings only took place for half a day 40 times a year, the number of vocal participants was inevitably limited not only to 'wholly active citizens', but to those with established reputations for political oratory. Even Ober (1993:484), the most erudite scholar to argue for the Athenian narrative of the *demos* overcoming the elite, admits that '[a]lthough in principle any Athenian could address the Assembly, in practice much of the debate was carried out by a cadre of skilled "politicians" who were well known to their audiences and referred to variously as rhetors, deamagogues or the "accustomed speakers"'. Furthermore, the methods by which the star performers maintained their share of speaking time was far from democratic: 'When the Assemblymen tired of listening to a speaker, they would shout him down' (Ober, 1993:483). The mood of the Assembly was set by arrogant demagogues prepared to mock and heckle anyone deemed unworthy of speaking time. According to Natali (1987:235), 'It seems certain … that in ancient Athens political democracy was not as closely associated with freedom of speech as it is today. Everybody was supposed to be free to express his opinions, but only if he was a morally acceptable person and his opinions were not too much out of harmony with prevailing views.' Here we return to a trope explored in the previous chapter: the exclusion of the morally incompetent and unacceptable from the sphere of public debate. Indeed, in cases of ostracism, such exclusion extended to the boundaries of the state: civic death by another name. We do not know how many hesitating proposers of motions were shouted down, how many stuttering sentences were never completed or how many potentially vocal citizens thought better of running the gauntlet and remained as 'standing participants': voters who did not open their mouths. Not only is this an empirically unknown aspect of the Athenian democratic experiment, but it remains an uncharted dimension of our own political culture. Chronicling silence, measuring trepidation and hearing the 'hidden transcripts' (Scott, 1990) of mumbled complaint calls for a sensibility not yet developed by political scientists.

A third appeal of the Athenian narrative focuses on ways of arriving at decisions without resorting to formal voting. Just as representation is seen by some modern theorists as a dilution of embodied presence, so voting is seen as a crude substitute for more consensual decision-making mechanisms. The two most common alternatives to voting employed by Athenian democracy were rotation of office and appointment by lot. Both of these were intended to prevent the establishment of a permanent oligarchy and were more common than appointment by public vote, which was largely confined to the selection of the generals (*strategoi*). The Athenian principle of sortition reflected a democratic aspiration to keep the powers of office in constant circulation, but it did not acknowledge the agonistic nature of politics, where competing interests, positions and values are embodied in candidates for election. Athenian democracy operated on the republican assumption that any citizen, selected fairly and behaving honestly, would work towards the same social good as any other. Those who could not be trusted to hold (any) office should be barred from citizenship, ostracised or shouted down in the course of debate. The narrative of Athenian democracy encourages the communitarian dream that all can be winners in every social decision; that all disagreement can be resolved through consensus; and that political interests can be overcome by the force of general will. In short, the Athenian narrative offers an alternative to the conflict, voting and majoritarian domination of what Mansbridge (1983:3) refers to as 'adversary democracy'. This escape from conflict presupposes a democracy of friends who share interests – or will eventually come to do so once they have deliberated together for long enough. The Athenian ideal of *homonoia* (unanimity, or the oneness of friendship) stands in mocking contrast with the disagreements, votes and compromises characteristic of the clash of political representations. Aristotle's claim that '*homonoia* ... is the principal aim of legislators' amounts to a declaration of war against agonistic politics, forever after cast as postlapsarian, morally suspect and anti-utopian.

The Athenian narrative persists into modernity as a romantic idealization of a democracy of friends. New England Town meetings, Swiss cantons, Israeli kibbutzim and anarcho-style workers' councils have all been depicted as higher forms of democracy, free from the vulgarities of mere head-counting. As friends, their members would not feel inclined to vote against one another's interests, preferring to talk things over, make light of awkward tensions and arrive at barely articulated decisions which embrace the homogeneous mood. But, as Mansbridge (1976:658) found in her empirical study of 'Conflict in a New England Town Meeting',

> For those who are *full members* of a community, the familial joking and informality, the attempts to cover up embarrassing incidents and the unanimous voting make a potentially frightening situation bearable. Each of these actions eases tension, dissipates possible conflict, and allows insecure members of the community to participate more fully. ... Unfortunately, the very devices which make participation easier for *full members* of the community serve to distant those who are *not yet full members*. (My emphases)

But of what exactly are full community members replete? What constitutes democratic satiety? The fantasy of the Athenian narrative suggests that the 'full member' (ignoring for the moment the Freudian pun) is a container for the affects of all members; that the citizen embodies citizenship. To speak as an Athenian-style citizen is to both express and echo public feeling. 'Those who are not yet full members' of a democratic community, like the 'standing participants' in the Greek Assembly who were present but rarely spoke and the participants in New England Town meetings who, for various reasons, were not part of the inner circle, could be easily 'humiliated, frightened and made to feel more powerless than before' (Mansbridge, 1976:663). They suffer the disquieting experience of being nominally within but affectively beyond the demos. As the directness of direct democracy hints not only at fully embodied presence, but fully acknowledged feelings, those who cannot unconditionally incorporate the repertoire of public affects are doomed to the awkwardness of bystanders.

The fictional narrative that most powerfully captures this inducement towards affective consensus is Sidney Lumet's classic 1957 film, *Twelve Angry Men*. The plot, devised by the eminent screenwriter Reginald Rose, centres around a jury vote in a murder case. The jurors are defined by a single affect. Their anger circulates around the jury room, verbally, bodily, morally, individually and collectively. Indeed, the thrust of the narrative is a drama of transition from personal to unified feeling. One by one, the jurors succumb to an irresistible sensibility out of which an apparently just decision is allowed to emerge. It is a warming tale of citizens coming to see an event through one another's eyes. There are four observations worth making about this narrative before we move on to consider a different theme.

First, these are not just any twelve citizens: they are men and they are angry. The subject of the film could have been twelve jolly women or twelve embarrassed boys or twelve procrastinating men, but it is twelve angry men whose deliberations we are invited to observe. According to the film's narrative, their anger is the problematic condition that stands between them and reasoned judgement. It must be tamed. It is tamed. The film is a dramatised account of how emotions must be repressed if consensus is to be reached. Outsiders are dragged inside; bystanders, intent on sticking to their own affective positions, are made to feel sufficiently uncomfortable to surrender their autonomy and subscribe to the unanimous feeling.

Second, there are only twelve of these angry men, not twelve thousand or twelve million. Their anger can be contained and constrained within face-to-face interpersonal discussion. Six thousand angry Athenians would have required a different taming strategy. Two million angry *Daily Mail* headline readers would present yet another challenge to those seeking to subdue emotions. In fact, researchers who conducted an impressive content analysis of the film transcript found that only three jurors contribute 45 per cent of all speech acts in the jury room debate and six out of the twelve contribute 73 per cent (Beck and Fisch, 2000). As in the Athenian Assembly and the New England Town Meeting, it is a minority of the participants who dominate the debate.

Third, the process of overcoming emotions dramatised in *Twelve Angry Men* relies on periodic voting to test its success. Beck and Fisch (2000) found that each turning point in the jury deliberation, from emotion- to reason-based argument, was followed within approximately four minutes by a vote in which the jurors came closer to unanimity. In short, voting served in this instance as the best way of checking 'progress' towards the normatively desired goal of an affect-free judgement.

Fourth, these twelve angry men were not just any old angry men who chanced to meet in a bar. They were jurors, locked into a room in a courthouse from which they could not escape without reaching a judicially legitimate decision. They had not entered this room freely and could not leave, despite the humidity and lack of air conditioning. This narrative of ideal deliberation is therefore doubly artificial: it depicts a forced discussion, framed by pressures that the deliberators could not control; and it is, of course, a fictional construction, devised by Rose and Lumet to play out one ideal narrative, but not others that might have transpired. Perhaps that is the main point to be made about the ideal voting narrative: if citizens could be forcibly locked into it and their actions then edited so that distracting affect is deftly eliminated, its plausibility as a democratic model would be greatly augmented.

Ritual

Moving backwards in time from one fictional voting narrative to another, we turn to an electoral contest in Eatanswill between the Honourable Samuel Slumkey, the Blue candidate, and Horatio Fizkin Esquire, the Buff candidate, as told by Charles Dickens in the thirteenth chapter of *The Pickwick Papers* (first published in serial form, 1836/7). Pickwick is introduced to Slumkey's agent, who asks him:

> You have come down here to see an election – eh?
>
> Mr Pickwick replied in the affirmative.
>
> 'Spirited contest, my dear sir,' said the little man.
>
> 'I'm delighted to hear it,' said Mr Pickwick, rubbing his hands. 'I like to see sturdy patriotism, on whatever side it is called forth – and so it's a spirited contest?'
>
> 'Oh yes,' said the little man, 'very much so indeed. We have opened all the public-houses in the place, and left our adversary nothing but the beer-shops – masterly stroke of policy that, my dear sir, eh? The little man smiled complacently, and took a large pinch of snuff.
>
> 'And what are the probabilities as to the result of the contest?' inquired Mr Pickwick.
>
> 'Why, doubtful, my dear sir; rather doubtful as yet,' replied the little man. 'Fizkin's people have got three-and-thirty voters in the lock-up coach house at the White Hart.'
>
> 'In the coach-house!' said Mr Pickwick, considerably astonished by this second stroke of policy.
>
> 'They keep 'em locked up there till they want 'em', resumed the little man. 'The effect of that is, you see, to prevent us getting at them; and even if we could, it would be of no use, for they keep them very drunk on purpose. Smart fellow Fizkin's agent – very smart fellow indeed.'
>
> Mr Pickwick stared, but said nothing.

Two themes of voting as ritual spectacle are introduced in this passage. First, the election is spoken of as a show which observers might 'come to see'. Not unlike a popular carnival, it was an event to be witnessed; quite in contrast to the closed-off sobriety of Lumet's deliberative jury room. Second, it was an event in which contenders battled for the affective attention of potential voters. In this account, both candidates had gained control of rival public-houses where they were aiming to win support through the traditional custom of 'treating': bribing voters with gifts including banquets, beverages, trinkets, concerts and parades. Dickens points to the antithesis of rational appeal: a drunken electorate that will follow whoever is prepared to keep them that way. But eighteenth- and early-nineteenth-century elections appealed to more than just inebriated supporters, and an argument could be made that 'treating' constituted an important part of the moral economy, forcing elites to distribute periodically some of their wealth to the less well-off, including ineligible voters whose support was regarded as essential in setting the local political mood.

Polling day in late-eighteenth-/early-nineteenth-century Britain was anything other than a dull, administratively dominated civic moment. It was a spectacle surrounded by elaborate social ritual. Indeed, in the late eighteenth century, there was no single polling *day:* voting often went on for several days on end. In 1785, an act was passed limiting polling to no more than a fifteen-day period. The 1832 Reform Act cut this down to two days. In *The Pickwick Papers*, Dickens provides a vivid description of the sights and sounds of a noisy and bustling election campaign:

> The beating of drums, the blowing of horns and trumpets, the shouting of men, and tramping of horses, echoed and re-echoed through the streets from the earliest dawn of day: and an occasional fight between the light skirmishers of either party at once enlivened the preparations, and agreeably diversified their character.

That this was no merely Dickensian exaggeration is evident from the writings of social historians who have charted the performative character of pre-democratic elections. O'Gorman (1992:92) describes the forms of 'tumultuous and widespread public participation' that characterised British election campaigns between 1780 and 1860. He identifies six key moments which served to draw both voters and non-voters into a collective performance of public representation. First, there was 'the ceremonial entry of the candidates into the constituency': 'The crowds would be waiting at some popular designated point in town. Then, in a carefully determined order of procession, and usually with musical accompaniment, they would march to greet the candidate' (ibid:83). Second, there was a canvassing period, which involved 'treating' potential voters to free dinners, breakfasts, picnics and public entertainments. All of this created a carnival atmosphere; people came to associate election campaigns with thrills and amusements. Third, there was the formal nomination of the candidates, which was 'the first occasion in the campaign when all the voters were officially summoned together' (ibid:86). The candidates and their leading supporters made speeches before the gathered crowd, following which there was a show of hands. If he believed he stood any chance of winning, the losing candidate would then demand a poll, which would lead to the fourth key moment of the performance. The poll, which could last for several days, was a far from silent affair. There would be hustings from which speeches would be given well into the night. Constituencies would be noisy with the sound of rival groups of supporters heckling one another, competing bands parading through the constituency and groups of people coming to and going from the open-air polling booths. Each citizen entering the booth was required to prove his entitlement to cast a vote, after which his right to vote could be questioned by the agent of the opposing candidates. Once eligibility was confirmed, the voter was asked to tell the poll clerk (verbally) whom he wished to vote for and this was entered by the clerk into an official poll book. The fifth key moment was the declaration of the result by the returning officer. 'This was followed by speeches of a non-controversial character from the various candidates, in which they thanked the returning officer, their friends and supporters, and complimented the electors on the good order in which the campaign had proceeded' (ibid:89). (This is the only one of the key dramatic moments that remains part of the contemporary voting performance.) Finally, the high point of the campaign was the chairing ceremony in which the victorious candidate was carried around the streets of the constituency. O'Gorman (ibid:91) describes this as a moment of political and cultural closure:

> Its long duration, the length of the procession, the numbers of people on the streets, watching from windows, carrying banners or colours, all indicate that the entire community, not just the victorious party, was witnessing and celebrating its new representatives. The community was coming together, binding its wounds,

purging its partisanship, preparing to return to social and political normality.

These symbolic occasions were not peculiarly British. Rural elections in post-Revolutionary France (Pourcher, 1991; Crook, 2002) were occasions for communal celebration and post-bellum U.S. presidential elections followed a traditional cycle of rituals:

> Political clubs organized marching companies to perform elaborate drill maneuvers in partisan parades. Often held at night, these drew tens of thousands of marchers with brass bands, glee clubs, processions of wagons, and seas of karosene torchlights. As Election Day neared, "monster rallies" attracted thousands more to large feasts and additional nighttime spectacle. ... The climax of these popular rites was Election Day, an official holiday in many states. This ritual timeout from routine time was an all-day affair devoted to food, drink, and socializing. (Marvin and Simonson, 2004:132)

To speak of these voting performances as rituals is not to denigrate them. Employed to describe practices that exceed the terms of rational explanation, the word 'ritual' too often connotes the merely affective, the culturally vacuous, the rationally inexplicable. On the contrary, it is through ritual that links are forged between quotidian expressiveness and political meaning. As Lukes (1975:301) states, ritual 'helps to define as authoritative certain ways of seeing society: it serves to specify what in society is of special significance, it draws people's attention to certain forms of relationships and activities – and at the same time, therefore, it deflects their attention from other forms, since every way of seeing is also a way of not seeing.' This last point is very important: the ritualisation of social performances cuts out other ways of acting, thinking and seeing. It affirms a conventional repertoire of available terms and gestures of performance. Tilly (2008) usefully reminds us that once a new repertoire becomes established, its mode of collective action appears to be the only one that could ever make sense, and earlier forms of collective action seem to be eccentric, archaic and senseless. Ritual, in this sense, not only establishes the contours of affective behaviour, but rules out those affects which would be disruptive or destabilising to conventional practice.

Enacting as well as reflecting democratic norms, ritual invests with affective substance forms, habits and events that might otherwise elude public significance. Durkheim's (1912) conception of ritual as a functional source of social solidarity is rather too simplistic to account for the various ways in which voting rituals open up space for the discursive contestation of representations (Alexander, 1989, 1992; Roth, 1995). It is the affective dimension of ritual that makes it open to unpredictable outcomes, sometimes cathartically resolving or concealing deep-seated conflicts and at other times arousing public emotions in ways that are symbolically irreconcilable.

As ritual performances, pre-modern elections evoked a popular narrative of public representation. As a response to the complexity and ambiguity of pre-democratic citizenship, ritual embodied a compensatory narrative, offering vocal roles for the effectively powerless and permitting saturnalian public display within a regime of institutionally primed affects. Enacting representation entailed constructing and making visible the public, determining the terms of public expression and ensuring the legitimacy of electorally established power. In situations characterised by stark social inequalities, political exclusions and limited institutional flexibility, the enactment of such narratives required appreciable dexterity.

The public has to be imagined before it can be represented (Warner, 2002; Coleman and Ross, 2010). Who counts as a citizen and what counts as the space of civic, rather than private, life are never ontologically given. Publicness emerges from contestation: the demand to be 'in' or 'out'; the claim that this issue is universally relevant, while that is a personal concern; the acknowledgement that some spaces are open to all, whereas others can be freely appropriated. As soon as political representation came to be even putatively democratic (as opposed to unquestionably dictatorial), the problem of representing the represented became a formidable challenge. The eighteenth-century concept of virtual representation rested on the notion of 'an aristocracy of virtue and wisdom governing for the good of the whole nation' (Pitkin, 1972:172). The claimed necessity for representative trusteeship was predicated upon the alleged incapacity of the mass of the public to reason for themselves. Burke conceded that 'the most poor, illiterate and uninformed creatures upon earth are judges of *practical* oppression,' but this does not enable them to understand the cause of or remedy for their problems; from discussion of such matters they 'ought to be totally shut out; because their reason is weak; because when once aroused, their passions are ungoverned; because they want information; because the smallness of the property, which they individually possess, renders them less attentive to the measures they adopt in affairs of moment' (Burke, 1854:512). Lord North, speaking in opposition to a failed motion for electoral reform, posed himself a rhetorical question which he proceeded to answer in terms of the conventional rhetoric of virtual representation: 'Did freedom depend upon every individual subject being represented in that House? Certainly not; for that House, constituted as it was, represented the whole Kingdom' (Dickinson, 1977:286) A key function of election ritual was to make visible this complicated logic; to show that non-voters, in being spoken for, were no less entitled than their enfranchised social superiors to share in the carnival of public embodiment. Indeed, as O'Gorman (1992:81) is at pains to emphasise, 'Election managers and their candidates aimed their theatre *and the substance of their political messages* at the non-voters as much as at the voters.' The number of people engaged by the electoral narrative far exceeded the number who could actually vote.

One way of maintaining the involvement of non-voters was through rituals of social inversion. Through the acting out of transposed social roles, rulers were forced to 'explain themselves' before the harsh court of their inferiors, and political subjects were free to disseminate 'social messages and political criticisms which might have been utterly unacceptable at almost any other time and in any other form' (O'Gorman, 1992:109–10). In such electoral moments in which power lost its usual intangibility, strategies designed to put people in their place were momentarily open to public inspection and contestation. Never is what Lefort (1986:279) refers to as 'the empty place' of power more obviously vacant and uncertain than in the brief instant between the courting, casting and counting of votes. The powerful have to flatter the individually unimportant. The crowd assumes a fleeting authority based on its dormant capacity to overturn hierarchy.

While saturnalian gestures, such as mock chairings of candidates and bawdy songs drawing attention to the vices and weaknesses of elite actors, may have been ultimately ineffectual, amounting to little more than 'the mummery of extravagant posturing' (O'Gorman, 1992:109), their affective significance should not be underestimated. Once a criticism is uttered openly, regardless of its ostensibly facetious form, its reverberations cannot be eradicated. Allowing ironic, satirical and vernacular political appraisals to circulate freely, even if only temporarily and under the guise of playfulness, exposes the taken-for-granted to the risk of being redescribed in new terms. The case of the Middlesex election of 1768, in which the radical, John Wilkes, was repeatedly barred from Parliament, despite winning more votes than the government candidate, Henry Lawes Luttrell, well illustrates how both eligible voters and the wider population could use a campaign to question the foundations of constitutional authority. As a result of the campaign, the Society for the Supporters of the Bill of Rights, led by John Horne Tooke, emerged as advocates of the secret ballot in elections and opponents of the right to bribe voters. Although this reform movement was not to gather steam until the next century, here was an example of the peculiar freedom of electoral inversion giving rise to an enduring radical agenda.

Despite the inherent risks posed by opening up the social performance of voting to popular participation, electoral ritual is primarily geared to securing political legitimation. Through public acts of embodiment, a narrative of the many becoming one is both played out and witnessed. When, after the declaration of the poll, the elected candidate claims to speak for everyone, it is as if society were being cured of its agonistic aberration. Having split into partisan fragments, the community is reconsolidated, politics is purged until its next permitted outing and the natural order is resanctified by the miracle of aggregation. In this sense, the ritual narrative points towards closure but not necessarily solidarity, in contrast to the ceaseless deliberation of the ideal narrative which depends on solidarity but not necessarily closure.

Whereas the ideal narrative seems permanently to hang over contemporary democracy, mocking the thinness of its civic culture and the dullness of its political dramaturgy, the ritual narrative appears to be deeply buried: a long-forgotten account of carnivalesque democracy. When interviewees (see Chapter 7) were asked to imagine the voting performance as a pleasurable experience, they strained their imaginations to think of innovative ways of injecting fun into a drab routine. Their thoughts focused on a fanciful future, but none looked back to an age when voting had been an occasion for entertainment and boisterous participation. This history had been forgotten. It was as if the ritual narrative could only be envisaged as subliminal fantasy rather than recalled as historical praxis.

Before dismissing the contemporary relevance of the ritual narrative, however, two important caveats should be made. First, the vivacity and spectacularity of electoral ritual persist in states that have not yet fully yielded to the logic of modernity (Aguilar, 2007; Fell, 2007; Foucher, 2007; Heder, 2007; Prasad, 2007). In many parts of Asia, Africa and Latin America, political culture remains sufficiently rooted in the face-to-face interaction for symbolic repertoires of representation and legitimation to prevail. To observers of modernised, Western politics, it is as if the price of modernisation is the demise of ritual; as if the exotic drama of somatic democracy is something to be written about anthropologically rather than being within the scope of political science; as if the price of modernisation is the demise of ritual.

Perhaps, however, it is only the form and locus of electoral ritual that have changed. As in many other zones of modernity, the embodied immediacy of the crowd is replaced by the virtual confluence of the dispersed public. Practices which once involved the co-presence of bodies that might touch, sounds heralding the socially extraordinary, smells infused with festivity and sights signifying civicness are now mediated through technologies that perform the conjuring trick of making the mass electorate seem visible in its vast diffusion.

In bringing together fragmented characters, locations and events through its own diegetic narrative, television and other electronic media are implicated in the construction of the electoral rituals they claim to be merely reporting. It is as if the nation somehow comes together, spatially and dialogically, through the distance-compressing rituals of mediaspace. On the BBC's election-night results programme, a flashing map of Britain in the studio represents the outcomes of millions of individual votes cast in thousands of specific places, all assembled within what Ferguson (1990:156, cited by Marriott, 2000:146) refers to as a 'space-without-space'. In her study of the BBC's coverage of the 1997 British general election results, Marriott (2000:134) observes how '[r]eporters and interviewees are invariably seen first on the studio screen before the programme cuts to a direct, unmediated shot of the OB [outside broadcast] location, and participants at remote sites on no occasion directly address each other, commenting always through the mediation of the studio, and of the studio presenters at the centre'. In playing out politics through the centralising prism of the television studio, a narrative of spatial and intersubjective connection is perpetrated. As in a ritual, there is a prevailing conceit that all expression will ultimately meet its intended target; that mediated democracy somehow fits together within a contained and expressible performance.

This same ersatz centre becomes the locus for the phone-ins, studio-audience discussions and, more recently, online forums intended to capture 'the public voice'. These are ritualistically structured mediaspaces, within which citizens are invited to perform particular roles such as 'The Voice of Experience' (the unemployed factory worker, the mother of a soldier killed in war, the anxious owner of a failing business, the pensioner who cannot make ends meet), 'The Pushy Voter' (who traps a leading politician with a devastating question – Diane Gould's phone-in attack on Thatcher and Joe the Plumber's encounter with Obama are the model scripts) and 'The Deeply Apathetic' (the first-time voter who needs to be persuaded that he or she is in need of political representation). Through this mediated centre the public gets to speak on certain terms, in certain tones and for certain lengths of time; the ritual is carefully managed, and neither 'bad television' nor 'bad citizenship' are allowed to spoil the show.

As a ritual narrative, repeated somewhat formulaically every few years, media coverage of elections appeals to what Couldry (2000:23) has called 'the myth of the mediated centre': the claim that the media provide 'an access point to society's centre' and that its rituals exhaust the repertoire of meaningful social performances. If it is not on the television, can it be real? Media producers have become expert in telling stories that fit in with their predictions and which they have themselves helped to construct. But they have great difficulty in dealing with deviations from the script. The unexpected can very quickly result in the collapse of the mediated centre and a breakdown of ontological security. The U.S. presidential election results coverage in November 2000 provides a striking illustration of such ritual discomfiture.

At 7 PM, EST CNN's co-anchor, Bernard Shaw, announced that polls had closed in nine states, including Florida, 'and CNN is looking at what is going on.' In fact, Florida, divided by a time zone, had not finished voting; people living in the west of the state still had another hour to cast their votes. At this point, Voter News Service (VNS), the company funded by the five networks and Associated Press to analyse the voting trends, gave Gore a 6.6 per cent lead over Bush in Florida. At 7:48 PM (before the state polls had even closed, and with less than 5 per cent of the votes counted), NBC announced that Gore had won Florida. Two minutes later, CNN and CBS made the same declaration. Then VNS re-examined its exit poll data and realised that in at least one county the estimated Gore vote has been seriously overstated. At 9:54 PM, CNN and CBS retracted their earlier call for Gore. CNN co-anchor, Judy Woodruff, stated that 'we don't entirely trust all the information that we have.' By 2 AM, with 96 per cent of the Florida vote, counted, VNS found Bush to have a lead of slightly more than 29,000 votes. At 2:16 AM,

NBC announced that Bush had won Florida. Two minutes later, CNN and CBS made the same declaration. At just after 3 AM, CNN announced that Gore had called Bush to concede defeat. At this point the reported majority for Bush in Florida had gone down from 29,000 to 11,000. Then began a new narrative of Bush's declining vote. Starting with a media-created projection, the next hours were devoted to reports of how the actual voters had deviated from the studio projection, as if by some act of mass recalcitrance. By 3:40 AM, VNS decided that Bush's majority had 'fallen' to 6,060 votes. At this point Gore withdrew his concession, preferring, we must suppose, to be guided by the votes cast rather than the votes determined by the media. By 3:57 AM, Bush's lead was slightly less than 2,000 votes. A little more than ten minutes later it was less than 1,800. Judy Woodruff was moved to observe that 'it's the news organizations that are frankly creating part of what's going on tonight – the atmosphere, the ups and downs' (Konner et al., 2001:18). The report commissioned by CNN to review this debacle declared that the news organizations had recklessly endangered the electoral process and their own credibility:

> Their excessive speed, combined with an overconfidence in experts and a reliance on increasingly dubious polls, produced a powerful collision between the public interest and the private competitive interests of the television news operations and the corporations who own them. (Konner et al., 2001:1)

Beyond the details of this journalistic failure lies a bigger problem: the sense that voters have a duty to play their part in a made-for-television event: a social performance that can only have legitimacy through being reported. The 'closeness' of the result was only exceeded by the distance between the casting of votes and the interpretation of their meaning by unaccountable 'experts'. Subsequent investigation by the courts was to show that it was at the point of voting that the most egregious confusion occurred; that the routine mechanics of voting were simply not geared to democratic moments in which citizens were consumed by indecision.

In Jose Saramago's (2004) satirical novel, *Seeing*, the citizens of an unnamed city go in large numbers to cast their votes, but the vast majority of ballot papers (83 per cent) are left blank. This is described by the author as a 'civic power cut' (ibid:5). As in the 2000 presidential election, the electoral supervisors are at a loss to understand how voters have acted: '[W]hat most confused the authorities, and was nearly driving them crazy, was the fact that the voters, with very few exceptions, responded with impenetrable silence to the questions asked by people running exist polls on how they had voted' (ibid:25). The prime minister insists that the country 'had been the victim of a vile assault on of the very foundations of representative democracy' (ibid:31), and the president appears on television to admonish the electorate:

> You are to blame, yes, you are the ones who have ignominiously rejected national concord in favour of the tortuous road of subversion and indiscipline and in favour of the most perverse and diabolical challenge to the legitimate power of the state ever known in the history of nations. Do not find fault with us, find fault rather with yourselves. (ibid:84)

Let us return briefly to Mr Pickwick whose sole desire was to see the show, to witness 'sturdy patriotism, on whatever side it is called forth.' It is not the victory of one party or faction that entices Pickwick, but the game itself – the ritual of conflicting interests coming together as if they were one. 'The beating of drums, the blowing of horns and trumpets, the shouting of men, and tramping of horses' which 'echoed and re-echoed through the streets' of Eatanswill were not significant in their support for Slumkey or Fizkin, but in their construction of an atmosphere fitting for both the rehearsal of difference and the embodiment of accord. Had the voters of Eatanswill decided to cast blank votes, the very foundations of the political order which Dickens so whimsically describes would be in jeopardy. For, as Lefort (1988:110) astutely observes, 'power belongs to the individual or individuals who can ... speak in the name of the people and give them their name'. Every political election is an exercise in doing precisely that.

Routine

On the surface, there may not seem to be much of a distinction between ritual and routine narratives of voting. Both refer to the repetition of taken-for-granted gestures, rules and enactments. But, unlike routine, ritual performs a displacement function, allaying anxieties about what might otherwise happen. Routine is culturally embedded to the point of appearing naturalised. A sense that nothing else *could* happen, that this is the only way of realising a social end, separates routines from rituals.

So much a default position, routine seems to have no story to be told; the strength of its influence lies in its latency. In focusing on voting as a routine narrative, Garfinkels's approach to understanding 'the routine grounds of everyday activities' is enlightening. Garfinkel (1964:227) set out to consider familiar, quotidian, inconspicuous scenes and social interactions, asking 'what can be done to make trouble'. Making trouble entails denaturalising them and identifying the ways in which the social is produced both as an effect and an affect. As Garfinkel (1964:37) puts it:

> The operations that one would have to perform in order to mul-
> tiply the senseless features of perceived environments; to produce
> and sustain bewilderment, consternation, and confusion; to pro-
> duce the socially structured affects of anxiety, shame, guilt and
> indignation; and to produce disorganized interaction should tell
> us something about how the structures of everyday activities are
> ordinarily and routinely produced and maintained.

In the context of voting, routines that seem at first to realise purely technical, instrumental ends (fair, accurate, efficient preference aggregation) turn out, upon critical examination, to be implicated in more extensive social enactments. That is to say, far from being mere instruments of political democracy, electoral routines constitute the political and the democratic, affirming certain practices and protocols and disavowing others. The success of a routine is to make any alternative virtually unthinkable. Two of these routine narratives of voting – one justifying the spatial separation of voting from everyday life and the other justifying the organised surveillance of voting as an act of normative appraisal – will help to cast light on the ways in which practice has come to define principle.

The UK Electoral Commission's *Handbook for Polling Station Staff* (2007:8) sets out clear instructions as to the affective figuration of the voting space: 'The atmosphere in the polling station should be business-like and friendly, and polling station staff should dress accordingly'. The mood-setting injunction is laudable, insofar as most voters would probably welcome efficiency and friendliness, but how exactly should it be interpreted? Could friendliness extend to something more than not being rude to voters? Are there ways of creating a convivial atmosphere that could be recommended as having worked in some polling stations – or other situations, such as public meetings or community events? Interesting research has been conducted in recent years with a view to understanding how some civic events succeed in generating feelings of inclusion and sociability whereas others do not (Goss, 1999; McComas, 2001; Rogers, 2004; Hajer, 2005; Harvey, 2009). Given the detailed recommendations in the Electoral Commission's *Handbook*, the rather meagre advice to be 'friendly' and 'dress accordingly' is of limited value. (What, after all, constitutes friendly dress?)

Perhaps this is explained by the subsequent injunction to avoid any risk of political expression within the polling station:

> Walk the route the voter is expected to follow, checking all signs and notices. Make sure that there are no party posters or other material that might be construed as supporting the views of any candidate involved in the election displayed in or on the premises. If any such materials are found, they must be removed or covered up. (UK Electoral Commission, 2007:10)

In constructing the polling station as an apolitical sanctuary which must be protected from the designing influences of organised interests, a sharp distinction is being made between forming and expressing a political preference. Earlier democratic spaces comprised dynamic interaction between a range of political settings: the clamour of the streets, the rhetoric of the hustings, the animation of public debate, the ironic gestures of satire, as well as the procedural order of casting votes. That contemporary voting spaces need to remain untouched by these affective flows is stated rather than defended, as if no other form of civic expression could possibly be compatible with democracy. The Electoral Commission would certainly be justified in objecting to some party materials being available and not others, but the blanket, unexplained injunction to remove or cover up all references to the competing options facing voters seems like a move to depoliticise the social performance of voting.

The *Handbook for Polling Station Staff* offers a map of how a standard polling station should be set up. Central to this geography is the preservation of secrecy:

> Voters must mark the ballot paper in the privacy of the polling booth *and then re-fold the ballot paper so that no one can see the way they have voted.* Voters should show the ballot paper and the unique identifying mark on the back of the ballot paper to the Presiding Officer or Poll Clerk before placing it in the ballot box. (Ibid:17) (emphasis added)

As a place of secrets, polling station becomes a space of risks. Secrecy always entails the hazard of exposure. What goes on between the counted citizen and the counting state must not be told to anyone. The ballot paper must be folded and refolded until the secret is wrapped so tight 'that no one can see the way they have voted'. There is history behind this preoccupation.

The Whiggish account of how the social performance of voting came to be cloaked in secrecy depicts the Parliamentary and Municipal Elections Act of 1872 (known as the Ballot Act) as a culminating moment in a long struggle by liberal-minded campaigners to protect the independence of voters in the face of attempted bribery. In 1819, Jeremy Bentham published his *Radical Reform Bill* which called for both universal suffrage and secret voting. In July 1830, James Mill warned in a *Westminster Review* article that '[t]he unfortunate voter is in the power of some opulent man; the opulent man informs him how he must vote'. The only way to prevent this would be by making voting strictly secret, thereby denying bribers the chance to verify the fruits of their investment. The cabinet considered introducing the secret ballot within the 1832 Reform Act, but decided against it,

not least because of the influence of King William IV who 'warned
his minister that nothing should ever induce him to yield to it or
to sanction a practice which would ... be a protection to concealment, would abolish the influence of fear and shame, and would
be inconsistent with the manly spirit and the free avowal of opinion which distinguished the people of England' (Park, 1931:56).
This criticism, which led to frequent assertions in press and parliamentary debates that the secret ballot was 'un-English', associated open voting with the transparency of hierarchical order. The
best way to maintain fear of social superiors and to attach shame
to the promotion of vulgar interests was to keep politics within
the purview of public surveillance. Between the 1830s and 1860s,
only a few enthusiasts agitated for secret voting – and these were
mainly liberals who believed in the autonomy of political judgement rather than democrats who favoured universal franchise.
The campaign for secret ballots had such little impact that as
late as 1865 the *Annual Register* could describe the secret ballot question as 'trite' and 'over-discussed' (ibid:73). Most liberal
opinion, led by John Stuart Mill (in opposition to his father who
had proposed it), was firmly opposed to making voting secret
on the grounds that participating in national decision-making
was a matter of civic trust rather than personal right and should
therefore be 'performed under the eye and criticism of the public'
(1861; 1960:300).

According to the Whiggish narrative, the tide of opinion
turned towards the secret ballot when the franchise was granted
to substantial numbers of working-class men in 1867. To protect
newly enfranchised electors from unacceptable pressures from
employers, landlords and social superiors, the Ballot Act was
passed and voting moved from the streets and market squares to
the seclusion of the polling station. In no other way, it is argued,
could political autonomy have been safeguarded against the consequences of social inequality.

That is one version of the historical narrative. An alternative
reading sees secret voting as part of a process of Weberian ratio-
nalisation, designed to strip away ritualistic traditions and aber-
rant passions from the democratic process and replace them with

the atomistic, impersonal, calculative logic of system-rationality. This is not to say that protecting voters against bribery and intimidation was an entirely disingenuous motive for the secret ballot, but that this stated rationale was ambiguously linked to other impulses intended to save the new voters from themselves.

The period in which the Ballot Act was passed was one of deep elite anxiety about the dangers of unmanaged collective action. From the organisation of trades unions to recurrent street demonstrations, the fast-expanding working class was seen to be moving away from its innocent carnivalesque role in pre-modern public culture. It was one thing for the lower orders to play the fool as candidates were cheered and jeered through the streets of a constituency, but quite another for the newly enfranchised to combine with a view to asserting common interests. Even before the extension of the franchise in 1867, there were prevalent fears of 'crowds' and 'mobs' that were becoming too expansive and unruly to discipline. The establishment of a Royal Commission in 1866 to examine the allegedly intimidating tactics being used by trade unionists reflected elite fears that neither established custom nor existing law could constrain the 'outrages' of the organised working class. As this ungovernable mass began to acquire political influence, elite tolerance of its public presence began to wear thin. In his clarion call for the defence of culture against anarchy, Matthew Arnold (1867:58) painted a horrific picture of a society besieged by 'tumult and disorder, multitudinous processions in the streets of our crowded towns, multitudinous meetings in their public places and parks' and appealed to his readers to 'encourage and uphold the occupants of the executive power, whoever they may be, in firmly prohibiting them'.

Mid-nineteenth-century election campaigns were becoming increasingly turbulent. The number of contested elections escalated (doubling between the 1859 and 1865 elections), and many candidates found the cost of 'treating' the increasingly demanding electorate exorbitant. Non-voters, who had always been central to the enactment of voting rituals, were becoming more organised, assertive and demanding, turning many election periods into occasions for mass disorder and menace (Richter, 1971).

A description in *The Times* (23 June 1868) of a typical nomination day on which 'no one gets a hearing', 'heads are broken' and
'blood flows from numerous noses' was something of a caricature, but reflected well the contemporary fear of out-of-control
mobs who would destroy hierarchy and property if allowed to
intervene at the key moment of political decision. These concerns
(both material and imagined) encouraged a belief that a new culture of meditative tranquillity and intramural seclusion should
replace the festive dramaturgy of the open-air election.

The 1872 Ballot Act marks a seminal moment in the prescrip-
tive codification of political space. It served to establish a boundary which closed off the officially political from the influence
of the informally social. This kind of spatial demarcation was
characteristic of industrial modernity which established a range
of social and physical boundaries designed to mark distinctions
between authority and the everyday, prescription and proscrip-
tion and inside and outside. Activities that had once been embedded within affective repertoires of popular culture were enclosed
within new official spaces such as parks, football grounds,
schools and centres of 'rational recreation.' In turning voting into
a secret act, to be performed in a designated, official building, the
state was not simply 'protecting' voters from corrupt influence,
but closing down options to behave in ways likely to release passion. As the rituals of democratic politics were evacuated from
the streets, the voter came to be

> cut off from all his roles in the subordinate systems of the house-
> hold, the neighbourhood, the work organization, the church and
> the civil association and set to act exclusively in the abstract role
> of a citizen of the over-all system: there will be no feedback from
> what he does in this anonymous role to what he does in the other
> roles and therefore no need for him to take responsibility for the
> act of voting in his everyday interaction in his regular environ-
> ment. (Rokkan, 1970:35)

The citizen-voter created by this new political architecture was
an atomised, clandestine figure, capable of saying one thing 'on
the outside' and endorsing something else in the privacy of the
polling booth. All sorts of emotions, from hot passion to deep

shame, are rendered invisible within the dark, secret refuge of this private space from which public consequences are stealthily determined.

Alongside this process of veiling and anonymising the democratic citizen, there emerged new, sophisticated technologies designed to monitor voters as a collective body. Twentieth-century democracy paradoxically combined an obsession with concealment of the voter and surveillance of the electorate. Beyond the regulated isolation of the polling station, there emerged in the 1930s an industry devoted to extracting political secrets. Utilising the new 'science' of opinion polling, the secret choices of vast numbers of individuals were systematically probed with a view to constructing an aggregate representation of the public conscience. Gallup originally conceived the opinion poll as a technology that could replicate across distance the model of the New England Town Meeting. It was, Gallup (1938:15) believed, as if 'everyone is in one great room', cohabiting a space of pooled political consciousness. As the polling station served to regulate voting within official space, polling came to simulate the impression of a single public sharing its views under the controlled auspices of science. In both cases, politics is somehow dragged within boundaries, put in its place, subjected to the counting scrutiny of experts. The architecture of routinised democracy is protective – of secrets, of disorder, of politics itself, regarded as a mode of intrusive influence. It naturalises certain forms of political expression while foreclosing others. It contains affective political action within institutionalised spaces while smothering those that were once sites of democratic animation.

As the social performance of voting has become routinised and managed, it has become standardised. Countries wishing to be recognised as democratic – which is now the greatest symbol of national prestige, having previously been considered a subversive threat to stable statehood – must demonstrate that they conform to universal norms and practices of voting. Scrutiny of elections has emerged in recent times as a vast international industry, conferring legitimacy upon compliant states and stigmatising those failing to meet the benchmarks of effective, well-managed democracy. Since the late 1980s, and what Huntington (1993) has called 'the third wave of democracy', there has been a rapid growth of international electoral monitoring. Between 1975 and 1987, 10 per cent of elections in non-established democracies were monitored by international bodies; by 2004, more than 81 per cent of such elections were monitored (Kelley, 2008:222–3). This has responded to a growth in the number of countries holding multi-party elections for the first time: more than fifty of these took place in the single decade between 1989 and 1999 (ACE Project, 1999: 9).

States are under increasing pressure to demonstrate to the rest of the world that their power derives from legitimate voting, which, generally speaking, means the adoption of standardised norms. As Kelley (2008:223) notes,

> Regardless of whether inviting monitors signals the intent to hold free and fair elections, inviting monitors has become a norm for governments not yet under established democracy. International monitoring is part of the collection of rules and practices that define *proper election behavior* for such governments. Importantly, however, the norm is that not all governments should invite monitors: the larger goal is for states to attain democratic maturity and therefore graduate out of the practice (my emphasis).

Openness to international surveillance might be understood as a mark of apprenticeship. Governments are observed to ensure that they are capable of managing the transition from ritual to routine, from democracy dependent on the mood of the demos to bureaucratically structured voting. Advice is offered to democratising states in the form of a widely used CD-ROM on *Administration and Cost of Elections* produced by the ACE Electoral Knowledge Network (ACE, 1999) and a handbook on *Electoral Management Design* produced by the International Institute for Democracy and Electoral Assistance (IDEA, 2006). The latter sets out twelve seemingly innocuous characteristics of 'good electoral processes': 'freedom, fairness, equity, integrity, voting secrecy, transparency, effectiveness, sustainability, service-mindedness, efficiency, impartiality and accountability' (ibid:2). Conspicuously absent from this list are efficacy (evidence that voting makes a difference) and emotional satisfaction (evidence that voting relates in any ways to affective needs or desires.) The former is a sticky problem, as we shall see in the next section, because arguably most voting is not efficacious at the individual level. Urging democratising states to ensure that casting a vote might lead to a reasonable chance of effecting policy outcomes would be to seek from 'immature' democracies what 'mature' ones have never realised. The second absence is even more problematic. One could imagine the authors of the IDEA handbook responding in one of two (and possibly both) ways to this criticism: (1) it is not the job of a voting system to make people feel good about themselves; (2) even if it were, there is no way that we could monitor this. Both of these imaginary responses are rooted in the routine narrative of voting, according to which the function of this social performance is purely instrumental and not open to the kind of scrutiny that might be applied to a visit to a theatre, or an audit of job satisfaction, or the experience of eating in a particular restaurant. Once voting is routinised as an impersonal act, only meaningful in terms of aggregate outcomes, the affective experience of participation can be easily discounted. But when Garfinkel's advice to 'make trouble' is followed, such formulaic displacements come to be seen as insensitive and deleterious to meaningful democracy. One is left asking why civic affectivity is so routinely abandoned in favour of administrative effectiveness.

This theme is taken up in Matt Charman's play, *The Observer*, first staged at the National Theatre, London in May 2009. The play is set in an unnamed democratising state, governed by a president with few scruples regarding human rights. The central character is Fiona, a professional election observer, well accomplished in composing reports about the fairness or otherwise of voting procedures in democratising states. In the very first scene it is made clear that the observers' role is purely technocratic; their job is to ensure that voting conforms to international standards, regardless of the outcome. Fiona's retiring boss declares, 'The wrong man is going to win in the first round and we are going to record that it was free and fair enough and then we are going to go home' (Charman, 2009:6). During the course of voting in the first round of the election, Fiona visits a rural polling station and witnesses voters being turned away, even though many of them have walked for six miles to get there. The result of the first round is too close to call and the election goes on to a second round. It is here that Fiona is faced with a moral dilemma. If she devotes huge energy to registering more rural voters, who are likely to support the more liberal Opposition party, she may be able to influence the result. To do so would be going beyond her remit to simply observe. She would be driven by her feelings to intervene:

FIONA: People walked for six miles to vote. I've been doing this job for twelve years and I'm telling you that for the first time in what *feels* like a lifetime we can do something real here. Something genuine. That opportunity may not come again. I don't *feel* bad about taking it and neither should you. (ibid:51) (emphases added)

There is rather more feeling going on here than is proposed in the IDEA handbook on electoral management design. In a conversation with Daniel, her local interpreter, Fiona explains her reasons for feeling as she does:

FIONA: I worked for Leeds City Council. As an Election Officer. Assistant Registration and Elections Officer, actually. I was responsible amongst other things for the registration of voters.
DANIEL: Like you're trying to do now?
FIONA: It's part of what I do now, but it's different, where I come from … People don't really want to vote.
DANIEL: No one?
FIONA: Some do. But we're used to it. Bored of it. Nothing changes.
DANIEL: You wanted to make a change?
FIONA: I wanted to register people who wanted to vote. Who want to do something with their vote. In the end, at home, it's a paperwork competition. A race between colleagues. Quotas, targets.
Daniel seems unsure. Fiona moves closer and breaks off a piece of bread.
What I mean is, you're registering people but not actual voters, because most of them just won't bother to turn up on the day and in your heart of hearts you know that they won't.
DANIEL: Why won't they?

FIONA: We don't have the contrasts that you have here. Two very different men, different ideas of what the future might be. Here, other places I've been ... if you register people in a first-time election – they use it. It's like you're putting a voting slip in their hand and they didn't have it there before. It's power actually in their hands.

DANIEL: You like the way it makes you feel?

FIONA: What's wrong with that? And even if we don't register, even if we're just brought in to observe, then at least you get to observe something changing right in front of you.

DANIEL: So you do want to make a change?

FIONA: A difference. They're not the same thing.

DANIEL: And when we get bored of being able to vote, bored like Leeds, then we know we are truly democratic?

FIONA: Something like that ... (Ibid:61–2)

Several aspects of Fiona's position are deeply problematic: her imperious belief that it is her role to place power in the hands of others; her belief that having a vote is equivalent to possessing power; and her overstatement of the alienation of Leeds voters. All of these are open to a challenge. But the most forceful part of Fiona's explanation is her attempt to outline an affective rationale for caring about voting. In Leeds, she claims, 'people don't really want to vote', but in this unnamed country she wants to register people who 'want to do something with their vote'. To want is both to acknowledge what is lacking and desire what is potential. (One way of interpreting this might be in terms of a dialectic between the Lacanian theory of radical difference as a structural failure inherent to signification and the Deleuzian theory of rhizomatic synthesis which ceaselessly propels new differences into being.) To speak of not *wanting* to vote or of *wanting* to do something with a vote refers to a choice that is not merely instrumental, but is coated in affect. I might, for instance, need to vote (to protect my interests) or have to vote (because it is compulsory), but not want to do so. The distinction is one of affective disposition to absence and promise. Fiona expresses this disposition almost as if it can only be experienced once; Daniel responds, ironically, by assuming that effective democracy entails the satiation of affect and the institutionalisation of boredom. As the play concludes (with Fiona's registration campaign paying off by the defeat of the president in the second round), a hint that the routine narrative is on its way to realisation is provided by Wink, a bartender, who describes his experience of voting: 'They gave me a piece of paper. I shut a curtain and took a pen and marked a cross on the paper. I put it into a metal box that was riveted. I walked outside after that and went straight to pick up my son from school' (ibid:94).

Normality intact, the monitors can publish a positive report. The technology of voting functions.

Pathological

Narratives of deviation and pathology often serve to illuminate norms. The football team with only nine players; the planetarium with no roof; the corrupt judge; the unhip rock band; the 'conversationalist' who bores everyone around him to death; these dysfunctions, by pointing to what is missing, cast light on the meanings and maintenance of what is deemed to be normal. Too often rendered invisible by their apparent naturalness, norms are made conspicuous through their partial or non-realisation. In the case of voting, there are numerous examples of social performances going wrong, both contingently and systematically. As these pathologies are lamented, described and occasionally repaired, one is able to see what the social performance was supposed to look like.

Written in 1947 by William Douglas Home, the brother of the Conservative politician who was briefly the British prime minister from 1963 to 1964, *The Chiltern Hundreds* offers a playful account of an anomalous political situation. Set in the aftermath of the 1945 British general election, in which Labour won its historic landslide victory, the whimsical, plodding plot revolves around themes of saturnalian class inversion. The imaginary constituency of East Milton has been held by the Conservative Lister family for as long as anyone can remember. In 1945 Lord (Tony) Pym, the Lister son, is defeated by the Labour candidate, Cleghorn. Almost immediately after his defeat Pym abandons Conservatism, concluding that the Labour platform is more appropriate for the post-deferential culture of the new world. When Gleghorn is offered a Cabinet role on condition that he accepts a seat in the House of Lords, Pym decides to stand in the attendant by-election, but this time as a Labour candidate. At which point the family butler, Beecham, incorrigibly loyal to the political tradition of his masters, determines to oppose him by standing as the Conservative candidate. This is the comic narrative of the play, thinly disguising a simmering anxiety about the fluidity of social boundaries and the risks of cultural renunciation.

The Chiltern Hundreds stands alongside other social-democratic post-war fantasies, including Noel Coward's *This Happy Breed* (1947), Warren Chetham-Strode's *The Guineau Pig* (1946), Bernard Miles's *Chance of a Lifetime* (1950) and Sidney Gilliat's *Left, Right & Centre* (1959), in using the irony of inversion as a mode of coping with forebodings of cultural instability. Had they been solely didactic productions, *The Chiltern Hundreds* and its like could have been easily dismissed. It was, however, in capturing the affective challenges surrounding the anomalies of class disorder that they were most suggestive. In *The Chiltern Hundreds*, Tony Pym's drift from the certainties of Conservatism is accompanied by a sentient distancing from his American fiancé, June. The latter is an Anglophile: a woman with a large inheritance and a yearning for traditional hierarchy. There is no little irony in her urging Tony Pym to feel the insult to his class to which he seems indifferent. Indeed, Tony's new-found commitment to Labour extends to domestic labour: he calls in the maidservant, Bessie, and interrogates her about her life, the degradation of which seems to enthral him. (There are shades here of the nineteenth-century fetishist, Arthur Mumby, who derived sexual thrills from observing impoverished and powerless working women.) This combination of collapsing social boundaries, political fortunes and affective entanglements is what gives *The Chiltern Hundreds* a meaning that transcends its narrow animus. Beneath the sordid divisions of power are emotionally forged attachments. The rather contrived ending, in which Beecham, having defeated his master by thirty votes, resigns the seat and announces his intention to marry Bessie, is Home's heavy-handed attempt to repair the anomaly: the traditional power-holder acquires the seat, albeit against the will of the local voters; the servants are bound in squalid romance; and, of course, Pym is reunited with June – a winning coalition of new and old money, ancient and modern empire, interest and feeling securely enfettered.

Were all deviations from the performative norm as easily resolved, the anomalous narrative of voting would not be nearly as significant as it is. According to most political theorists, however, voting as a way of determining social choice is inevitably blighted by the impossibility of devising a mechanism that converts individual preferences into a fair and meaningful representation of the popular will (Buchanan, 1954; Black, 1958; Arrow, 1963; Sen and Pattaniak, 1969; Breton, 1974; McLean, 1982; Hardin, 1982; Riker, 1982). Thus problematised, vote-counting approaches to democracy can be seen as trapped within a series of paradoxes: Why should anyone bother to vote if individual votes hardly ever make any difference? Why become an informed voter when the costs of doing so are high and other citizens are likely to express your will just as well as you could yourself? Why should voting be regarded as fair if the method of ordering and counting preferences is more important in defining the general will than are voters' original preferences? As Coleman and Ferejohn (1986:13) have succinctly put it, 'The meaning of social choice can be reconstructed in terms of the interplay of the data base and the decision rule... the "will" that is revealed by a social choice is as much a function of the method of choice as of the initial profile from which the choice emerges.' Given that individual voters have control over neither the database (to which they contribute just one datum amongst many) nor the decision rule (which is decided before an election is called), why should they think of the act of voting as a path to empowerment?

There are two common theoretical responses to the question of why citizens bother to vote in the face of these barriers to democratic outcomes. One, most famously argued by Downs, is that rational citizens realise that mass abstention would result in the breakdown of electoral democracy, so they participate in order to maintain the democratic political system as a collective good, even though they might have no faith in the procedures by which the popular will is determined (Downs, 1957; Riker and Ordershook, 1968). This rationale seems odd: Why would people value a regime which they do not believe to represent their interests, preferences and values? And yet, when we turn to the empirical evidence in later chapters (especially Chapter 5), there does seem to be a good deal of such thinking amongst voters. Many citizens feel an obligation to vote, even though they do not expect their votes to count for much.

A second common response to the so-called voting paradox is to assume that many citizens do not really intend to act instrumentally when they cast a vote. They are engaged in an expressive act. As Schuessler (2000:91) puts it, 'An expressively motivated individual ... performs *X* not to generate or do *Y*, but to be an *X*-performer'. The benefits of this kind of expressive voting performance are existential rather than instrumental. Rather than seeking to realise a tangible objective, such as the rule of a particular party or higher expenditure on certain services, expressive voters act with a view to asserting their own political identity or uniting with a community of imagined others who share their values. Dowding (2005:12) has criticised this response, suggesting that if voters really were expressively motivated, it would surely not matter to them whether their votes were counted or not, and very few voters manifest such indifference. Nonetheless, the empirically charted rise of what Inglehart (1977 and 1997) has called 'post-materialist' voters, who are less interested in pursuing their own interests than expressing their social values, could be understood as evidence of declining plebiscitary instrumentalism.

Both of these responses to the paradox of rational-choice voting suggest that something more is going on at the ballot box than the uncovering of a pre-existing general will by electoral technologies of excavation and revelation. Indeed, it may be that, rather than disclosing what is there, within the 'public mind', the function of voting is to construct what is not there: the public itself. In this sense, the social performance does not serve to show what the public thinks, but that there is such a thing as the public. It is a means of conjuring the public into existence, of constructing that which can then be disclosed. According to this theory, most famously propounded by Lefort, the main function of the social performance of voting is the formation of a mass subject which comes to imagine and recognise itself through the quantifiable process of aggregation. In such situations, people find themselves curiously sucked into a collective imagined status (the British electorate, 'my fellow Americans', Northern Irish Catholics, Kashmiri Muslims) through which they are revealed 'on the level of phantasy' as 'an image of the People-as-One' (Lefort, 1986:303).

So conceived, the social performance of voting presents citizens with a number of risks: of being made to appear part of a univocal public which does not represent who they really are or how they really feel; of being given a name to which they do not wish to answer; and of being misled into opposing their true interests. In no historical moment were these dangers disclosed more vividly than in the electoral victory of the German National Socialist (Nazi) party in 1933. That such a criminal and genocidal regime could have been legitimised by millions of vote-casting citizens calls attention to the risk that electoral majorities might sanction forms of self-imposed tyranny. Historians have shown beyond doubt that, after they were street thugs and before they were dictators, the National Socialists ran a well-oiled electoral machine, dedicated above all else to winning votes from a population with diverse problems and interests (Brown, 1982; Childers, 1983; O'Loughlin, Flint and Anslein, 1994; King et al., 2008). The party's strategic appeal to voters in the 1930s was highly sophisticated, ensuring that different messages reached key interest groups and that its most sinister visions were concealed from voters who would be disturbed by their radicalism. The Nazi election victory in 1933 was by no means a clean affair – violence and fear were by then pervasive features of Weimar politics – but neither was it a coup d'état. After Hitler, democratic theorists were compelled to reflect on the potential pathologies of mass public judgement, and doubt began to be cast upon the normative claim that majority rule was a secure guarantor of pluralistic liberal democracy.

Since the late nineteenth century, social theorists, witnessing the rise of mass, urbanised, enfranchised populations, had been fearfully reflecting on the extent to which unrestrained public emotions could undermine rational collective action. Most famously, Gustave Le Bon (1895:5) had argued that '[t]he substitution of the unconscious action of crowds for the conscious activity of individuals is one of the principal characteristics of the present age'. The condescendingly defined 'masses' came to be the focus of a deep sociological anxiety. Depicted as a moving bundle of raw emotions, mesmeric in their suggestibility, contagious in their viral irrationalism and irresponsible in their collective anonymity, crowds and masses evaded the disciplinary ethos of hierarchical rule by feeling themselves to be beyond control. Coinciding with the emergence of the mass franchise, these anxieties can be read two ways: as a generalised fear of the politically emergent *demos* or as the expression of an imagined dichotomy between the dutiful, peaceful, rationalised electorate and its doppelgänger – the affectively charged, inchoate crowd. Understood in this latter sense, plebiscitary democracy performs the function of maintaining emotional continence.

Post-fascist political theorists have been haunted by the spectre of mass irrationalism. The untamed affectivity of the multitude has led some political theorists to sense a permanent tension between democracy and liberalism and even to argue for forms of qualified or managed democracy, whereby the will of voters is only allowed to become mandatory if it satisfies stipulated conditions of public reason (Habermas, 1996). More than any other critic of majoritarian pathology, Carl Schmitt (1985:15) has argued explicitly that liberalism, with its emphasis on parliamentary deliberation, and democracy, as the expression of a mandatory popular will, are antithetical conditions: 'Against the will of the people, an institution based on discussion by independent representatives has no autonomous justification for its existence'. Schmitt's argument is based on a particular definition of democracy – one in which the public arrives at a consentient and univocal status, akin to Rousseau's notion of the General Will. Schmitt sees democracy, in this specific sense, as a threat that liberalism cannot withstand, for its claim that the legitimate source of political authority can only be derived from those over whom it is wielded denies the possibility for institutions such as parliament to perform an intermediary role in the movement between public will and public policy.

In dichotomising liberalism and democracy, Schmitt (1985:9) is proposing that the latter depends on 'homogeneity and ... elimination or eradication of heterogeneity'. If, as I have suggested, the point of the democratic vote is not to discover the will of an ontologically pre-existing public, but to construct the public as a democratic entity, the need to found such a construction on the principles of liberal pluralism is surely essential. For, as Mouffe (1999:51) has argued:

> Democratic politics does not consist in the moment when a fully constituted people exercises its rule. The moment of rule is indissociable from the very struggle about the definition of the people, about the constitution of its identity. Such an identity, however, can never be fully constituted, and it can exist only by multiple and competing forms of *identification*. Liberal democracy is precisely the recognition of this constitutive gap between the people and its various identifications.

Schmitt's conception of democracy as an illiberal political pathology is more applicable to what most political theorists describe as populism. As Canovan (1999) has astutely demonstrated, populism emerges from a tension within democratic thought between what she calls redemptive and pragmatic perspectives. The former sees politics as a means to salvation, whereas the latter sees it as a mode of coping with disagreement through rules and practices; the former focuses on popular power as the source of legitimate authority; the latter places greater emphasis on democracy as one particular way to administer a polity; the former is romantic and anti-institutional; the latter sees power as constituted by and within institutions. Populism, argues Canovan, operates within the inevitable gap between these two aspects of democratic ambiguity. Pathological narratives of voting, framed by fears of populism and illiberal majoritarianism, assume that publics cannot resist the allure of populism, that electorates are embryonic crowds of the Le Bonist imagination, under constant pressure from affective urges liable to disrupt or overthrow political reason. In its extreme form, this narrative becomes neurotic, seeking to defend democracy against the recklessness of the *demos*, in the spirit of Brecht's wry observation that perhaps the government ought to elect a new people. It is ultimately a shaming and degrading narrative, a relentlessly chiding whisper in the ear of citizens, reminding them of just how often they have got it all wrong.

3

Memories of the Ballot Box

> Memory, insofar as it is affective and magical, only accommo-
> dates those facts that suit it; it nourishes recollections that may
> be out of focus or telescopic, global or detached, particular or
> symbolic.... Memory takes root in the concrete, in spaces, ges-
> tures, images, and objects; history binds itself strictly to temporal
> continuities, to progressions and to relations between things.
>
> (Pierre Nora, 'Between Memory and History: *Les Lieux de
> Memoire*, 1989)

> Memory (the deliberate act of remembering) is a form of willed
> creation. It is not an effort to find out the way it really was – that
> is research. The point is to dwell on the way it appeared and why
> it appeared in that particular way.
>
> (Toni Morrison, 'Memory, Creation and Writing', 1984)

To be a democratic citizen is to belong to a community of memories. There is much to remember: what is law, what is custom,
what is taboo; the professed differences between political parties;
acknowledged repertoires of protest and affirmation; the names
of the historically iconic and demonic; and countless mundane
enactments of civic fidelity. Less explicitly, there also is much to
forget: the routine amnesia around which the stability of shared
statehood revolves (Renan, 1882/1990:11).

The heavy burden of civic memory is painfully illustrated in
the UK government's *Life in the UK Test* which all applicants to

become British citizens are required to take. Amidst a range of 'facts' that would-be citizens are called upon to memorise are the year in which married women gained the right to divorce their husbands, the name of the French protestant sect that fled to Britain in the sixteenth and seventeenth centuries to escape religious persecution, the date of St George's Day, the role of parliamentary Whips, the title of the monarch within the Church of England, the number of member states of the Commonwealth and the purpose of the Council of Europe. (How many Home Office ministers, justices of the peace, public school headmasters, newsreaders, professors of political communication or immigration officials could answer these questions 'correctly' is a matter for speculation.) Test applicants are informed that they will have 45 minutes to answer 24 multiple-choice questions and that they must correctly answer 18 (75 per cent) to pass.

In making the assimilation of random knowledge a qualification for national membership, citizenship is effectively constituted as an act of memory. To be 'one of us' is to enter into an imaginary relationship with an acquired past. The community of shared affinity becomes a community of adopted reminiscences in which official history is severed from experiential biography. This is precisely the phenomenon to which Nora alludes in his magisterial account of the historical disjuncture

> between true memory, which has taken refuge in gestures and habits, in skills passed down by unspoken traditions, in the body's inherent self-knowledge, in unstudied reflexes and ingrained memories, and memory transformed by its passage through history, which is nearly the opposite: voluntary and deliberate, experienced as a duty, no longer spontaneous; psychological, individual and subjective; but never social, collective or all-encompassing.
> (Nora, 1989:13)

Late modernity is pervaded by a casual forgetfulness. Institutionalised commemoration, in the form of 'invented traditions' (Hobsbawm and Ranger, 1992), public museums, televised reconstructions and kitch souvenirs, has come to displace collective memory as the social repository of affective experience. Halbwachs (1992:38), who famously observed that 'it is in society that people normally acquire their memories' and 'recall, recognize and localize their memories', set out to distinguish collective memory from other notions of individual cognitive or psychoanalytical memory. Rejecting the idea that memories are preserved 'in some nook of my mind to which I alone have access', Halbwachs regarded memories as relational effects, irreducible to internalised notions of mind or soul. As Connerton (1989:36) has put it:

> Every recollection, however personal it may be, even that of events of which we alone were the witness, even that of thoughts and sentiments that remain unexpressed, exists in relationship with a whole ensemble of notions which many others possess: with persons, places, dates, words, forms of language, that is to say, with the whole material and moral life of the societies of which we are part or of which we have been part.

The relevance of this conceptualisation to the social performance of voting need not be laboured. When people try to think of voting as a practice and themselves as voters, they are drawn to resources of recall that are both deeply personal (often secretive) behaviour and culturally transmitted. Images, feelings, smells and idioms evoked by memories of the vote reflect a curious intermingling of the barely experienced, the mediated, the imagined, the inferred and the unconsciously ingested. Both pregnant with symbolic meaning and abated by vacuity, memories of voting layer social narratives upon discrete biographies, engendering alchemies of affect that exceed any formal definition of what is being recalled.

Not so for those taking the UK government's *Life in the UK Test*. They are required to memorise a number of 'facts' about voting, in preparation for their admission to the ranks of the counted. When are local government elections held? Which voting system is used to elect the Scottish Parliament and Welsh Assembly? When were women over thirty given the right to vote? What must a candidate achieve in order to win their constituency? These multiple-choice questions studiously avoid matters of feeling. Like the very worst kinds of sex education, they stick to the technical by abstracting the motive from the act. The result is a form of mnemonic citizenship which locks the initiate into an embrace with a borrowed past.

Memory, as a mode of orienting personal sensibility and sense-making to the contingency and indeterminacy of time, mediates between personal experience and the lived experience of others, many of whom we shall never meet and could never meet because they are distant from us or dead. As Ricoeur (2004:58) puts it, 'With remembering, the emphasis is placed on the return to awakened consciousness of an event recognized as having occurred before the moment when consciousness declares having experienced, perceived, learned it'. But why do some memories endure and not others? Ricoeur (2003:427) suggests that this is because of 'the passive persistence of first impressions: an event has struck us, touched us, affected us, and the affective mark remains in our mind'. We know too little about how these 'first impressions' endure and are erased, how 'affective marks' inscribe the act of voting in particular (and democratic citizenship more generally), and how the extent to which democracy, as a political system, is sustainable without full acknowledgement of these visceral traces.

The remainder of this chapter explores these questions by focussing on two themes: the nature of the multifaceted relationship between memory and voting, and the ways in which talk about voting can be read as a civic performance, *involving both onstage and offstage actors.*

Voting and/as Memory

Forgetfulness and False Memory

The 2008 U.S. election, culminating in the victory of the country's first black president, was a landmark event. Yet more than a third of the eligible population (36 per cent) did not cast a vote. Asked in a post-election survey why they abstained, 2.6 per cent of non-voters stated that they had *forgotten* to vote. Similar acts of forgetfulness are regularly reported in most other countries. For example, the UK Electoral Commission found that 6 per cent of abstainers 'forgot to vote' in the May 2003 local elections. (Forgetting is only one reason given by non-voters; others include not being 'interested in politics', not having 'any information' and seeing 'no point' in voting.)

At the same time, in the aftermath of most elections in most countries, significant numbers of people claim to remember having voted when they actually had not done so. That is to say, the number of people accounting for how they voted when asked after the election exceeds the number who actually cast votes. Karp and Brockington (2005:825) have noted that 'the gap between official turnout in presidential elections and reported turnout in the American National Election Studies (ANES) is over 20 percentage points'. The gap between actual turnout and post-election survey claims is around 26 per cent in Britain, 35 per cent in Norway and 42 per cent in New Zealand (Karp and Brockington, 2005:830) These are significant acts of forgetfulness and false memory, suggesting that complex issues are at stake which cannot be explained by the conventional paradigms of political science. It is to the intricacies of affectivity that we must turn if we are to understand what is going on.

When non-voters say that they 'forgot' to vote, some will mean that they had an intention which went out of their head (rather like forgetting to buy an item when out shopping), whereas others will really mean 'I didn't *feel like* voting.' They were aware that it was an option and may or may not have intended to take it up, but when it came to it, the intention was of such low salience that no action was taken. Like people who 'meant' to give blood or write a letter to a newspaper, negative feelings at the time that the action could have been taken were more powerful than original intentions. Feelings are not easily captured by political science research methods. Consider the following (fictitious) statements in which the phrase 'didn't feel like' can be substituted for 'forgot':

> I recorded the final of *Britain's Got Talent*, but I forgot to watch it for a month and finally deleted the recording.
>
> I keep forgetting to look at the poster in the local library to see who won the local election. I've been in there several times, but I just keep forgetting about it.

I promised to go on the demonstration. When I woke up that morning, I forgot all about it.

These are not statements about cognitive recall. The first is not claiming that the task of remembering to watch a recorded talent show was more than the brain could manage. A critical response to all three of these statements would be something like: 'But you could have remembered if you really wanted to'. In the case of the Obama election, eligible voters were subjected to more media messages than had been transmitted in any previous election. It would have been almost impossible to have missed the symbolic significance of Election Day. But for those non-voters who 'forgot', a statement was being made – a performance enacted, one might say – suggesting that their feelings outweighed their intentions or others' intentions for them. Survey research cannot capture these feelings. Only expansive, open-ended interviews of a kind that political scientists rarely conduct could hope to get at the nature of these feelings. It could be, for example, that 'forgetfulness' was a defence against the likelihood of disappointment; far from having little interest in the election, those who 'forget' about it feel a need to guard against the intensity of their frustrated desires. Alternatively, it might be that 'forgetting' refers tacitly to the shame of being under-informed – that the dutiful intention to vote was overcome by a dutiful forgetfulness as a means of preventing irresponsible voting. These are speculations about forgetful voters. The only way to know more is to ask them. Even then, memory is slippery, and it may be that what people did not feel like doing on Election Day is re-articulated as something else after the event. Indeed, even at the time of acting or non-acting, it is not easy for any of us to be wholly clear about our motives. But once the object of investigation moves from the linear rationality of instrumentalist actions to the messy performativity of affective explanations, there is at least some scope for arriving at a more nuanced account of political motivation.

Rather more has been published within the political science literature about over-reporting: non-voters who claim to have voted. Two explanations are commonly offered, both entirely dependent on affective motives. The first is that people do not

tell the truth to survey researchers about having voted because
they are embarrassed; their reputation as a good citizen is at
stake, so they claim to have performed a dutiful civic act when
they had not really done so (Presser, 1990). Such face-saving
strategies make sense, although it seems odd that over-reporting
even occurs in on-line surveys, when there is no direct contact
between the respondent and an individual questioner. A second
explanation for over-reporting is that people imagine that they
have voted because they are thinking about voting in general
rather than a specific vote cast in a particular electoral context
(Belli et al., 1999). Social psychologists refer to this phenomenon as source-monitoring, whereby 'events that are only imagined may become remembered as actually having occurred, when
particular aspects of the imaginary experience are not reliable
indicators of its source' (ibid:91; see also Johnson et al., 1993).
It is quite likely that a combination of both factors – social desirability and source monitoring – are combined in the case of vote
over-reporting: non-voters are concerned to be seen to have done
'the right thing' and, in recalling past occasions when they had
actually voted or intended to vote or talked about voting, they
feel as if they have engaged in the social performance of voting.
From the perspective of affective interpretation, this is a compelling phenomenon because it suggests that voting is rather
more than an isolated, instrumental act. For vote over-reporters,
the generalised cultural experience of being counted as a voter
might be more memorable than the singular moment of casting
one vote.

There is one further social-psychological phenomenon that
might add to our understanding of the ways in which people
remember or forget about voting. Political events are remembered best when they are the subject of shared emotions. If an
event is (1) emotionally affecting and (2) discussed with someone
else, it is much more likely to be remembered for a long time
afterwards. People are most likely to talk to others about events
that impinge upon them emotionally, and the more they engage
in such emotional sharing, the longer the event is likely to stay in
their memory. One kind of event that social psychologists have

found give rise to particularly vivid and enduring memories are referred to as 'flash bulb memories' (Brown and Kulik, 1977; Finkenauer et al., 1998). These are events, usually learned about through mediated news, that are shocking, world-changing and collectively acknowledged, such as the assassination of JFK or the attacks of 9/11. A key to such memories is that people recall where they were at the time in relation to other people; they are intersubjectively constructed and rehearsed through social repetition. The act of voting possesses none of the characteristics likely to produce such an enduring memory: it is rarely emotionally affecting at the time; it is often not discussed with others, even after the event; and it is unlikely to be conceived as shocking or world-changing. In short, the social performance of voting is almost the opposite of a flash-bulb memory; it is highly forgettable. The end result of voting – the election of a government – is sometimes more like a source of flashbulb memory. The 1945 Labour landslide; Margaret Thatcher quoting Thomas Aquinas before she entered Ten Downing Street in 1979; Tory ministers losing their seats in 1997 – paradoxically, voters are more likely to have a memory of 'being there' when they had watched these events on film or television than when they were physically present in the vicinity of the ballot box. Dayan and Katz's (1992) account of 'media events' captures the sense in which memories such as these are not simply records of behaviour enacted, but accumulated stories of feelings experienced, often through 'mediated quasi-interaction' (Thompson, 1995:84).

Memory as a Political Resource

Election campaigns are rhetorical assaults on memory. Political strategists compete to claim responsibility for positive and popular historical developments and associate their rivals with all that was wrong in the past. The British Conservative leader David Cameron's attempt to 'decontaminate' his party's image by distancing it from the spectre of Thatcherism and Tony Blair's earlier project to exorcise his party's proletarian origins by rechristening it 'New Labour' are illustrations of the importance that politicians attach to the shaping of mnemonic connections.

Voters are called upon to perform prodigious acts of memory in judging the validity of the countless claims and counterclaims, records and fabrications, images and caricatures that are cast before them. Despite the vast media resources devoted to the dissemination and explanation of political news, however, the findings of much empirical research suggest that few citizens can remember very much about what candidates, parties or governments stand for or have done (Berelson et al., 1954; Markus and Converse, 1979; Converse, 2000; Bartels, 1996; Delli Carpini and Keeter, 1996; Schudson, 2000; Mutz, 2002; Gilens, 2005; Prior, 2007). Ferejohn's (1990:3) observation that 'nothing strikes the student of public opinion and democracy more forcefully than the paucity of information most people possess about politics' would not be disputed by many political scientists.

Making choices as voters entails evaluative information processing – the selection, recall and judgement of stored evidence about policies, parties and candidates – but this is often undermined by cognitive and evaluative constraints (Lodge et al., 1989:400) which serve to rationalise recall to fit in with prior beliefs and current attitudes. In short, far from information processing comprising the rational sorting of dispassionate memories, it involves a response to affective signals which define the terms of recall. Although most of the early studies of political information processing tended to have a pronounced cognitive emphasis, seeking to explore how much voters can remember and how heuristics might create conditions of low-information rationality, there has been a recent move towards understanding the evaluative process as a product of affectivity. As Lodge and Taber (2005:256) put it: 'Feelings become information. Affect imbues the judgment process from start to finish – from the encoding of information, its retrieval and comprehension, to its expressions a preference or choice'.

The most influential theory of affective information processing to date is the impression-driven voter choice model – also known as the on-line model. In contrast with the memory-based model, which suggests that voters collect a vast repertoire of information which they weigh up rationally when deciding how to vote, the impression-driven model assumes that most political information people encounter will be forgotten – that is to say, buried in long-term memory and rarely recalled. While specific items of information do not endure, the affective memory of the feelings evoked by them do endure within what Lodge et al. (1989:401) refer to as an 'evaluation counter' or 'judgment tally'. The cumulative impressions left by these affective responses remain within short-term – or working – memory and serve as an efficient guide to the formation and expression of personal voter choices. So, according to the impression-driven model, the cognitive failures that are so lamented by psychologists and political scientists who equate citizenship with mnemonic accomplishment do not matter very much because affect-laden memory provides voters with all that they need to arrive at meaningful decisions. Far from undermining or displacing cognitive rationality, argue Lodge and Taber (2005:476), the impression-driven model 'may provide *high information rationality*' in the sense that affective memory encapsulates and distils the most impressive and poignant traces of personal experience, and it is these that enable voters to act upon their most important thoughts and feelings. Indeed, Marcus and Mackuen (1993:691) contend that, 'Rather than being antagonistic or detrimental to citizenship, emotion enhances the ability of voters to perform their citizenly duties'.

Whether or not the 'duties' of citizenship are enhanced by reliance on affective memory (a question that can only be answered simply if such duties are deemed to be clear and enhanced quality an uncontested effect), the results of a series of experiments conducted in the past two decades seem to have confirmed that when voters use memory as a political resource, they rarely do so in a rational-instrumentalist fashion. On the contrary, voters act upon a range of stimuli ranging from the neurophysiological (messages of anxiety or enthusiasm generated by different parts of the brain's limbic system) to the degree of congruence between message perceivers' moods and the affective tone of message senders. Dependence on stimuli such as candidates' facial expressions or their 'likeability factor' is vulnerable to the derision of cognitivists who regard affective memory as a pathway to incidental and superficial information, far from the rich combinations of historical data and ideological perspective stored in the mind of their idealised voter.

However, even when considering those motivational factors which drive the ideological attachments and investments of more politically sophisticated voters, there is strong evidence to suggest a correlation between subscription to belief systems and powerful affective dispositions. Adorno et al.'s (1950) intuition that an individual's belief system 'reflects his [sic] personality', and that there is a 'structural unity' between affective propensities and ideological convictions, is supported by a wide range of psychological research, mainly conducted in the past two decades (Haidt, 2001; Duckitt et al., 2002; Block and Block, 2006; Jost, Ledgerwood and Hardin, 2008; Federico and Goren, 2009). In a comprehensive review of this research, Jost, Frederico and Napier (2009:315) point to the limitations of theories of political communication which focus on the top-down flow of ideological messages from elites to citizens. Ideology, they argue, 'can be thought of as having both a discursive (socially constructed) superstructure and a functional (or motivational) substructure'. Put simply, the discursive superstructure comprises a range of social representations offered to voters, typically by political elites, and the motivational substructure refers to the 'ideo-affective resonance' (Tomkins, 1963) evoked in particular people by the messages they receive. Jost et al. (2009:318) suggest that 'at least three major classes of psychological variables comprise the motivational substructure of political ideology: epistemic, existential and relational motives'. Summarised rather simplistically here, epistemic motives for ideological take-up include the needs for clarity, certainty and closure in a complex and confusing world or a desire for sensation seeking and political experimentation; existential motives give people a sense of value in the world, help them to come to terms with their own mortality and cope with perceptions of personal danger; and relational motivations explain ideological beliefs absorbed during childhood, transmitted by parents to children and local environment to individual actor.

The relevance of all of this to the relationship between memory and the social performance of voting is twofold. Firstly, by abandoning a narrowly cognitivist conception of civic competence, which, as Schattschneider (1960:136) notes, dwells upon 'the ignorance and stupidity of the masses', it becomes possible to see voter memory as a psychologically cavernous, intellectually protean phenomenon rather than something reducible to a quiz score. Secondly, in line with Bourdieu's important notion of *habitus* as a system of transposable dispositions which mediate between social structure and personal behaviour, affective political memory can be seen as a means of constituting and inscribing the citizen. The cognitivist reduction of memory to a record of empirical data (that which the citizen needs to recall in order to vote correctly) has limited value compared with the recognition that individuals are shaped as citizens by conscious and subliminal memories of their own political socialisation. In this sense, the voters' memory has less to tell them about how they should vote than why or how they should vote. For it is through the imperceptible inculcation of civic belonging that the voter is actualised.

Being Re-membered

Although voting appears to be a furtive, muted, atomistic act, intended to be inconspicuous and untraceable, the very point of the exercise is to be noticed. Fears of votes being cast and then lost, ignored or untallied, frustrations about electoral systems that 'waste' votes or attach more weight to some than others and suspicions about 'smoked-filled rooms' in which deals are made behind the backs of the voters are all manifestations of a tacit anxiety underlying democracy: that power, while seeming to be up for grabs, is in reality impervious to the public's will. The democratic imagination inhabits a metaphorical space, marked by the axial boundary between 'inside' and 'outside'. Only those fortunate enough to be 'within' rather than 'beyond' can hope to be counted.

To be an outsider is to be forgotten, to be denied access to the enfranchising code of citizenship. Outsiders are those deemed to be too incompetent, immoral, immature or exotic to achieve the rights of citizenship. The failed applicants for UK citizenship, who score less than 75 per cent on the government's *Life in the UK Test*, become certified outsiders, free to linger at the fringes of citizenship but never to cast a counted vote. To be an insider is to be named as a member of the public, to be issued with the two most precious symbolic tokens of citizenship: a passport (Torpey, 2000) and a vote. Insiders are counted: counted in with a birth certificate and passport; counted out with a death certificate; and counted while in through periodic votes – the heartbeats of vital citizenship.

This affective bond, which links the individual body to the body politic, depends on regular maintenance for its stability. Most of the time, citizenship is sustained at a banal cultural level (Billig, 1995), through prompts and allusions towards the nomenclature, symbols and protocols of belonging. But there are also extraordinary moments of civic affirmation, and voting is surely one of them. Voting is an act of civic remembrance: it is to be re-membered in the sense of renewing one's subscription to the polity in the confidence of being recognised and counted. Without this recognition, both the individual and the culture are damaged; the former through the insult and injury of misrecognition; the latter through the collapse of an intersubjective foundation for arriving at common meanings and resolutions. For voting to succeed as re-membering, an expectation of reciprocal recognition must obtain.

What leads people to believe that voting will result in recognition? What happens when it manifestly does not? Does the desire to be recognised overcome the experience of being misrecognised or disrespected? In what ways does casting a vote have the effect of making one's preferences, interests and values count? How do people learn to value this social performance as an emblem of self-worth and democratic significance? What is the relationship between the spaces and rituals of voting and the cultivation of feelings of recognition and political dignity? How do people cope when they cease to be charmed by the efficacy of voting? Are there modes and subjects of voting that people yearn to experience? How does it feel once the vote has been cast, the result announced and history resumes its regular beat? Are there other ways of counting than having one's vote counted? These rarely posed, but vital, questions are the subject of the interviews reported in the following chapters.

Deciphering that testimony calls for an approach to memory that focuses less on the linearity of indexical recollection than on the circulation of affects. The political scientist's ideal mnemonic citizen, who always remembers to vote, makes decisions based on a synoptic appraisal of the political record and can respond to the searching interrogations of opinion pollsters, is a rare beast. When people are encouraged to reflect on their experience of voting, their memories are expressed in fragmentary, enigmatic, hesitant, confused and counterfactual ways. The image of the voter that emerges is always half-formed and overshadowed by surrounding moods, events, desires and regrets. In short, talk about voting is rarely just talk about voting; for, as Toni Morrison (1984:235) reminds us, 'Because so much in public and scholarly life forbids us to take seriously the milieu of buried stimuli, it is often extremely hard to seek out both the stimulus and its galaxy and to recognise their value when they arrive'. The task of interpretation is to appreciate how particular milieu inflects specific acts; how the dialectic of stimulus and galaxy shape memory and flavour affect. It is this interpretive project to which we now turn.

The Interview as a Performance of Citizenship

'The Road to Voting' is the title of a three-year research project funded in 2007 by the UK Arts and Humanities Research Council (AHRC). The rationale for this research was that moments of mass voting are central to the experience of being a contemporary citizen, but little is known about this experience. While the right to vote remains the most symbolically significant characteristic of contemporary liberal democracies, we know little about the affective and aesthetic aspects of voting as a social act. The research project was conceived as having two stages: the first would entail talking to voters – gaining access to their memories, stories, anxieties, pleasures and aspirations; the second (reported and enacted in other published, performed and exhibited works) was to produce four artistic outputs (a play, a film, an installation and an archive), each intended to translate and reflect on the data gathered during the first stage.

This two-stage division of labour carried with it an implicit risk: that the social-scientific phase would somehow be expected to deliver a corpus of scientifically legitimate, reality-revealing data that could then be illuminated, embellished and aestheticised through the mysteries of the creative imagination. If we were to resist a banal dichotomy between social scientificity (facts) and the creative arts (imagination), it was vital to confront the illusion that the interviews conducted in the first phase could encapsulate raw or objective truth. Given that a fundamental intention of the project was to render traditionally estranged disciplines more legible to one another through the development of intertwined and porous research practices, it was important from the outset to acknowledge the sense in which attempts to access public memory are performative, insofar as they enact representations that come to shape social reality. Social scientists can never simply describe the world as it is, but, through their choice of questions, methods and interpretations, contribute to the construction and classification of social reality. Law and Urry (2004:391) claim that research methods are inherently performative: 'they have effects; they make differences; they enact realities; and they can help to bring into being what they also discover.' In saying this, they are not suggesting that social reality is merely a by-product of methodology, but that 'reality is a relational effect' which 'is produced and stabilized in interaction that is simultaneously material and social' (Law and Urry, 2004:395)

A principal aim of 'The Road to Voting' project was to illuminate these relational effects by making it apparent that the collection and analysis of voting memories are dependent on forms of enactment; that both creative artists and social scientists act on the representations that they seem to be apprehending, interfusing empirical and aesthetic strategies in their pursuit of the real.

Rather than seeing this as a disruptive blurring of boundaries, I found that I gained most from these interviews in moments when personal memory and social performance were most weakly distinguishable. Schechner (2002:22) describes these as moments of 'twice-behaved behavior' – or 'restored behavior': 'performed actions that people train to do, that they practice and rehearse'. These reiterations and repetitions are improvised through memory, never quite the same each time they are enacted, but bound together in their variation by a performative commitment to working on what has already happened. Restored behaviour is, in Shelley's (1821) terms, 'the curse which binds us to be subjected to the accident of surrounding impressions' – those feelings that are 'blunted by reiteration.' The remainder of this chapter reflects on three senses in which interviewees' memories of voting discussed in the following chapters were characterised by restored or twice-behaved behaviour. First, the interview, as a means of disclosing raw and authentic experience, will be problematised. How far can the direct testimonies of interviewees be understood as representing the real? This question is confounded by the use of such testimony in 'The Road to Voting' project as a basis for a 'verbatim theatre' performance. If the first recording of memory is already rehearsed and restored, what is its retelling as a stage performance? What are the implications of these repeated performances for claims of realism? Second, the ways in which interviewees, when asked to speak as voters, came to perform as citizens, will be explored as an example of the performative power of memory. Third, there is the glaring question of the interviewer's presence, a performance that has been years, perhaps decades, in subliminal rehearsal.

Enacting the Interview

Memory-based research is beset by the myth of mimetic representation. The belief that there is an original moment, sensation, image or idea that can be conjured into existence through the power of recall sets up an ideal that is always bound to be unrealized, because 'memory, so far from being merely a passive receptacle or storage system, an image bank of the past, is rather an active, shaping force' (Samuel, 1994:x). Even the most 'scientifically rigorous' techniques for capturing and analysing memories are destined to produce stories that create rather than reproduce the past.

Research interviews, as rhetorical situations in which people meet artificially and verbal exchange is dominated by the pre-meditated intentions of an interviewer, are performances in which telling and listening take place, with the teller's agenda shaped by the listener who will later become the reteller of what he thinks he heard. While scrupulous attention to representa-tive sampling, ethical consent, accurate transcription and critical analysis are essential to both evidential plausibility and scientific credibility, the interview is always an event set up and conducted with a purpose in mind – a purpose which is far clearer to the interviewer than to the interviewees. As techniques for eliciting public experience and knowledge, interviews have to be pro-duced. Somebody has to think of organising them, decide to ask particular questions, select the interviewees, set up the room in a particular fashion and determine when the event has performed its purpose. However chatty and sociable the interview atmo-sphere may seem to feel, it is not a naturally occurring conversa-tion and should not be mistaken for one.

Conducted insensitively, the research interview can become an exercise in memory plunder. Once given, interviewees' tes-timonies are no longer their own, but are reduced to data to be tagged by the standardising codification of tacit positivism. Interviewees are turned into compound entities, describable as types rather than as inhabitants of particular times, places and bodies. Qualitative analysis software, employed crudely, as it too often is, confounds this degradation by coding only the relation-ship between stimulus (interview questions) and memory (tran-scribed responses), without acknowledging the ways in which both are dialectically co-produced through the contingencies of communication – and also miscommunication.

From the outset, it was clear that the project of interviewing people about their memories of voting was surrounded by risks. Firstly, this was not a subject that most people would have chosen to talk about of their own accord. There was a sense in which the subject was imposed upon them. (Interviewees were paid to participate). Even those who were interested in politics were more likely to be interested in talking about how they arrived at their voting *choice* rather than how they experienced the voting *act*. It was important not to force a singular meaning upon the topic of 'voting', rewarding interviewees with encouragement when they 'got it' and steering them back to base when they dared to make unanticipated connections. When people tell their own stories they never start from scratch. They offer citational narratives, replete with rehearsed utterances. Bakhtin's (1981:293–4) understanding of the socio-ideological dimensions of imposed meaning is relevant here:

> The word in language is half someone else's It becomes 'one's own' only when the speaker populates it with his own intention, his own accent, when he appropriates the word, adapting it to his own semantic and expressive intention. Prior to this moment of appropriation, the word does not exist in a neutral and impersonal language (it is not, after all, out of a dictionary that the speaker gets his words!), but rather it exists in other people's mouths, in other people's contexts, serving other people's intentions; it is from there that one must take the word, and make it one's own.

Making this happen entailed allowing interviewees to find their own way to the subject of voting. Rather than coaxing from them reiterative performances in which the taken-for-granted nature of voting translates into prosaic expression, the interviews were structured with a view to opening up dialogical spaces in which reflections on voting could emerge in unforced ways. Most of the interviews began with questions about the areas in which interviewees lived, their feelings of local attachment and their thoughts about how they would respond to harmful and unwanted policy interference by government. This usually led to a series of questions about the resources available to people who felt that they were being wronged – and the extent to which interviewees felt that they could make a difference to the world around them. By this stage in the interview,

voting was sometimes mentioned – although it was striking
that few people spoke of the vote as a political resource; more
often they would imagine themselves signing petitions, writing
to elected representatives or contacting the media. By the time
that questions about voting were finally introduced, interviewees had had an opportunity to position themselves in relation
to both their homes and neighbourhoods and the flows of power
they recognised as affecting their lives. Of course, the agenda
was still being set by the researcher, but the aim of allowing
the interviewees to work their own way towards establishing
the meanings of key terms resulted in a set of responses that
sometimes approached the inventiveness (and instability) of
the poetic.

A second risk facing these interviews lay in the hubristic delu-
sion that verbatim testimonies collected from 'ordinary folk'
might constitute an uncorrupted representation of reality. The
allure of realism, promising that uncut actuality can escape the
oscillations of interpretation, has contributed to a range of exag-
gerated claims, from nineteenth-century novelists through to
documentary producers and oral historians. In the case of 'The
Road to Voting' project, this conceit was brought into sharp
focus by the awareness that a group of dramatists were proposing to use the transcripts as a source for a verbatim theatre production. As its name suggests, proponents of verbatim theatre
claim that, by basing their content entirely on the authenticity
of documentary material, taken directly from interview record-
ings, court transcriptions and official documents, they are able
to produce representations of social reality that escape the usual
distortions of literary mediation. Through attention to mimetic
detail rather than creative artifice, verbatim theatre sets out both
to simulate and problematise the real. The pioneers of verbatim
theatre – or documentary theatre, or docudrama – such as Erwin
Piscator in the 1920s and Peter Weiss, Rolf Hochhuth and Heinar
Kipphardt in the 1960s, tended to exaggerate their capacity to
render text and production commensurable. More interestingly,
it is the incommensurability of the theatrically translated verbatim that raises important questions about the performativity of

both the 'original' data and its dramatised enactment. Verbatim theatre has flourished in the past two decades, partly as a consequence of the increased availability of inexpensive recording technologies which make it possible to capture events and debates 'in the raw', but also as a response to a sharp decline of public trust in official and journalistic narratives, which has impelled people to seek out alternative sources of credibility (Coleman, Morrison and Anthony, 2009). As David Edgar (2008) has observed, 'much verbatim theatre is double-coded, not just sourced from interviews, but about the interview process, questioning how retrospect recasts the past'. Martin (2006:14) notes that verbatim performance 'does not necessarily display its quotation marks, its exact sources'. Rather, it

> takes the archive and turns it into repertory, following a sequence from behavior to archived records of behavior to the restoration of behavior as public performance. At each phase a complex set of transformations, interpretations and inevitable distortions occur. In one sense, there is no recoverable "original event" because the archive is already an operation of power (who decides what is archived and how?). (Ibid:10)

This is not to say that attempts to reproduce the recorded utterances, pauses and micro-gestures of people encountering their own memories is a pointless exercise; nor should it be taken as a refusal to engage with the ontological challenges of representing the real. As Bottoms (2006:57), my collaborator in the project of re-enacting the 'Road to Voting' interviews, has put it, 'Without a self-conscious emphasis on the vicissitudes of textuality and discourse, such [verbatim] plays can too easily become disingeneous exercises in the presentation of "truth", failing (or refusing?) to acknowledge their highly selective manipulation of opinion and rhetoric'.

Acknowledging the pervasive iterability of *all* performance, both in the interview situation and in theatre, calls for a critique of 'restored behaviour' that begins not with the dramatised reproduction of the archive, but with the 'original' reproduction of memory within the interview. In this sense, verbatim theatre might be classed as thrice-behaved behaviour, the interview as twice-behaved behaviour and the whole project as an exercise in citational restoration.

In the course of conducting the 'Road to Voting' interviews, it became important to think of them as symbolic performances in which remembrance was revealed as imagination – in which interviewees' apparent search 'within' the recesses of subjective memory for voting-related anecdotes, sensations and beliefs was framed by narratives, images and values derived from a range of sources and stimuli emanating from beyond their individual experience. These indistinctive boundaries between personal and cultural performance were indicative of how it feels to be a citizen in a society characterised by a semi-scripted notion of citizenship. Making sense of the fragments and fractures that constitute this civic script came to be the most important challenge of the interview research.

Enacting the Citizen

Modes of address reflect and shape expectations about what a person is capable of telling; they contribute to the constructivist enterprise that Hacking (1999) calls 'making up people'. In interviewing people as 'voters', they were being invited implicitly to speak and act in ways consistent with culturally recognized performances of citizenship. For most of them, this was an unusual kind of performance. They were used to acting as shoppers, employees, local residents, television viewers and family members, but how exactly were they supposed to behave when their civic selves were on display? In many cases, the task of responding to questions and telling stories became itself a performance of citizenship, an acting out of the subjective dilemmas entailed by the search for democratic recognition. The interviews therefore took on a double role (although the split was generally imperceptible) of disclosing memories of voting while at the same time attesting their status as citizens.

Addressed as voters, interviewees began to reflect on the question of what it means to live together with strangers who are one's fellow citizens. For some of them, in the spirit of Rorty's (1989:73) 'metaphysicians', a 'final vocabulary' prevailed; they felt bound by a civic script which determined the connections and boundaries of civic activity. So, for example, they spoke vigorously about their obligation to vote in elections, while at the same time insisting that voting in TV talent shows or reality series was 'not real voting' – an adulteration of the truly civic. In these cases, the interview became rather like the UK government's *Life in the UK Test*, with the ironic twist that interviewees were trying to give 'the right answers', while the interviewer was attempting to throw them off course by suggesting imaginative distractions from the official script. But these cases proved to be a small minority. As the interviews went on, it was striking to observe the inventive and latitudinous ways in which memories and experiences of voting were framed by resonant discourses and images. These were introduced by interviewees without prompting, as linkages and boundaries which defined the symbolic map of talk about voting. Identifying and deciphering these frames provided an important key to recognising the sense in which interviewees were enacting their own roles as citizens.

A prevalent frame connected voting to a vague and amorphous notion of power, usually spoken of as a semi-tangible force wielded by remote others. The interviews opened up opportunities for people to position themselves in relation to power. Interviewees would speak of a set of overarching and inviolable social forces, often defined by the third-person plural: *they* want us to believe this; *they're* more likely to take notice if you do that. The act of voting, rather like tribal rituals in which gods are addressed, was seen as a means of encountering, and sometimes influencing, these mysterious repositories and flows of social power. Part of the sanctity and solemnity attached to voting can be attributed to this sense of hallowed proximity; perhaps a trace legacy of earlier acts of representation in which petitioners would have to appear physically in the presence of the divinely anointed.

As they spoke of power, interviewees would reveal their own sense of political efficacy, both in terms of their capacity to make a difference to the world around them and their beliefs in the willingness of political authorities to listen to and learn from them.

Generally speaking, these perceptions seemed to be reasonable: very few people believed that they could do very much, with their vote or otherwise, to affect social structure or public policy. Most believed that representative institutions were not answerable to them; some had evidence of not having been appropriately acknowledged when they had tried to make their voices heard; a few had personal contacts with councillors, MPs or officials and felt more confident about their chances of receiving a positive hearing. Overwhelmingly, however, interviewees identified a source of potential power in their friends and neighbours. When asked how they would respond to a totally unacceptable policy imposed on their locality, very few responded with reference to their vote or elected representatives. The power inherent in 'we' was spoken about quite differently from that ascribed to the extrinsic third-person plural. With we-power there was a default assumption that justice would be recognised, even if it could not be realised; with they-power it was the other way round. A generalised sense of political inefficacy led interviewees to speak of voting as both a sublime and duplicitous act; a route to power and a tool of power.

At the end of each interview I drew a map – a simple dot (E) placed closer or further from a centrally placed dot (P) – to describe where I thought interviewees felt themselves to stand in relation to power, as they conceived it. As I went on with this inexact exercise, it became clear that not only did E need to be moved after each interview, but so did P, because each person imagines power differently and speaks of it in ways that both internalise it and give it an estranged character unique to their own political cartography. A key determinant of the latter was the way in which people framed voting within a strong and affective context of place.

Despite all that is commonly asserted about the overwhelming effects of globalisation, attachment to local space persists as a vital factor in people's civic identities. In talking about memories of voting and experiences of citizenship, interviewees returned again and again to the local and the familiar. Both the context and consequences of voting acquired meaning for them through the particularities of place and belonging. So, the act of voting, often written about as if it were an abstract convention, was usually recalled in its material specificity. Voting places were described, sometimes in great detail, in terms of their conversion from other uses; their sound and smell; its distance from home; their energy or emptiness. The consequences of voting were rarely described as having national or global effects, but were recalled in terms of their affective impact; people feel the result of a vote before they witness its social impact. Here was a paradox: voting brings together the dispersed through institutionalised aggregation, but at the point of vote-casting and vote-impact (so to speak) it cannot escape the lifeworld of the corporeal individual. Personal memories do not tell the story of aggregation – of swings and cycles and marginal majorities. These are the subject of political science and then history. The disappointments, pleasures, embarrassments and compromises of the voting act belong to discrete memories that are rarely spoken and more rarely still articulated without reference to the ambient and biographical contours of its scene.

This locational specificity of voting as a social performance strengthened my decision to conduct the 'Road to Voting' interviews in and around a single northern English city. Interviewees were selected to represent the diversity of the city and its rural surroundings, but it seemed important – and proved to be so – that their testimonies could be as free from abstraction as possible. If they said that they lived in an area that nobody ever listened to, I wanted to be able to go and see with my own eyes what an unlistened-to neighbourhood looked like. If they described their local polling station as a dingy place, otherwise used as a sweaty school gym, I wanted to be able to visit it in all of its olfactory grimness. When a small-town golfer explained that he could never tell his fellow golfers that he was a non-Conservative voter, I wanted to be able to peer through the windows of the clubhouse and imagine the strength of that enforced silence. While these distinct experiences could not provide a reliable basis for generalisation (qualitative data rarely can), they illuminate the sense in which memories are rooted in place and civic acts are always concrete in their execution. The interviews helped to make this linkage vivid.

The interviews tended to be framed by a rationalistic aesthetic, resembling the look and tone common to current affairs discussions on television or public meetings intended to consider civically important matters. This aesthetic disposition led many interviewees to behave as if, having been addressed as voters, they were bound by an aura of deadly seriousness. They spoke about their voting memories in the manner that Bakhtin (1981:5) describes epic literature: 'It is given solely as tradition, sacred and inviolable, involving a common evaluation and demanding a pious relationship with it.' Rather than speaking directly about their own experience, they would search their minds for references to 'the way elections work' and 'what every voter needs to know.' As twice-behaved behaviour, the interview became a stage on which enactments of civic competence and responsibility were played out. Unsure what the interviewer's questions might be testing, responses sometimes took a hesitant, interrogative form. (Is this what I'm supposed to remember?) The adoption of this civic discursive tone constrained spontaneity and sometimes led to approval-seeking responses to questions. At the same time, other interviewees reacted against the paramount nature of the conventional discourse by expressing indifference and even derision towards the language of political citizenship. In some cases, this accorded with what Eliasoph (1998:203) has called 'cynical chic': the strategy whereby estranged and disengaged people distance themselves from official discourses as a way of asserting 'that they do not care, that they have not been fooled into wasting their time on something they cannot influence and cannot be held responsible for whatever happens'. Some interviewees made a point of expressing their belief that, either as voters or abstainers, they were vulnerable to ruses that would draw them into a self-defeating political game. Even being asked questions about voting was regarded by some as an attempt to drag them into a form of talk that it would be safer for them to avoid. These two apparently antithetical responses to the rationalistic meta-framing of talk

about voting led to similar outcomes: a tendency for interviewees to be guarded at times about tensions between direct testimony and official discourse, and a suspicion of invitations to
reflect on affective responses to voting that were not rationally
explicable.

As all of this started to become clear, I began to conduct the
interviews in two new ways. First, I tried to explore openly these
dispositions towards the rational bias in civic discourse, by asking overt 'rationalists' why they felt that voting needed to be
spoken about in a special way and asking 'cynics' to share with
me their tacit apprehensions about the hidden traps of civic discourse. This direct approach generally worked well, allowing for
more candid interactions. Second, I made a point of explicitly
casting aside rational expectations in some of my questioning,
urging interviewees to think about what might at first seem
ridiculous. (For example, I was eager to spark their imaginations
about ways of making 'the voting experience' more like a 'restaurant experience' than a 'taxpaying experience'.) The further the
interviews strayed from what Nichols has called the 'culture of
sobriety', the more original and evocative responses became.

My role as interviewer came to be dominated by two seemingly contrasting aims: to elicit the frames that helped interviewees to make sense of voting, and then to encourage them to
transcend those frames with a view to releasing them from the
burdens of prosaicism. The aim of the interview was to hear
what the interviewee had not come to say – had, perhaps, sur-
prised themselves by knowing or feeling or expressing or repress-
ing. The momentary, hesitant silence which follows a rejected
cliché is the effervescent space within which expressive memory
thrives. Small, technical strategies were adopted with a view to
opening up such spaces: pausing at some length after immediate answers were given, in the hope that second thoughts would
reveal more; asking supplementary questions about small details,
allowing interviewees to exercise their memories and stray from
conventional narrative paths; and inviting interviewees to consider political scenarios and reflect on the resources available to
them in trying to exercise influence. As the interview analyses in

subsequent chapters will hopefully demonstrate, the process of listening to voters' memories, stories, anxieties and aspirations resulted in something more than a chronicle of polling-day experiences. A rich picture of the complex relationship between the demos and democracy began to emerge, one which exceeded the terms of the narrowly political and reverberated with affects that are irreducible to the old terms of power.

Enacting the Researcher

That research interviews are sites of asymmetrical power has been widely acknowledged, for example by Kvale (2006:485), who states that 'a research interview is not an open and dominance-free dialogue between egalitarian partners, but a specific hierarchical and instrumental form of conversation, where the interviewer sets the stage and scripts in accord with his or her research interests'. (See also Gubrium and Holstein, 1995; Limerick et al., 1996; Denzin, 2001; Enosh and Buchbinder, 2005.) Others argue that research interviews entail interactive contestations of meaning, in which both interviewer and interviewee arrive with their own moral agendas, articulated through self-presentation and negotiated through such questions as 'What are the moral and identity implications of what is being said here *for me*? ... What should we define here as important, and what should we overlook? Who is leading this interview and in what direction? and What meaning will we make for the agreed-upon construction of reality?' (Enosh et al., 2008:463).

To see the interview as a stage for the enactment of research, in which the roles of interviewer and interviewee are played out through the drama of performance, goes beyond the simple acknowledgement of power asymmetry. It raises questions about how these uneven relationships are accomplished and reproduced, and whether the use of different words, gestures and rhythms of interaction might subvert the didactic script. Performance is never an innocent act, devoid of interests and motives. In laying these bare, one begins to see how the interview is created as a scene for the construction of subject positions and the framing rather than mere capture of memory.

It is clearly the case that before, during and after every interview, the intentions, assumptions and uncertainties of the researcher fill the air, determining much more than her own interrogative performance. The almost subliminal manner in which both the Said (*Dit*) and the Saying (*Dire*) of the interview exchange are tinged by the relational effects of power is complex and routinely under-explored. The Said, according to Levinas (1991:5–7), comprises the routine transmission and reception of messages, while Saying refers to the manner in which the recipient of communication is approached and addressed. The Saying is an ethical event, insofar as it conveys the speaker's sense of proximity and responsibility to the addressed. As a tone or manner that determines the reading of what is Said, the researcher's disposition towards Saying is a vital determinant of the integrity of the interview and the relations of the subject positions within it. For, as Williams (1977:411) has argued, 'Reciprocal recognition is possible only if each side renounces its attempt to steal the other's possibilities, acknowledges the other, and allows her to be. ... Allowing the other to be means to renounce attempts to control and master'.

Allowing the other to be entails making oneself morally reachable and addressable – not claiming the right of invisibility as one weaves narratives out of strangers' words, and making a responsible appearance, in the manner that both Bakhtin and Levinas demand of ethical dialogue. This must surely mean in practice that an effort has to be made to bring the researcher's presence to the fore; to make conspicuous what is so commonly obscured by the spurious enigma of academic objectivity.

It was not until the 'Road to Voting' interviews had been conducted, transcribed and analysed that I came to consider the role of the interviewer (myself) as a performative actor. Like most researchers, I felt able to ignore the transcribed words of the interviewer, which seemed merely to repeat a scripted set of questions designed to test pre-determined hypotheses (Wengraf, 2006). Some months into the analysis of the interview data, a writer and directors from the verbatim theatre company came to show me how they were planning to dramatise the data. They had produced a first draft of a script, based entirely upon what was said in the sixty interviews. We sat in my office and read it out; it was too long to be staged in its raw, unedited form, but nonetheless striking in its nuanced capture of the diverse narratives and moods of the dialogue. As I listened to the restored accounts that I had first heard as a co-present actor within the research situation, I experienced a heightened sense of witnessing the cryptic undercurrents of testimony; a capacity to hear the rhythm as well as the melody; the silences and evasions as well as the meditated messages; the throwaway metaphor which illuminates the mundane account. Greedily (all researchers are omnivores), I congratulated myself on the fruitful outcome of this productive interdisciplinary collaboration, thinking about how I could use these dramatic insights to present a richer account of the data. Upon further reflection, and after discussion with my theatrical collaborators, it became clear that this acute sensitivity to interviewee responses was rather like an account of a one-sided telephone conversation: penetrating in its attentiveness to the other, but strangely silent about the interviewer's role in the intersubjective dynamic.

After all, the interviewer (me) was the most consistent presence across all the interviews. With my excellent research assistant, I was there before, during and after each of these interviews; no mere mechanical asker of set questions, but a participating actor with his own story to tell – or withhold. Understanding the contingent and localised ways in which research is enacted demands an engagement with the particularities of performance. This means that, as well as recognising the reality of communicative imbalance between interviewer and interviewee, an attempt must be made to apprehend the habits, strategies and constraints that shape each apparently spontaneous act and utterance in an interview situation. The work of making visible, both in this analysis and the theatrical representation of the interviews, the interviewer's tone, responses, hesitations and numerous ad libs which hinted at motives, anxieties and yearnings raises important questions about how distant the memory of the researcher can be allowed to remain from the pursuit of other people's memories.

In the interview analyses that follow this chapter, the research-er's presence is emphasised by a series of scene-setting para-graphs – part field notes, part reflexive meditations – which serve not only to set the scene of the interviews, but to problematise the diverse ways in which the scenes could be read or even coun-terfactually constructed. For, as Back (2007:16) has argued in his excellent study of *The Art of Listening*,

> More often than not research findings are presented in the form of long block quotations from research respondents. These excerpts are expected simply to speak for themselves. The portraits of the research participants are sketched lightly if at all and the social location of the respondent lacks explication and contextual nuance. Sociological data is reduced to a series of disembodied quotations.

Avoiding this kind of social-scientific disembodiment entails not only giving flesh and colour to the portraiture of interviewees and their surroundings, but working hard to describe and explain the flows of historic energy that surround and give meaning to their every utterance. Rather than thinking of the interview as an event, I am inclined to theorise it as a space in which differ-ently conditioned and positioned subjectivities are both at risk of exposure and in hope (not always the same hopes) of rec-ognition. These performances of risk and hope are inflected by histories that exceed and feed back upon the space of interaction. The space of the interview is charged by multiple, invisible cur-rents – recent, distant, unforgettable, subconscious, counterfac-tual, material, symbolic, wishful, dreadful, shameful – that flow around and through and beyond everything that is said or asked. The researcher's craft is to make them visible. I am reminded here of a reflection of Harold Pinter's:

> I am dealing a great deal of the time with this image of two people in a room. The curtain goes up on the stage, and I see it as a very potent question; What is going to happen to these two people in a room? Is someone going to open the door and come in?" (Harold Pinter, *New Yorker* interview, 25 February 1967)

As a researcher, I found myself sitting often at this half-opened door, wondering who or what will come in and who or what they are coming in to. What is going to happen to these two people in a room? The indeterminacy of that question, combined with the over-determinacy that history confers upon the people and their imaginable range of actions and interactions, frames everything that follows in the next four chapters.

4

Acquiring the Habit

Unsure Starts on the Road to Voting

The taxi draws up to a grim-looking estate at the furthest edge of the city. Its driver, who has spent the entire journey from the city centre talking on his mobile phone, turns around to tell me that this is a part of town to which few people ever ask to be taken – and he, for one, wouldn't drop anyone off here after dark. The estate is strikingly austere, neglected and peripheral: row after row of utilitarian dwellings, balanced precariously between the sanctuary of domesticity and the incessant disturbances of poverty. We have stopped in an empty car park, in front of a functional building which could be a community centre on a good day or a probation office on a bad one. The sign tells us that we are in the right place: Sure Start. These two words appear incongruous, perhaps even ironic. With the confident air of an ad for breakfast cereal or breath freshener, Sure Start seems to be declaring an intention to its bleak surroundings: 'Believe enough and we shall break the legacy of deprivation and disempowerment that reproduces social inequality'. Well, perhaps.

Inspired by the U.S. Head Start programme and the UK Plowden report, which called for the creation of a 'compensating environment' (CACE, 1967:57) that would 'innoculate children against the harmful effects of growing up in poverty' (Zigler and

Styfco, 2000:68), Sure Start was a flagship social programme introduced soon after the election of the New Labour government in 1997. Setting out the rationale for Sure Start in a speech to the Joseph Rowntree Foundation on 6 September 2006, Prime Minister Tony Blair observed that

> about 2.5 per cent of every generation seem to be stuck in a lifetime of disadvantage and amongst them are the excluded of the excluded. Their poverty is not just about poverty of income, but poverty of aspiration, of opportunity, of prospects of advancement.

From 'the excluded of the excluded' to a 'sure start' is a huge leap. Evaluations of the Sure Start programme have been mixed, with some concluding that 'children from relatively disadvantaged families (teen mothers, lone parents and workless households) appear to be adversely affected by living in an area with a Sure Start programme' (Ormerod, 2005), and that it 'seemed to have beneficial effects on the least socially deprived parents and an adverse effect on the most disadvantaged families' (Welshman, 2008), while others found that the programme promoted 'new relationships between professionals, parents and other members of the community.' (Myers et al., 2004:2)

Through the windows of the modest Sure Start centre, I observe parents playing with their children, although they might just as well be children playing at being parents. Watching them, heady rhetoric about 'breaking the cycle of deprivation' feels just as remote and intangible as talk of 'democratic empowerment' or 'civic renewal'. What lies between these grandiose objective-slogans of high-level policy and the mundane exigencies of everyday survival? Through what language, gestures and customs can people shape the world that shapes them and their children? What sort of dispositions enables or inhibits a will to make a difference? How do such dispositions come about? In what ways does upbringing delimit thought? In what ways is it ever transcended?

But what on earth makes me imagine that talking to people about voting will help to answer these questions? There is

something seductively suggestive about the notion of a democratic sure start. Democratic citizenship – and voting in particular – is based on the ideal that everyone has an equal voice within
the public sphere. What is it about contemporary democracy
that confounds such an ideal? What would need to happen for
people to feel sure of themselves as democratic citizens? Once
these teenage parents have been taught how to change nappies,
who will teach them how to change health policies, or the government, or the economic system?

The interviews take place in a room that is usually a crèche.
We are surrounded by toys that have seen better days. The chairs
are all child-sized, bringing a certain kind of equality to the
conversations. (It's less easy to be academically pompous when
your elbows are six inches from the floor). Beyond the door, the
humdrum clamour of babies crying, kids fighting over toys and
receptionists chasing up missed appointments betokened a world
of familiar disorder. But as the interviewees (five females aged
between sixteen and twenty and one seventeen-year-old male)
entered the room, they seemed apprehensive, as if prepared for
some kind of official encounter that might be beyond their control. Rather like stepping into the hermetic realm of the polling
station, in which codified practices, terms, motifs and prohibi-
tions prevail, the research subject is thrust into an unfamiliar
space and asked questions about unfamiliar themes. Quite how
unfamiliar the theme of voting was to some interviewees was a
surprising finding.

There is a thin line between cognisance and imperception.
When shown a visual prompt to see what thoughts might be
evoked by images of ballot boxes, voting booths and election
counts, some interviewees were clearly perplexed. Even when
told that these were images of voting, Hayley (a sixteen-year-old
single mother) responded with some uncertainty:

> I've never heard about these voting things … they've had them err
> different… votes what've been goin' around, but I can't remember
> what they are. Do you know what? Sticky Windows? Some'at for
> public or some'at like that? I've seen those.

And when asked whether she had ever come across people voting, Sara (an eighteen-year-old single mother) said:

> I know they do because on my Mum's street they've got, they have like a ... voting, is it a voting poller thing? Like a big like thing ....
>
> *{A polling station?}*
>
> Yeah, they have one just on the end of street.

The hazy ways in which 'these voting things' and the 'voting poller thing' were spoken about served as an important reminder that for some people the very concept of voting, let alone its affective texture and political repercussions, simply does not register. Even when the concept of voting was recognised, interviewees were often uncertain about *how* they knew what it was. When presented with the visual prompt, Becca, a seventeen-year-old single mother, was unsure how she came to recognise it:

> I'll have seen it somewhere, I don't know where.

In Becca's case – and many others after the Sure Start interviews – awareness of voting derived from overhearing family talk:

> *{Did your parents vote?}*
>
> I think my dad did. I don't know about my mum. I know my dad did.
>
> *{Did your dad ever talk about voting?}*
>
> Yeah, but it went over the top of me head. [laughs] He did talk about it.
>
> *{What sort of thing would he have said?}*
>
> I don't know. He were talking about something that ... about years and years ago, when someone else were voted in and some'at went wrong – but I honestly don't know because me dad does talk. [laughs]
>
> *{He talks a lot?}*
>
> Yeah, he talks about all sorts.

The impression here is of voting as one of those themes that is only ever half-articulated and vaguely registered. Interviewees strained to recall moments when voting had been the subject of other people's talk: the ramblings of the aggrieved or the passing comment of the overburdened. Nobody from Sure Start reported having sat down with their parents or friends with a view to making sense of what voting entails. In Becca's case, non-voting is a direct consequence of not knowing what is at stake:

> More like ... I wouldn't know who to vote for than anything – because there's that many people promising different things and not keeping promises. I just don't understand. I don't know, I might sound thick, but I don't understand who's going to do what and what would be best, so I just don't bother.

Asked what she would need to know in order to become a voter, Becca says:

> I don't know: What's going to happen after we've voted, say ... A certain person's voted in. What exactly they going to do? And, basically, what they're promising they're gonna do which they're not.

Five of the Sure Start interviewees had never voted. The one who had – Lisa, a nineteen-year-old single mother – had gone to the polling station with her mother:

> I just sort of went along and, you know, because you watch news and you hear about all like Tories, Labour, everything else and it's like, Phew, there's that many though, you don't realise ... It felt weird because it were all closed in; and it was like ... well, there's a list and it's like twelve different ones, and you have to think, 'Well, which one do I choose?'

Asked to describe the experience of casting a vote, Lisa talked about the voting place itself:

> It were just ... erm it were just a big green cabin ... and there were just people, just going in, ticking, folding the bits up, putting a box and leaving ... it was like ...
>
> *{Was it in a school or a community centre?}*
>
> No, it was just in a damp street.

But despite the dampness and drabness and mystery of all this ticking and folding and closed-in uncertainty, Lisa was strangely exhilarated by the experience:

> It was really weird. It was like, I voted ... Labour. I just ticked it. And first time I did it I thought ... I said, 'Mum, what do I do

now?' And she was like 'Just fold it up and put it in box.' And you just folded it up and put it in box and I thought 'I've voted and that's first time I've done it'. I got right excited!

I needed to know more about this excitement. And I needed to relate it to three other questions that emerged strongly from the Sure Start interviews. First, how do people learn that they are 'voters' before they ever come to vote? Hayley's uncertainty about what voting was served as a reminder that social performances have to be imagined before they can be enacted. How are the sensibilities of citizenship assimilated? Second, how does the physical space in which voting takes place shape its affective reception? If there can be an aesthetic design that makes restaurants pleasurable to eat in and courtrooms conducive to truth telling (or fear of lying), what sort of designs produce what sort of feelings when it comes to the most common act of democratic participation? Third, what does it feel like to have voted for the first time? Lisa's excitement, combined with her question to her mother, 'What do I do now?', seemed somehow to capture the mixture of accomplishment and anxiety that follows a social performance which is neither instantly consequential nor immediately disappointing. Drawing on responses from the whole range of interviewees (rather than only those conducted at the Sure Start centre), the remainder of this chapter attempts to address these three questions with a view to understanding what it means to become a voter, to participate in a social performance that is both pre-scripted and replete with contingent promise.

Awaiting the Opportunity

Oh yes, I ... I think ... I think I awaited the opportunity of being able to vote, which in those days was 21 presumably. Erm and so as soon as the opportunity arose I ... I took it.

This was George, a retired businessman in his late sixties. His first vote was a long time ago, but he recalls – or thinks that he recalls – waiting for the opportunity to cast it. What was this waiting like? In one sense, childhood is one long experience of waiting – the fullness of adult rights deferred. 'Wait until you're older'. It seems as if the life of the democratic citizen is one of endless anticipation. Waiting to be old enough to vote. Waiting for the election to be called. Waiting in line to cast a vote. Waiting for the result, which will never be directly communicated to you. Waiting for politicians to deliver on their promises. The deferred moment, in which the represented desire and its representation coincide, is forever anticipated but rarely reached.

And yet, for many interviewees, this wait seemed pregnant with possibility and value. Explaining that he 'came to love democracy', Bill, a retired textile merchant in his seventies, spoke of voting as 'a thing you did ... part of growing up' and 'a good thing to do.' Stephanie, a housewife in her mid-forties, explained that casting her first vote was

> a duty. Something I was brought up to do. It wasn't like a big special event or anything. It was just a part ... I've turned eighteen. Now, this is what you do when you're eighteen.

Through what hints and signals does a child come to 'love democracy' and think of voting as 'a duty' and a 'good thing'? How does the notion that 'this is what you do when you're eighteen' come to be internalised? How do norms of voting come to make such sense that at the precise moment of reaching the age of eligibility people are ready to perform as millions of others have done before them? And what is it that leads some people to regard their first vote as a climactic moment of entry into a world of being counted?

These are not new questions. Easton and Dennis (1967:38), in their seminal study of political socialisation, noted that 'from a tender age children are able ... to mirror adult feelings of mastery over their political environment'. The embryonic citizen learns

> to carve out a small piece of political authority for himself – at his own level of consciousness. He is still far away from any actual role that he normally would have in the political process. Even so, he begins to feel his political power when it still involves a high degree of projection to those around him and to his future role as an adult member of the system. (Easton and Dennis, 1967:33)

Projection, in this sense, precedes the performance of citizenship; it comprises the subjectively shaped stage directions for
the future enactment of a routine social performance. In imagining themselves and others around them as wielders and subjects
of power, pre-citizens learn to internalise feelings about where
they stand in relation to others, how they expect to be perceived
and received, how far they feel able to cope with and contest
unwanted interferences, and how they go about displaying these
dispositions through word, gesture and silence. Cultivating these
civic proclivities entails a sustained period of rehearsal that
is inherently performative. As people talked about how they
came to think of themselves as voters, two narratives began to
emerge: the vote as an act of nature, found rather than made;
and the vote as a creative accomplishment. As with Winnicott's
(1974:104) account of the baby's comfort blanket, where the
infant will never be challenged to answer the question, 'did you
create that or did you find it?', the emerging citizen, while both
inheritor and maker of one's civic identity, experiences it through
the prism of a subjective projection.

Many of the people I interviewed described voting as a
passed-down habit, imbibed almost imperceptibly. For Simon,
a gay retired school teacher in his late fifties, voting was 'just
something you did, really.' But why did he just do it?

> Well, my parents voted. My grandparents voted. And it was some-
> thing that you sort of, in a way, saw.

Ali, who was in his early twenties, could not really remember
when or how he first voted, but knew that

> it's mainly through my father ... He said, like, oh, what do you
> call it ... 'You need to support ... so and so' ... So, from that age
> we used to, like, 'Oh, OK' and take it from there really.

Others were physically taken to the polling station, long before
they ever became voters:

> Yeah, erm, my mum took me to the polls every year when I was
> growing up ... er was very sort of 'People died and people pro-
> tested to give you the right to vote, so use it'. So it was something
> I was brought up ready to get prepped to do, if you like.

Indeed, there were many accounts of parents – particularly mothers – seeking to impress upon their children – particularly daughters – the sanctity of voting as a right that others had died to gain or preserve. People would recall the passion of their parents in disseminating this sense of historical debt – an intimately related historiography passed on from generation to generation, but only within the relative seclusion and safety of family relationships. Perhaps, like Eliasoph's (1998) community activists who wanted at all costs to avoid being seen as political animals, there are many apparently 'non-political' people who feel strongly about the normative values of democratic citizenship, but prefer not to express them in the estranged language of civic politics – prefer not to take them beyond the sphere of intimacy.

Many interviewees spoke about how their first act of voting was almost an extension of family dynamics. Aysia, a sales assistant in her late thirties, described her first vote as something of a family affair:

> We went ... couple of us sisters went together. And we voted for ... I voted for the person my eldest sister were voting for, to be honest with you.

Voting is one way of conforming to parental values. Edward, a retired lawyer in his late sixties, explained:

> My parents were Tories. I am. And we just did it. It was part of the social fabric.

Edward knew that his parents were Tories because 'they threw other people's literature away. [Laughs] So it was you were pointed in that sort of direction'. Martha, a rural housewife in her fifties, cast her first vote in the knowledge that her father, a miner and parish councillor, whom she described as 'always on his soapbox', was at the door of the polling station checking off the names of Labour voters. While she voted then (and still now) as her father would have wished, Martha was eager to affirm the independence of her vote:

> Me dad was actually on the door as I went in. Yes, just outside. They weren't allowed inside. They were just ticking people off as

they went in … and I remember there were policemen about then as well. That's what I remember about that. Yes, I do remember.

Schools provided some future voters with an 'imperceptible apprenticeship' (Bourdieu, 1973:82) through which the rules of the democratic game were absorbed. Bill, the retired textile merchant, explained that he was 'brought up in an age where [voting] was thought to be a sensible thing to do'. But long before he cast his first vote at the age of twenty-one, he had been exposed to a series of rehearsals, preparing him for the performance:

> Well, we used to have erm citizenship talks at school, erm mock elections, that kind of thing.

Other interviewees lamented the absence of such background information. For example, Raji, a twenty-six-year-old bank worker, said she 'didn't have a clue' who her local MP was and stated that 'I think you only know if you know somebody who knows'. Asked how she might become a better-informed voter, she seemed disconcerted:

> I don't know … I don't know how I would. Yeah, I don't know if I would, to be honest. I don't know how I would. I never hear about it.

Tales of bewilderment and uncertainty were common. Interviewees complained that nobody had posted election leaflets through their letterboxes - or that those received were too complicated to decipher. The jargon of electoral politics was offputting and the game-playing of politicians encouraged immobilising suspicion. People knew what they themselves stood for, but felt unsure about how their values and preferences connected to the promises on offer.

But for many interviewees, the mystery of what it all meant was overcome by the routine of following the well-marked footsteps of others. Ella, a secretary in her early thirties, summed up this sense of becoming a voter as both a rite of passage and a beaten path:

> I would have probably just turned eighteen. I don't remember how old I was exactly … but I remember going with my mum and dad,

going to the polling station and just sort of looking round and thinking 'OK, well', watching what everybody else did, because there's no real instructions as to what to do. You just sort of see people going in, you know. You're signed off your list. You're crossed off. And then going in and making me choice. And then thinking 'Well, what do I do with this now?' Obviously, turning round and seeing the ballot box, erm. And then going to the pub with my mum and dad. I was like, 'Right, come on, we've had a night out. We've been to the vote, you know, been to polling station – let's go and have drink'.

For other interviewees, however, the act of voting had less to do with adhering to social custom than with forging a personal identity. It was as if becoming a voter allowed them to engage with historical and intimate dynamics that went far beyond the constitutional domain. They spoke of how casting a vote offered them a long-awaited opportunity to contest values that had been imposed on them by their families ('You have a reaction against your parents.... You know: with them or against them.... Having been away to public school, which was fairly right wing, in terms of my erm contemporaries, I was erm bit of a rebel ... so, I would vote Socialist or Liberal just for the hell of it', recounted Bill). Those who had fought in the war against fascism spoke of democracy as if it were a personal accomplishment ('I feel it's something that I won myself. It's a very personal thing to me', explained Theo, a retired solicitor in his late seventies). And those who came from places where they had been denied the right to vote spoke about how casting their first vote as British citizens gave them an intangible sense of belonging ('You know, it is going to sound ridiculous, but do you remember when ... they voted in South Africa, it felt a little like that', was how Lakyta, a retired schoolteacher in her mid-sixties, put it).

Apart from prisoners who had lost their right to vote (discussed in Chapter 7), the only interviewees who could speak with any authority about feelings of disenfranchisement were those who had come to Britain from other countries. Amadi, who had been brought up in Nigeria under the military regime of General

Ibrahim Babangida, spoke of how the president's motorcade had
passed through his village:

> His enteourage ... speeding motorcycles and ... err the whole
> bling bling and limousines.
>
> *{Did you go and see him?}*
>
> Well, people were just shouting at the roadside. So you tend to
> join in. I was, oh, 6, 7 then ... and, you know, that particular
> president, if he had any opposition he would just erm expel them,
> because he had so much power.
>
> *{How did that make people feel?}*
>
> Erm ... without a voice. Without. A bit helpless. A bit hopeless. If
> you weren't happy with something and you criticised erm the rul-
> ing powers, then you know there could be severe repercussions.
> Like, you know, a few beatings here and there.

Surely, it was this to which people were alluding when they spoke
frequently about how using their vote at least entitled them to raise
public objections; as if it were a permissive gesture, a right-affirming
rite that sanctioned future complaint. Conversely, interviewees
would insist that those who 'couldn't be bothered' to cast their
vote should not feel free to criticise the elected government. In
this sense, the act of voting appears to serve a double function: as
an expression of choice between competing representatives, often
weakly or grudgingly given; and as a signal of minimally active
citizenship – enough at least to justify subsequent expressions of
reproach and disgruntlement. The empty space of the ballot box
becomes both a repository for the storage of private preferences
and an admissible conduit into the arena of public claims-making.
This latter role explains the anticipatory excitement that people
recalled when they spoke of voting for the first time. While the act
of putting a cross against a candidate's name leaves most voters
feeling like responsive subjects – shoppers in the political supermarket – it also marks a rite of passage into the public sphere
where, as registered citizens, the right to make claims, hold representatives to account and rehearse for a potential speaking role in
the drama of democracy comes to feel justified.

And yet, the polling station as a portal into the public sphere
is the oddest of entrances: a space that checks and subdues the

noisy vivacity that is the public sphere's most promising feature. The rightness of Habermas's (1989:177) observation that in opening the public sphere to universal access there emerged 'an interlocking of state and society which removed from the public sphere its former basis without supplying a new one' is vividly apparent within the space of the contemporary polling station. Much as those who venture within may imagine that they are entering a domain of expressive citizenship, memories of voting are pervaded by images of languid detachment from social intercourse; the voting space remembered for its hushed tones and affective barrenness.

A 'Sombre Hall' with 'Nothing Much in It'

Margaret Kohn (2003:3–4), in her astute study of political space, observes that

> space affects how individuals and groups perceive their place in the order of things. Spatial configurations naturalize social relations by transforming contingent forms into a permanent landscape that appears as immutable rather than open to contention.... The social dimension of space reflects the way in which places encourage or inhibit contact between people. Linguists have identified the 'phatic aspects of speech', terms like 'hello', 'how are you?' which initiate, maintain, or interrupt contact. Particular spaces serve a similar function. They aggregate or exclude, and they determine the form and scope of the interactions.

Writing about the opening of the new New York Criminal Court building in 1941, Chief Judge Brietel observed how the new surroundings affected the behaviour of witnesses who entered them: 'No one told these people that they should keep their voices subdued. No one told them that they should abstain from food and drink while waiting. They just did so' (quoted in Blanchard, 2004:17). But nobody 'just does' anything. Actions are structured and constrained by design. Inventive and dissentient ways of behaving as citizens are 'abstracted out' and 'smothered' through what Allen (2003:162) describes as 'the social coding of space': 'the closing down of possibilities, the restriction of alternative uses, so that others have little choice but to acknowledge the construction of a singular space – even though they may imagine themselves moving within and around it'. Rogers's (2004:28) study of public attitudes to British town halls reported one interviewee who said that 'I feel like I am doing something wrong if I come in here.' As people began to tell me about their memories of going to vote, memories of place seemed to evoke strong feelings of awe and nervous circumspection. From 'walking in' to 'going out', they would describe a series of moves that were neither autonomous nor controlled, but somehow consistent with a narrow range of available options. Masud, an Asian-British college student in his early twenties, sounded like he was describing the first day of a job apprenticeship rather than his coming of age as a democratic citizen:

> I can remember my first time when I did it. You know, I went in there and said 'What do I do here?' Erm, I go up to that lady first and tell her, you know, who you are, so she'll, tell you, she'll cross you off on that register. So you go up to her nervously, thinking, you know, 'My name's Masud', 'Right, what's your address?' and you tell her, and like she gets a ruler and she crosses you off and she, like 'Here's your piece of paper'. 'Where do I go from here?' She says 'Well, go to any of those boxes there and just put a cross, and you think 'I can just stand on here and do it and just put it back into box', you know.

Tina, a childminder in her early thirties, recalled how

> we all trotted along to the community centre and, yeah, I found my name and it's like 'Ooh, what do I do now?' and then ... it was quite exciting really in a strange kind of way. It was ... you know ... was exciting because I didn't really know, you know, what to do ... and I'd read everything ... and it was like Going in, put my little cross. And that was that.

Martha's recollection was similarly characterised by uncertainty and a sense of needing to do 'it' the right way:

> It was something you've not done before, so you'd go in and you go up and, you know, what do you do? They usually direct you to where you want to go ... and the little curtains ... I think then, I think there were curtains up then ... but I think there were curtains and a pen, a pencil at and a bit of string.... And you just look down. And there weren't many to choose from then.... Oh yeah, you knew what you were going to do.

Stephanie, a council administrator in her late thirties, described how her mother had taken her along to the polling station to show her what to do, even before she was old enough to vote:

> I remember ... the people asking who you're going to vote for on the way in, and sitting behind the counter with the all those bits of paperwork and a ruler and crossing your name off and er ... then me mum took me over to the little booth and showed me, explained what the people were, and all the different parties, and showed me how to put the cross, and then sometimes I'd actually go and put it in the ballot box when I got a bit older.

There are two kinds of public place: those that are occupied by a self-generating public, such as raves and street demonstrations, and those in which the terms of publicness are shaped by rules, structures and mores that preclude undesired and unanticipated actions. Polling stations epitomize the latter. The ambit of democratic opportunity is predetermined by an ordained route: entry into an officially designated hall; being checked off a register; receiving a ballot paper inscribed with already printed choices; the solitude of the polling booth; the minimal size of the box to be marked by a pencil tied to a string; the narrowness of the slit in the ballot box. One proceeds from one to the other in an order that is invariable and non-negotiable. Novice voters learn the ropes, follow the trail, get in and get out without making a fool of themselves. When they recall the experience of first-time voting, they rarely speak of spontaneity or creativity. The curiosity of the fledgling citizen soon gives way to the anxiety of the nervy neophyte. This sense of rote behaviour is reinforced by the places occupied by polling stations for their short lives as prefab edifices of democracy: school and church halls, with their never-far-from-the-surface threats of punishment for improper conduct, remind the novice voter that there is an order to be followed. Denise, a cook in her early forties, described going to the polling station as 'a bit frightening at times'. Describing her first time, she said:

> I think I were a bit nervous when I went. I needed a wee ... you know?

Whatever it is that awes first-time voters into feeling that they have to follow the unclear rules of an opaque game, it is not the aesthetic design of the polling station. Far from experiencing them as grand or imposing places, most interviewees were struck by their dowdy austerity. Rose, a college administrator in her early fifties, was distinctly unimpressed by the environment in which she was asked to cast her vote:

> It's like something from the Communist era really ... I mean, they've got wooden billboards, a table with nothing on it, and er, then they've got a box that looks like it's come from Morrisons or somewhere and ... It's not very enticing, is it really?

Angus, a retired research scientist, was almost thirty before he cast his first vote. He had watched election night programmes on the television and, 'seeing all the razzmatazz,' had expected the act of voting to be more exciting than he found it: 'a bit more banging of drums'. He recalled

> walking into the building and somebody accosting you in the foyer and saying, er as you came out, actually asking for your address or something. They would be the agents or, you know, the activists. And then walking into a sombre hall, which had nothing much in it apart from a few, erm, a few booths and erm a couple of senior citizens at a table writing, drawing ruler marks through the electoral register.... It was a rather arid kind of experience, and I hadn't realised that it was er, [pause] well, such a spartan kind of exercise ... I just felt it was very ah, hmm, no, mysterious isn't the right word, just just er devoid of erm paraphernalia. With er, I mean, that was probably a good thing but erm it, it, it just impressed me with how sort of frugal everything was.

Ella was regularly disappointed by her visits to the polling station:

> You go in, do your bit and leave. You always tend to find there are school halls or, you know, portacabins or somewhere stuck somewhere.

As for the polling booth:

> Just a box, basically. A tiny little ... well, there's two, made out of MDF or whatever they can throw together. Erm, no real privacy. It's just an enclosure. (42)

The severe functionality of the spaces in which people are invited to vote is largely a reflection of their ephemeral and inexpensive existence. They are forgettable places. Recollections of voting reflected this aesthetic scarcity, as if speaking of a film in which the set always fell short of the projected action.

Making Representations

I had listened to a wide range of accounts of voting as a dimly recalled experience. The script was becoming familiar:

> Do you remember the first time you voted?
> *Not really.*
>
> Had you been looking forward to it?
> *Yes – I suppose so.*
>
> Was it an interesting occasion?
> *Not really.*
>
> What about the polling station – nice place?
> *A bit dull.*

Not, on the face of it, the sort of experience that people would choose to give their lives for, to cherish as their most inviolable right, to pass on to their children as the institutional guarantee of future freedom. The apparent disconnection between what people recalled themselves doing as voters and what they thought they were doing by voting led me to wonder whether the surface act itself was something of a distraction; whether more attention should be paid to the intentions, projections, sensations and impressions that frame the idea of voting than to substantive moments in time and space in which votes are forgettably cast.

As I conducted more interviews, now listening less for the circumstantial details of vote-casting than for the affective sensibilities of would-be represented citizens, a distinction began to emerge between voters as subjects, adhering responsively to officially stipulated practices, and voters as actors, pursuing claims to speak and be spoken for in ways that do justice to them. These are quite contrasting experiences. The voter as subject is bound by the scene of the election – a scene that she has not made for herself. The voter as actor is defined by not only maintaining their own civic claims, but endeavouring – in whatever ways possible – to have them recognised. This contrast bears some resemblance to Isin's (2008) theorisation of the distinction between action (as the behavioural expression of *habitus* and settled order) and acts:

> To act ... is neither arriving at a scene nor fleeing from it, but actually engaging in its creation. With that creative act the actor also creates herself/himself as the agent responsible for the scene created. (Isin, 2008:27)

To act as a citizen is to make something happen, to employ agency towards the generation of a desired end. In this sense, the civic act is performative. The *act* of voting is more than a mere reflex response to an existing order of power. It is a declaration of sorts, a call to be represented as a certain person on certain terms. It is, at the very least, an assertion that one considers oneself to be a person who should count in the world.

In their most positive moments, interviewees captured this feeling of counting as something within the great reckoning of representation, sometimes speaking of voting as a rite of passage: a coming of age (eighteen since 1969, or twenty-one for older interviewees) and a dawning realisation that the right to be represented was now fully theirs. Masud spoke of the excitement of being old enough to vote:

> Yeah, I was excited. [laughs]
>
> {*Because you thought you could make a difference?*}
>
> No, I just turned eighteen and I was allowed.
>
> {*Did it feel like that was one of your moments of becoming an adult?*}
>
> Yeah, it did. It really did. Because when you turned eighteen, you know, you think 'Oh, what can I do now that I'm eighteen?' Middle, smack bang middle of the exams, not exactly gonna be going out anywhere. 'Oh, I'll vote.'

Timothy, a retired council officer, recalled his feelings about his first-ever vote: 'It was novel, it was cool, it was the 'I'm allowed to vote. My voice counts for something.' He elaborated: 'it's a little bit er ... like er all the coming of age bits, isn't it? You can go for a drink. You can vote. So it was er ... it was novel.'

Looking back with a sense of bitter nostalgia at the enthusiasm he felt as a first-time voter, Jethro recalled how it felt like a moment of emergence as a person of consequence:

> You felt as though you'd come to an age and that you were going to influence what went on. There's a naivety there. I actually believed that I was going to influence what went on.

However much Jethro subsequently felt beguiled by this initial feeling (an impression we shall return to in the next chapter), there is no doubting the power of this memory of entering the sphere of political influence. Daisy, a schoolteacher from a village on the outskirts of Bradford, encapsulated it quite beautifully when I asked her why her vote meant so much to her:

> Because it's my vote. I know that's my name. That's my number. Whatever, you know, that's my cross. Nobody's accidently put it in a different ... nobody's lost it. It's gone into that tin. I know that tin's locked. You then hope the tin doesn't get lost or whatever and you know your vote's going to be counted.

I asked her whether all of that made her feel counted:

> No, not that I'm being counted; that my views are being counted on.... So somebody, they've no idea who I am, 'Oh, this person's put a cross in A, therefore that's A.' You know, so it's like, it's not me; I'm a nonentity; it's what the cross I've put stands for.

For others, the vote signified the prospect of realising hopes and dreams that might otherwise remain internalised and impotent. Lisa, from the Sure Start centre, explained: 'I think people gotta vote to get their opinion across, because if you don't vote you don't ... get ... everything sorted'. Sana, a receptionist from Leeds, told me that 'in my heart, I think if we vote we will get what we want in life – and if people don't vote it's the people up there are making all the decisions' Interestingly, Sana's sense of involvement extended to a feeling that she is somehow part of the government she elects:

> I've been part of whichever party wins. I was part of that. And, unfortunately, if the party if I vote for loses, I was part of that as well.

What do these sentiments mean? In what sense are people's being counted when they vote? How exactly does casting a vote influence what goes on? What is it that voters feel that they are 'part of'? These should be interpreted as neither literal accounts of what voters thought they were actually doing nor merely symbolic or metaphorical allusions. More than to just the mechanical act of representation, statements of this kind refer to the complex relationship upon which all representative claims rest. To be represented is to be spoken or acted for by others. For political representation to be deemed democratic, there must be a chain of accountability between representatives and represented that results in the latter feeling at least recognised and, ideally, well served.

While political representation has sometimes been conceived rather simplistically as a matter of creating 'an exact portrait, in miniature, of the people at large' (Adams, 1776), the notion of mimetic representation, whereby an actual body politic is brought to life through the ventriloquising force of democratic simulation, has few adherents within contemporary political theory. Political representation, it is now widely acknowledged (Ankersmit, 1996; 2002; Saward, 2003), is not a matter of faithfully replicating a fixed object, but rather comprises a claim to speak and act for others in ways they find credible. Making representative claims plausible entails an aesthetic project of both reflecting and constituting an electorate's view of itself. While there is no singular 'people at large' that can be reproduced exactly, voters do play a crucial role in shaping the terms on which they will agree to be spoken for. Representation depends, then, on the credibility of claims made to speak or act for others – and these can only ever be the outcome of a communicative relationship between representatives and represented of which voting is a part.

Daisy's affirmation of her powers as a voter – to possess a vote, a name, a number and a cross that prevent her from being forgotten – is tinged with anxieties about the ballot box being lost or her being thought of as a nonentity. Both her confidence and her apprehension are largely symbolic in their articulation, referring to the vagaries of the representative relationship and the burdens facing individual voters in their quest for recognition. Daisy wants to maintain the vote as a guarantee of her being remembered, acknowledged and respected, but her figurative allusions to being abandoned or nullified serve as a reminder that representation can go wrong, that the performative act offers assurance but not certainty.

When Masud, Timothy and Jethro spoke about their feeling of being allowed to exercise political influence as first-time voters, they were invoking a claim to be addressed and acknowledged in a new way: as adults rather than children; as citizens rather than as outsiders. As well as being allowed to do something that they could not do before they were eighteen, and having a chance to vote with or against their parents and elders, they were, perhaps more importantly, signalling their entry into a representative relationship that depended for its success on how they acted and what they were prepared to believe. When they spoke of how becoming voters would alter their powers in the world – 'my voice counts for something', 'I was going to influence what went on' – they were engaging in a performative act, intending to make happen what they were appearing to describe. While all of them admitted to some scepticism about the empirical force of their claims that voting gave them a voice that counts or an influence on what went on, they were describing how they had invested their agency in the scene of voting with a view to taking responsibility for its outcomes.

Sana's characterisation of voting as a way of getting 'what we want from life', while at the same time preventing 'the people up there' from 'making all the decisions', captures nicely the double-sided nature of political representation. On the one hand, to be represented is to make a claim for certain interests and values to be articulated and promoted. Embodying a spectrum of demands from the fantastically utopian to the modestly pragmatic, the vote comprises a manifesto of historical aspirations. On the other hand, the act of being represented is an agonistic rejoinder to the reality of unequal influence, an attempt to level the geography of power so that 'the people up there' are slightly

or momentarily weakened in their capacity to dominate, manip-
ulate and disrespect the represented. Neither of these two aspects
of representation is meaningful without the other, for desire is
hopeless without strategy, which in turn is empty without normative motivation.

There is a further duality within the representative relationship: because the object of representation is not a fixed reality
that can be mimetically captured, the position of the represented
is never stable. As Ernesto Laclau (1996:87) has rightly observed,
'it is the essence of the process of representation that the representative contributes to the identity of what is represented'. So,
when Sana speaks of being 'part of whichever party wins' or
'loses', she is acknowledging the reality that, as a represented
voter, she is not only a contributor to the outcomes of her representation, but is in an important sense reconstituted or redefined
by the unpredictability of political aggregation. She is part of
what is being represented, even when the representation is incongruent with her preferred outcome.

The habit of being represented turns most of us into gamblers,
speculating on the prospect of being counted in ways that will
save us from being lost, forgotten and disrespected. As citizens
strive to evaluate the claims of others to be acting in their best
interests, and live in hope that what ends up being represented
bears some resemblance to themselves, their confident accounts
of voting as efficacy are repeatedly undermined by inflections
of nervous anxiety. For all of its rhetorical vigour, democracy
is fraught with uncertainty: less a sure start than a stumble in
the dark.

5

The Burdens of Being Represented

Between Duty and Refusal

It was the morning after the local council election, and Lucy and Jo had not managed to vote. 'I really really meant to go and vote, but I didn't. No, I really wanted to, but I just … didn't', Lucy explained as I sat with her in one of the over-cheerfully yellow-painted cubicles at the young people's drop-in centre. Jo explained that she had recently moved and had mistakenly assumed that she was registered to vote at her mother's address. I had come to interview some of the regular visitors at the drop-in centre (described on its Web site as serving 'young people who may not have had the best start in life') because I was keen to find out whether, and how, the election of the day before had impinged upon their lives.

Making my way to the centre, through an inner-city high street with its depressingly familiar Poundsaver, Burger King, betting shop, newsagent selling groceries and grocery shop offering to cash welfare cheques, no signs of yesterday's election were apparent. The polling stations had already become invisible; no party colours, logos or graffiti were to be seen anywhere; not a single poster adorned the windows of any houses or flats and there was no publicity to suggest who had won or lost the election. It was as if this area, like so many others, had fallen through a vast aperture in the democratic universe, abandoned to a nebulous space of unrequited representation.

Lucy, a twenty-one-year-old single mother, had left school at sixteen and was now taking a university access course. She was eager to point out that she had known about the previous day's election: 'Well, I got one of the cards in my door and I'm registered and stuff', but

> I was out all day. That's why I ended up not voting ... because I was ... toddler groups, then parenting group, and then I was at uni till 9. Then I had to walk home. And the voting, the little booth things shut at 10, so by the time I got home it was shut.

I asked her whether she had simply been too busy to vote:

> Er, I don't know. I mean, I had all day, so I don't ... it was ... you know, I could have done it had I sort of just taken like a few minutes out.

So, what had stopped her taking the few minutes to do what she said she had really wanted to do?

> Well, I don't really know that much about the parties and stuff ... I did get a few bits of paper through the door from different parties, but ... I sort of scanned them briefly and then just put them in the recycling bin.

As she spoke about throwing away the election leaflets, Lucy told me about 'a huge argument' that she'd got into with some party canvassers who had approached when she was sitting on her doorstep:

> They were just these middle-aged, middle-class white women who didn't have the first, you know, they didn't live in ... round here. You could tell they were from, like, R***** or somewhere. And they were just coming round and handing out the leaflets and ... I can't relate to them ... Well, they dominate everything, so ...

I asked Lucy whether she believed that her vote could help in some way to redress the power of middle-aged, middle-class white politicians. She was pessimistic:

> Most of the people I know that are my age don't bother voting because they think, 'Oh, its not going to affect ... you know ... we

can't change things. It's not going to affect us and nobody's looking out for us', that sort of attitude, you know.

Lucy's friend, Jo, another single mother, told a similar story.
She was registered at a different address; she was preparing for
her daughter's christening at the weekend; she'd 'had nothing
through my door' from the candidates, so she came to feel that
voting was too far removed from her immediate experience to be
of high importance:

> It's ... to me, it's not compulsory in my life because I've got a lot
> of things going on. I've got my child. I've got, you know, a house
> to keep and everything like that. So voting is not as important to
> me because bills are more important. You know, because they're
> deadlines, whereas ... I don't know, it's not going to affect my life
> directly if I don't do it, whereas the other thing will ...

And then she gave me an example of a political act of which she
was proud:

> When I was pregnant, I had a lot of issues with the midwives at
> the [hospital], a lot of issues ... erm because of the fact I'd gone in
> and said, you know, 'My waters have broken' ... and she tried to
> say that I'd wet myself, you know, and it was just like that. And
> because I was, well I was nineteen and I'd got pregnant when I
> was eighteen, so they just presumed, 'Oh, she doesn't know what
> she's talking about. We can fob her off with this'. And I was 'But
> I know, I'm not a two-year-old. I know there's different feelings,
> you know' and she just wouldn't listen to me. And I actually got
> to the stage where I refused to go back to that hospital. I refused.
> I said I'm not going to be spoken to like that ... because she tried
> to justify it and say, 'Well, I had a baby at seventeen, you know. I
> can appreciate how hard it is for you', and I was just like, 'You're
> not listening to anything I'm saying. I'm telling you my waters are
> broken. I know something different is in my body. Something is
> happening. And you are not listening to me. And I just refused.
> And I told my midwife I'd much prefer to ... have my baby in
> my bed by myself with nobody there because I don't want them
> sorts of people delivering my child. I don't want their hands on,
> you know, my children. So I got a transfer ... in the end because
> I just refused.

Just as Lucy sensed that the people seeking to represent her in
the election were remote from her lifeworld, Jo's example of

speaking up for herself in the face of experts who thought they understood her body better than she did focused on the terms of representation. Both Lucy and Jo believed they could tell the difference between being taken seriously and being ignored or discounted. They were neither dutiful voters, who felt that they had an obligation to be spoken for by someone else, nor committed abstainers who expected any attempt to represent them to end in betrayal. For them, being represented entailed more than an act of surrender to a substitute voice; it involved an ongoing struggle for just recognition.

In the final section of this chapter I suggest that this precarious balance between the civic obligation to become part of the public body that is represented and the ethical refusal to be misrecognised or disrespected is at the core of the dilemma facing democratically inclined voters. But before that, we must consider two other forms of ambiguity that were persistent across the interviews that I conducted. First, there were interviewees who spoke of having a duty to vote – a sense of obligation that seemed to transcend self-interest, pleasure or convenience – and who then proceeded to tell me that they had little or no faith that their votes had ever made any real difference. These we might refer to as dutiful voters. They regarded being spoken for by others as an inevitability. And then there were those who insisted that they would never vote, but would protest vehemently if any attempt was made to take their vote away from them. These were the committed abstainers who could not envisage terms of representation that would not be beguiling. What does it mean to be driven by an obligation to act repeatedly in a manner that seems to be bereft of impact or to abstain from an act that one nonetheless regards as a sacred right?

If, as was suggested in the previous chapter, the feelings we are exploring here have less to do with the thin and fleeting action of expressing an official preference for this or that party or candidate than the act of consenting to being represented, this apparent antithesis between obligation and abstention begins to evaporate, Because in both cases representation is conceived as a kind of possession by the mediating power of a ventriloquial voice. While duty-bound voters seem to feel that they cannot have a voice unless another speaks for them, abstainers seem to fear that any attempt to speak for them might rob them of their own voice. The next two sections of this chapter explore the congruities and expectations surrounding duty and abstention. The final section considers how voting is seen by some people as but one move in a struggle to reclaim the representative relationship.

'It's a Criminal Thing to Waste a Vote'

Dutiful citizens vote, even when they are unconvinced by the parties or candidates on offer or the prospect of achieving any positive outcome. They do it because they feel that they should do it. 'I think it's part of my constitutional duty so to do', explained Teddy, a retired textile manufacturer in his late sixties, and then went on to say:

> Yeah, well, er you could argue that one person's vote doesn't make any difference one way or the other to the outcome of an election. It's the mass, isn't it, that makes, that makes the difference ... I mean, I never believe that whether I vote or not actually makes any difference to the outcome ... I just sort of feel that I should vote, that, you know, constitutionally I should vote.

I pushed Teddy further: did he really feel that he had a duty to vote, even though he did not think it 'makes any difference'? He smiled, acknowledging the apparent oddity of his position:

> But I felt better for doing it.... I don't for a minute think that my vote made any difference as to whether she got in or not, but it was more for me than it was for her if you like. I felt I was participating in the exercise.

This was far from being a unique feeling. Alasdair, a teacher and party activist from Wakefield, explained that he regarded voting 'as a kind of ... citizen's duty', but then went on to say that he was

> conscious of the ... powerlessness of one vote. I mean, I'm conscious that, you know, hundreds of votes and thousands make

a difference, but, you know, my individual vote ... I suppose I
sometimes argue it's neither here nor there.

Edward, a retired lawyer, told me that 'it's a criminal thing to
waste a vote', but he too was highly dubious about the efficacy
of this duteous action:

> I would though say that voting nowadays, and the colour of
> a government ... is now down to about 100 constituencies ...
> the other 500 or whatever it is can't make a change. There are,
> I think, as you well know, there are a number of constituencies
> which hold the country in their hand.

Edward, Alasdair and Teddy seemed to be making a separation
in their minds between the act of agreeing to be counted as part
of the represented citizenry and the less consequential action of
entering the aggregatory lottery of electing a candidate or government. While resigned to the relative inefficacy of the latter,
they remained committed to what they saw as a symbolic duty to
affirm their membership of the body in whose name representation would take place.

But this was no abstract sense of obligation, driven by blind
loyalty to a remote state. The duty to be represented encompasses two pragmatically formulated beliefs. The first is that the
opposite of being represented is not to be independent from ventriloquial encroachment, but to be wholly subsumed by unaccountable power. The duty to vote, therefore, is less about feeling
obliged to allow a representative to speak or act on one's behalf
than retaining the moral right and political capacity to determine
whether the act of representation comprises meaningful recognition. Non-voters, argue the dutiful, have no right to contest the
values or outcomes of representation. As Alasdair put it, 'if you
don't vote, you haven't got the right to criticise or, you know ...
complain about other people who have, who have voted.' Ella,
a secretary who described herself as being not very political,
said that she was a 'firm believer that you can't sit and complain
about something if you've not even bothered to get up off your
backside to go and vote'. This notion of vote-casting as registration for access to the public sphere was widely articulated.

Edward saw voting as justification for feedback on the quality of representation:

> We are supposed to be a democracy and voting is part of that process. And their not using that power, their individual power … they are really short-changing themselves. And they actually… they have not any right to come back because of anything happening, if they have not used their vote.

Imran, a twenty-two-year-old community worker, said that he felt he had to vote in order to be in a position to hold government to account:

> If no one would be voting then … the people wouldn't have … there would be no rights for people. They wouldn't have their say, basically. The, you know, the country would be run, you know, maybe like a dictatorship, in a way.

Often, interviewees would combine in a single statement a combination of acceptance that their vote would make no difference to the electoral outcome and a claim that voting is a duty because it allows one to speak as a represented citizen. Herman, a builder in his early forties, explained:

> If you don't vote, if you don't say your piece, then you can't complain about anything erm … you know. I'm in one of the biggest Liberal places you can be at the moment … so I know that my vote – even though I don't vote Liberal, but wont go into that – I know it's not gonna make much difference. But you still got to do it.

Indeed, such was the distinction between duty and outcome in the minds of some interviewees that even casting a blank vote was seen as constituting a fulfilment of civic duty. As Simon, a retired teacher, put it:

> Going and committing a spoilt paper act … or er … or 'none of the above' act … or leaving it blank, but actually going through the process, the physical process, I think can be useful.

To speak of casting a blank ballot paper as a 'useful' act is intriguing. It signifies absence by presence; that the voter counts and yet cannot be counted. It is a potential space in which citizens consent to be represented without subscribing to any specific regime of representation. (The function of zero as an empty signifier serves a similar function in mathematical theory to the 'blank' or 'spoilt' vote).

Avoidance of stigma was the second rationale for the duty to be represented. Feelings of pride in 'doing the right thing' and shame in being seen in the eyes of others as less than worthy citizens led some interviewees to regard voting as a means of affirming their civic identities. Rita, a housewife in her early fifties, described how she felt when she voted:

> I went along and voted last time in the elections and I thought, 'Ooh I've been and voted'. Yes, I felt right proud that I'd been and, you know, I actually walked to my polling station.
> *[It made you feel it was the right thing to do?]*
> Yeah. 'I've done it. I've done it. I've been and done what I should be doing'. And, you know, I've done it, so yeah.

Daisy, a schoolteacher, described how 'the first thing I do when I come out the library or the school is feel very smug ... nobody can say I can't do it, so yes, there is an element of smugness there'. Christine, a housewife and mother of four, told me that 'I did feel guilty when I didn't vote'. Other interviewees described feelings of virtue after they had been to the polling station and of shame about forgetting to vote.

Constable (1999:6) suggests that experiences of shame offer 'an intrapsychic and intersubjective lens through which a sense of belonging is magnified and or shattered, an affect intensely linked to what it means to belong, to the process of fitting in, as well as to those of becoming a misfit'. She refers to Sylvain Tomkins's conception of shame-inducing situations that arouse 'feelings of being out-of-place, strange, a stranger, and small and unworthy, as a result of communication interrupted by the very person, people or ideals one has grown to trust and from which one expects intimacy and mutuality' (ibid:10). To place oneself beyond representation, then, is to become vulnerable to the stigma of non-recognition – a state in which the shamed feel exposed as inadequate citizens, while the shamers are free to fortify their sense of bonded righteousness.

'My Opinion Is Not on That Piece of Paper'

And then there were the committed abstainers, vigorously eschewing the ballot box lest it swallow up their identities. Not for them the tepid simulation of the spoilt vote or the blushing shame of civic inadequacy. Residing within the long shadow of representation, but resisting its seductive reach, these obstinate refusers seemed to regard any attempt to speak or act for them as the first step down a slippery slope towards misrecognition and disrespect.

When committed abstainers explained to me why they would not vote, few of them mentioned the deficiencies of the voting system as a fair means of aggregating preferences. Rather, they spoke of an abiding sense of disrespect that they associated with the experience of being represented. 'Moral injury', says Honneth (2007:71), occurs when 'contrary to their expectations, human subjects are denied the recognition they feel they deserve'. The terms of political representation, as committed abstainers perceived them, entrapped them within a relationship in which they were spoken for and about, but not with and to, leaving them feeling enfeebled, unacknowledged and without voice.

Too often – too easily/lazily – abstainers have been labelled as *apathetic* – a misnomer if ever there was one, for the word derives from the Greek term *apatheia* (ἀπάθεια), meaning a lack of feeling or passion. In contrast to the insensible indifference of the apathetic, committed abstainers seemed to be even more affectively laden than their dutiful counterparts. I wanted to understand what led some people to repudiate voting and whether they believed that there were any ways in which the representative relationship could be made to work for them.

Sabrina was a twenty-eight-year-old office worker, brought up in a suburb of Leeds by her West Indian grandparents. She had only ever voted in one election and that was because she was taken to the polling station by her grandmother: 'I was actually forced to. My grandmother is a true believer in voting … and she said, you know, I had to do it. She took me down.' As the granddaughter of a dutiful voter who believed that 'every vote counts and ... you really need to do it to make a difference', the eighteen-year-old Sabrina found it almost impossible to resist the pressure to participate. But since that first time she has refused to vote because

> I believe that my vote really doesn't make a difference. I think we just do it because we're told to do it and we're told that 'Oh yes, every vote counts' and I don't truly believe that every vote does count. So that's why I think it's a waste of time and it's, erm yeah, it's just a waste of time.

Taking this view has placed Sabrina in conflict with her grandmother:

> I said I'm not doing it. I put my foot down and I said I don't believe it makes a change. It doesn't make a difference and so I really don't want to. Even this vote this year, erm, you know, she asked me if I'd done it ... and she got the forms through the post. I tore it up. I tore it up and put it in the bin.

Asked to explain why she felt so sure that her vote would make no difference, Sabrina said that it's 'the people with money' who are 'always at the top' and 'they're the ones that tell the little people down below ... how things are going to be'. Democracy, she argued, was little more than a popular illusion:

> I think they portray it to be like that, so we can live all happily ever after and, you know, we all count and ... No, the top dogs rule the country. They always have done and this is how it's always going to be. You know, it's just made to believe that we live in a free world, free society. We don't. .

I wanted to understand how far this feeling was based on direct experience. Sabrina told the following story of a neighbourhood consultation that had convinced her of the inefficacy of expressing her preference by casting a vote:

> A while ago they were coming round and asking if, erm, if you wanted gates on the streets ... on the backstreets.... There's a certain area which is actually kinda cordoned off. It's like a little prison where they've got these big metal steel gates and you need your key to get in and out, whereas before ... you were free to go, cut through if you like. People used it as a short cut. They came

and asked ... and the majority said No, but they still put it up in
this ... area ... and on a couple of the backstreets they put it up.
Now, to me that was, erm, the majority didn't want it, but they
still put it up.

Believing that local people knew what was best for them, but that
their votes against the gates were quite simply ignored, Sabrina
came to think of voting as a kind of fraudulence. She spoke about
her voting experience in the tone that one would use to describe
a personal insult. This was not just a lost vote, but an affront to
her dignity – a humiliating dismissal of her lived experience that
amounted to a profound failure of recognition:

> I said I didn't want to ... have the gates up. It was a simple 'Do
> you want them or not?' and I said No, I don't want the gates up
> in my street ... I know other streets in the same area had them up
> and I find it to be quite dangerous, you know ... a rape happened
> in the area and the girl couldn't get out ... she couldn't get out
> of the gates ... and that's why she ended up getting raped. And
> still, you know, even after this, and crimes have happened, they
> did it to try and stop the crimes but more crimes have happened
> because they know that people can't get out. An you say you don't
> want it. but still it doesn't matter what you say: 'We're gonna do
> it anyway'.

Political scientists have studied the effects on voters of being on
the winning or losing side of an argument (Anderson et al., 2005;
Craig et al., 2006; Clarke and Acock, 1989). But Sabrina's story
suggests that voting is not just an instrumental activity. Before
they are ever voters, people accumulate expectations about what
it means to be acknowledged as an individual, what constitutes
personal respect, and how far their life experiences should be
taken seriously. When such expectations are disappointed, the
trauma of misrecognition has effects that transcend the contingent context of the moral injury. One can feel more diminished
by being asked and not listened to than by not being asked at all.
This seemed to have been the case with Sabrina. Her response to
being ignored was to refuse to place herself in a position where
she could be either recognised or overlooked. Like Eliasoph's
(1998:154) 'cynical chic' respondents, who made a virtue of not

caring about what was going on in the political sphere as a way of avoiding the embarrassment of not being taken seriously within it, committed abstainers seem to be seeking a kind of civic invisibility that might protect them from the abuses of representation.

If Sabrina experienced political representation with an increasing sense of distrust, Jethro, a senior prison officer in his mid-fifties, seemed to regard the entire political system as a stultifying force, constraining his autonomy by perpetuating an atmosphere of public unease. It had not always been so: Jethro had taken part in mock elections when he was at school and voted as soon as he was old enough to do so, trusting that he was 'going to influence what went on'. But for many years now he had come to believe that he is living in an unfree society; that the public expression of his own feelings could do him harm:

> I think that in the last thirty years, whether it's because I've become more politically aware or whether it's circumstances, but I feel that the land, the freedom of speech, the sense that we are being watched, and everything is being monitored, has increased to such a level that I began to question whether I do live in a free society ... I can imagine what it must have been like to live in Eastern Germany where everything you say or everything you do ... Anything from your political views to comments on immigration to comments on equal opportunities to your comments on ... even humour, where certain things have become ... you cannot mention them anymore.

Jethro's account of representation as a process whereby, far from political elites being elected to speak up for voting citizens, governing elites project their values *upon* citizens in a way that inhibits their capacity to speak up for themselves, conjures an image of democratic dystopia. The empirical veracity of this position is less important than its rhetorical construction. The question is not whether Jethro is objectively caught in the trap that he describes, but how such feelings come to support a belief that representation is a means of normative manipulation. When Jethro spoke of 'a sense of feeling' that 'I can't change anything', his response was to see the act of abstaining as his only remaining option:

> It's my little way of saying, 'Listen you lot in there, I am not going to vote to give you credibility'. I have to earn my credibility.

> Don't you dare make me vote for you because I would destroy it.
> I would write on there some vulgar and disgusting thing and say,
> You ain't going to make me vote.'

Refusal to confer legitimacy upon those who would refuse him the respect and recognition he feels he deserves is Jethro's way of asserting a resistant autonomy. 'You lot in there' are addressed by an outsider who must 'earn credibility' in ways unknown to them. Their final assault on his sense of freedom would be to demand that he votes, but his response to that prospect is to resort to the abject: to debase and defile the very technology of collusion. The suspicion that Sabrina had derived from her local experience, Jethro had generalised into a disposition of permanent disbelief.

I met nineteen-year-old Cass at the drop-in centre. She was unemployed, but hoping to take a course that might help her to become a news journalist. She explained that her grandparents, who are interested in politics, 'tell me that I should read the news. I should watch the news. I should keep up to date with things'. And she does. But she will not vote. Like Sabrina and Jethro, Cass did not believe that voting made a difference: 'Our opinions are meant to be taken on board and I don't feel that they are. They just go ahead and do what they want to do'. But her committed abstentionism went further; she regarded the idea of being represented by someone else as, quite literally, a waste of time:

> Well, I suppose it's a form of communication, but it doesn't really get you anywhere. If you're going to spend a whole year sitting and waiting for someone to do something they said they were going to do, and they don't do it, and the only thing you can do is vote them out, then you've got to wait another year and see if the next person does it, it's pointless. You're just constantly sitting and waiting.

Through her description of representation as a frustrating and potentially futile waiting game, Cass drew attention to a discrepancy between the tempo of official politics, hampered by the constraints of institutional and deliberative proceduralism, and the more spontaneous rhythm and pace of the lifeworld, in which things can be made to happen without the will for change having to be re-presented and re-enacted. This may be what Wolin (1997:2) alludes to when he writes of 'political time' being 'out of synch' with the temporalities of culture. Cass's objection to voting for others to say or do things on one's behalf is that it undermines the spontaneity and inclusiveness of self-representation. As she puts it:

> Everyone should be involved in one way or another. We all live in this world. We all cause chaos. We all have our own beliefs. We are trying to get somewhere. So everyone's involved, whether they like it or not.

While voting seemed to Cass to be founded upon temporal and spatial distancing (separate constituencies, agendas and discussions), which inevitably results in the fragmentation of public voice and the deferral of public action, she was more attracted to the direct democracy of the *agora*. Cass's alternative to attempts to boost voter turnout was to

> make people more aware. Just ask more questions. Bring more people together.... Bring people together ... instead of pushing them apart, which is what is being done. You've got everybody in little ... in their own little age groups and their own little communities. There's ... I'm not sure exactly what you can do, but you need to bring more communities together.

In contrast, the act of voting for Cass felt like an abnegation of direct engagement and a muting of meaningful voice:

> But that's not me saying ... anything to them. That's me putting my name on a piece of paper and posting it in a box. I'm not giving my opinion. I'm just posting a piece of paper. I could have gone and not written anything I could have gone and draw a little picture, posting my piece of paper it's not going to make no difference. There's no words on it, there's you know, my opinion is not on that piece of paper. I'd have just have been voting for voting's sake.

Much as committed non-voters spurned the ritualistic notion of 'voting for voting's sake', they were surprisingly reluctant to reject the value of their vote as a symbolic resource. Asked how she would react to having her vote taken away from her, Sabrina responded without any pause: 'I'd probably be annoyed, even though I don't do it' [laughs] because 'when that choice is taken away … then, you know, it's like "Well no, I'm going to fight to vote then".' For Jethro, much as he had come to doubt the positive value of his vote, he had come to regard it as a means of testing the unworthiness of the representative relationship of which he felt himself to be a victim. Almost masochistically, Jethro related how, 'One year, I says "Whoever knocks on my door and asks me to vote for them, I'll vote for them. I don't care who". And nobody came'. By committing to vote for anyone who would bother to communicate directly with him, Jethro was affectively fortifying his resentment: his unused vote became an active symbol of the insult he felt himself to endure.

However we might want to judge the political merits of these rationales for abstention, it will not do to regard them as simple manifestations of apathy. If anything, the affective sources of abstention were even more heartfelt than those revealed by committed voters. The struggle to deny representation entails no less emotional energy than the struggle to be represented in a particular way. However, both dutiful voters and committed abstainers both seemed to be immobilised by the deterministic nature of their expectations of representation. The former spoke as if they were organically bound to the forces that claimed to act in their name, while the latter seemed to feel utterly vulnerable in the face of any collusion with representatives, however negotiated. The fragility and vulnerability of this imagined relationship was summed up by Patrick, an office worker in his mid-thirties:

> I'm just a vote. All it is is a vote to keep him in where he is. So he'll say whatever he needs to say to me, get where he wants to go, then not do owt about it. That's the way I see it personally.

To be represented, in this sense, is to enter a hierarchy of respect in which citizens were left with the paltry hope that 'the men at the top … remember the little people at the bottom' (Joan, a forty-eight-year-old local government employee).

'To Organise a Feeling'

In a most penetrating critique of electoral representation, Hannah Arendt (1963:237) argued that

> representation means that the voters surrender their own power, albeit voluntarily, and that the old adage 'All power resides in the people', is true only for the day of election. In the first instance, government has degenerated into mere administration, the public realm has vanished; there is no space either for seeing or being seen in action.

Thus displaced by permanently legitimised authority, the electorate is left muted, incapable of asserting a collective view of its own:

> The most the citizen can hope for is to be 'represented', whereby it is obvious that the only thing which can be represented and delegated is interest, or the welfare of the constituents, but neither their actions not their opinions. In this system, the opinions of the people are indeed unascertainable for the simple reason that they are non-existent. Opinions are formed in a process of open discussion and public debate, and where no opportunity for forming opinion exists, there may be moods … but no opinion.

For some interviewees, however, voting was conceived as something more than the appropriation of the benumbed electorate by an omnicompetent surrogate. Seeing voting as only one move in an endeavour to be recognised on their own terms, they sought to project on their political representatives a sense of who they were and how they experienced life. As retired businessman, George, put it, 'I think it is possible to, as it were, organise a feeling' (8). He was speaking about a protest that had taken place against the construction of a giant supermarket in the small market town in which he lived. The idea of organising feeling – or making feelings heard – is common to representative politics, yet we know little about how such feelings are projected, how they circulate or what it means for a feeling to be taken into account (or to count). Political constitutions, founded on the conflict of indurate interests, are largely impervious to amorphous feeling. Adhering to the Aristotelian division between *logos* and *pathos*, political commentators have tended to assume that feeling is at best 'grafted on' (Walton, 1997:166) to rational motivation – and more commonly distracts from it. But this polarity has been challenged in recent times by scholars who argue that emotions are the object rather than the effects of rational argumentation; that dispositions to feel can be argued over, in much the same way as we might debate any other claim (Plantin, 2004; Micheli, 2008). Organising a feeling, within the context of representative politics entails four moves. First, a particular feeling needs to be articulated in a form that has meaning to others: there is a call to attention. Second, others must accept that the feeling (quite literally) makes sense. Third, as in any other form of collective action involving the promotion of interests or opinions, ways must be found to circulate the feeling, ensuring that it reaches others with whom it might resonate. Finally, it must be made known to representatives with a view to ensuring that the ensuing representation of the group in question will reflect and do justice to this feeling.

Sabihah, a twenty-two-year-old trainee solicitor, provided an interesting example of this happening. She came from Blackburn, where her MP was Jack Straw, the former Labour Foreign Secretary. Sabihah voted whenever she had a chance to do so:

> Well, every person makes a difference to the result.... No matter how much people say 'Oh, I don't think my vote's gonna be counted', everybody that votes should, I think, have at the back of their head that there is that little inkling of hope that 'Oh, maybe if I vote, it could make that difference'.

When I asked her whether she felt that there was a relationship between her and her MP, she was emphatic that there was. Indeed, she believed that most people in Blackburn would agree that he speaks for them. But in relation to the direction of British foreign policy under his leadership, Sabihah described how the feelings of the local Asian community had been hurt by Straw's action:

> When he brought back Condoleezza Rice to Blackburn, erm my sister's high school went into riot, cos obviously there's a

huge Asian population there ... of whom, like say, 80 per cent
are Muslims. And that was right after the war in Iraq. And he
had erm the gall to bring Condoleezza Rice who, you know, was
one of the key players in the war to a 90 per cent Asian high
school. It's kinda, like, it takes the mick, if you get what I mean. I
don't know how else to put it. If he ... if he ... if he was senseless
enough to do that, then surely he wasn't taking into account how
his constituency feels.

But how does a constituency come to feel? That is to say, how
does an inhabited political space generate feelings and how do
such affects become communicable and intelligible? The kind of
localised collective feeling to which Sabihah was referring might
best be understood as a structure of expectations through which
social performances are judged. When political representatives,
such as Jack Straw, satisfy such expectations, the constituency
'feels' at ease. When they disappoint, there is a feeling of hurt
within the constituency, which exceeds a simple disagreement
of interests or opinions in at least three ways. First, such feelings possess a subjective core. They cannot be externally invali-
dated. Much as one can try to show a group of people that the
interests they imagine themselves to have are not their objective
interests or that their opinions on a certain issue are unreason-
ably erroneous, any attempt to deny a feeling simply compounds
the original injury. Second, whereas interests and opinions are
quantifiable and can be traded commensurably, feelings possess
intensities that are not easily measured, impossible to aggregate
and rarely nullified by the offer of equivalence. To affront intense
feelings about a single issue within a constituency could well be
more politically damaging than to confront a whole range of
local opinions that do not arouse the same affective sensitivi-
ties. Third, whereas interests and opinions fit comfortably within
the conventional political lexicon, feelings are porous, moving
fluidly between contexts that seem quotidian and non-political
and situations that are manifestly politically charged but lack a
language that can name or respond to the heat of affect.

How does this help us to understand Sabihah's claim that her
constituency's feelings were somehow disrespected? She began

by making it clear that she voted because she expected to make a difference. The person elected to represent her was someone with whom she felt she and her fellow constituents had a relationship, however indirect. On a key matter of policy – Britain's support for the U.S.-led wars in Iraq and Afghanistan – Sabihah found herself to be in disagreement with her representative, but this did not stop her or her fellow constituents from believing that he continued to speak for their town. It was when he brought into the constituency a leading architect of the U.S. foreign policy – indeed, brought her into their children's school, exposing them to the very symbol of his disagreement with their parents – that Straw was accused of behaving senselessly and without regard for the constituency's feelings. The failure here was not of re-presentation, for the constituents were present when the offence occurred. It was, on the contrary, a failure of projection: an expectation on the part of the citizens that, however much they might differ with their elected representative, he would recognise their presence as opponents of the war. It was precisely because they did recognise him as their representative that this act of misrecognition was so hurtful. Unlike dutiful voters or committed abstainers, who imagine themselves to be absent beyond the point of voting (and then virtually re-presented by a surrogate), these voters saw representation as a means of asserting their presence. To speak for them effectively, one had to respect their affective presence – to take account of feelings that had a vivid immediacy.

Political theorists have paid close attention to the relationship between expressed public interests and preferences and representative responsiveness. Voting is the principal mechanism for realising such democratic correspondence. Rather less attention has been paid to the ways in which constituent feelings are (or are not) recognised and respected by political representatives. How can public sentiment be represented when it is so clearly amorphous and intangible? But how can public feeling be ignored if political representation is not to be reduced to an insensible promotion of abstract interests? Ironically, these questions were most pertinently addressed by the anti-democratic political philosopher

Edmund Burke in his defence of the patrician principle of 'virtual representation'. According to this principle, while the majority of the population possessed too little property to qualify as voters, those who were entitled to vote had a moral duty to give voice to the feelings of those who could not:

> Virtual representation is that in which there is a communion of interests and a sympathy in feelings and desires between those who act in the name of any description of people and the people in whose name they act, though the trustees are not actually chosen by them.... Such a representation I think to be in many cases even better than the actual. It possesses most of its advantages, and is free from many of its inconveniences; it corrects the irregularities in the literal representation, when the shifting current of human affairs or the acting of public interests in different ways carry it obliquely from its first line of direction. The people may err in their choice; but common interest and common sentiment are rarely mistaken. (Burke, 'A Letter to Sir Hercules Langrishe', 1792)

For Burke, then, it is the duty of representatives to acknowledge and reflect not merely the interests and preferences of those for whom they act, but the 'feelings and desires' that might not be articulated as political ends, but constitute an underlying foundation to public consciousness. When politicians describe themselves as being 'in touch' with their constituencies, they probably mean more than that they visit them regularly; they are referring to a 'sympathy in feelings' that is both intangible and highly conspicuous when it does not occur. In this sense, as well as speaking for the interests and preferences of the represented, it is the task of democratic representatives to honour the projected presence of those in whose name they have been allowed to speak. Voting entails both the crude transmission of a public will and the moral permission for a surrogate to speak for one's feelings. The burden of granting such permission is carried by voters and non-voters alike, not only on election day, but long before and well beyond.

6

Spaces of Disappearance

Sana described herself as an invisible citizen. She was in her early thirties and had never voted, but desperately wanted to. I asked her how she thought she would feel the first time she was able to vote:

> Good, it's my first vote. It will mean that I've been part of which-ever party wins. 'I was part of that!' And unfortunately, if the party if I vote for loses, 'I was part of that as well'. You know, could have done more, encouraged more people to vote for the same party.

Sana wanted to be part of it all: engaged, acknowledged, counted. But circumstances had forced her into the shadows. Fearful of being followed, she arrived at my office with her baby in its pram, having travelled to the university by a circuitous route, avoiding busy thoroughfares, careful to lose anyone who seemed to be taking too much notice of her. I offered her an armchair opposite my own. The baby broke wind. We both laughed. This somehow cleared the air.

I showed her a picture of a polling station and asked whether she recognised it. She did: 'I remember that one – the curtains – when I were younger and I went with my mum ... in a local school ... I reckon I were about eleven'. She not only went with her mother to the polling station, but helped to deliver leaflets:

'We used to sort of help the local er Labour party ... knocking on doors ... it were fun ... they used to have the big sign: Vote for Labour'. Did she and her friends boo the other parties when their vans came round, I wondered? 'No, we were civilised'. And when she was old enough to vote, did she do so? 'I'd love to' she said. Then she told me her story:

> I left home because I were beaten up a lot. I were knocked about a lot and erm ... child abuse really ... physical, mental abuse. And it got to a point where I were sixteen years old and life just ... there were no way out. I were just this Muslim girl who followed the religion ... never cut my hair, never put make-up on, never went out with boys ... I followed it all and I went down that path and then, erm, when I were beaten up a lot I realised that this can't be my life. It can't go on forever. I used to go to my local shop where I worked, and erm ... manager picked up on the fact that I were being ... I didn't want to take my annual leave at work ... I were worried if I were at home, what would happen at home. So I were trying to spend as much time at work as possible.... They took me to office and personnel said 'You need to take your annual leave'. I told 'em I didn't want to take my annual leave. Told em to keep it, didn't want it. And then they asked me. And eventually it all come out. Then they got in touch with NSPCC. Then they got in touch with hostels and basically they told me what to do. Get my passport, erm, just get whatever I wanted to ... and we planned a day where I would ... they would put me on a train and somebody would meet me at other side of the train. And then I would be transferred from there to a hostel. But [the family] found me.
>
> They used to follow me. And I didn't know that they were there. So there've been two attempts to kidnap me ... erm, and then I've moved from one hostel to another hostel. I think I moved to three hostels all in all. They found me in all three hostels. They would park the car outside the accommodation and then ... it's the intimidation. Well, they know that I get frightened really quickly, so they thought the more they do it, eventually I will give up and go back. They found me at [names several local places]. And I always thought it were to do with my national insurance number, tax or insurance. And I've even phoned them up to see if there's a way to block the information, but people do these things, don't they ... backhanders ... and they will take the money. And, unfortunately, they don't realise they're ruining somebody else's life.

Sana explained that she had never been able to vote because she dared not register as an elector in case it led to her being traced by her family: 'I do watch my back a lot.... I do keep my, you know, keep an eye out who's behind me'.

Sana and her husband often argued about who she ought to vote for if she could. He supports one party, but she remains attached to the party she campaigned for as a child. I ask her what she thinks about people who are free to vote, but choose not to:

> What a shame. What a shame.... They are deciding ... they're basically leaving it to others to make a decision. I mean, I don't know what happens to the people who don't vote. Where do their votes go?

I tell her that that strikes me as a quite profound question. The baby farts again. Sana says she ought to be on her way. She leaves the university by the back entrance – we've arranged for a taxi to take her home safely. I'm left wondering whatever happened to Sana's vote. How many unregistered preferences, submerged opinions and stammered intentions disappear into the political vapour of democracy as it is currently institutionalised?

Hannah Arendt, whose insights are central to the themes of this chapter, argued that, rather than to be found within a territorial boundary, the *polis* is constituted by 'the organization of people as it arises out of acting and speaking together'. The true space of politics, according to Arendt (1958:198–9), 'is the space of appearance in the widest sense of the word, namely the space where I appear to others as others appear to me, where men exist not merely like other living or inanimate things, but make their appearance explicitly'. The image of a democracy in which interests, preferences and values appear openly for all to see and contest contrasts vividly with the closed-in, tight-lipped voting process that we have come to know and expect. The aim of this chapter is to explore how and why so many citizens of contemporary democracies have come to believe that political freedom lies in *not* having to appear explicitly to one another; how, indeed, the right to express political preferences secretly, implicitly and without discussion has come to be regarded as an inviolable pre-requisite of democracy. Historically, political democracy arose out of making things public that had once been exclusive; out of making seemingly unassailable things challengeable; out of freeing up speech so that truth could no longer be established from above and handed down as all that could be sayable. As the production of meaning became increasingly shared, the power of words and their discussion became central to political freedom. For Arendt (1958:4),

> There may be truths beyond speech, and they may be of great relevance to man in the singular; that is, to man in so far as he is not a political being.... Men in the plural, that is, men in so far as they live and move and act in this world, can experience mean-ingfulness only because they can talk with and make sense to each other and themselves.

In short, politics is either rooted in what is social or buried in what is not. So, can secretive behaviour constitute a social act? Can a political culture in which citizens *do not appear to others as others do not appear to them* perform the work of producing the mutual recognition upon which democracy depends?

'It's Not Something That's Talked About'

It is within the intimate sphere of the family that people first encounter the strange dynamics of politics. They become famil-iar with the asymmetries, injustices, legitimations and silences that surround the distribution of domestic power and learn that some things cannot be spoken about, at least at certain times and in particular places. While there is much evidence to suggest that people are more likely to discuss their political views within the familiarity and safety of their own homes (Huckfeldt and Sprague, 1995; Pattie and Johnston, 2008; Hatemi et al., 2009; Settle, Bond and Levitt, 2010), even there accepted protocols of equivocation commonly prevail. Families are contradictory spaces of unconditional openness and selective reticence. People who will regularly expose their unclothed bodies and private languages to one another can be peculiarly coy when it comes to disclosing their political identities. For example, retired textile merchant, Bill, recalled that voting was never discussed in his family when he was growing up:

> In fact, there was a family thing not to discuss politics in the house because my grandfather lived in the house and he was very socialist. And so, erm, there was always a problem with talking politics because the clash between my father and my grandfather was always ... rather interesting.

When he became an adult, Bill maintained this taboo within his own family:

> I don't think I discuss it with my children. It's up to them to make their own minds up. I don't discuss it with my wife, Ruth. She makes her own mind up.... She doesn't tell me who she votes for. And I might not tell her either.

Joan, a twenty-eight-year-old waitress, never tells her husband how she votes and has never asked him how he votes: 'I don't ask. I could probably guess'. I asked her whether he could guess how she votes: 'No, he couldn't guess at owt I do' she said, 'I'm a law unto myself'. Neither Bill nor Joan seemed to be keeping a secret from their families, in the way that one might conceal a love affair or an offensive habit. A curious kind of discretion seemed to be at work in these cases, closing down the scope for indelicacy rather than disagreement. It was not so much that voting preferences would cause bitter conflict, but that existing fractures within ossified relationships might be allowed to leak out. Daisy, a schoolteacher, explained why she would never discuss voting with her third sister:

> Well, you see, there's history with my sister, isn't there. There's other issues as well. And they, you know ... I remember those and they come into play and there's only a certain point you can go before ... I won't. On any subject but politics. I won't go beyond that with her. But with a total stranger I could go on all day, and have a discussion all day.

At stake in these cases seems to be less a sensitivity to potential disagreements about how to vote than a fear of political talk itself – for, in making the distribution of state power a matter for debate, power dynamics that are closer to home (indeed, within the home) might be raised to the surface. Rarely exposed to direct scrutiny, the mundane power play of family life resonates within the everyday experience of the intimately acquainted. Questions about who gets what, when and how (from control of the television remote to priority use of the bathroom) pervade the domestic sphere, but usually in whispers, sporadic rows and enduring resentments.

It is less the act of voting itself than the power relationships lying behind it that curtails political talk within the family. The political theorist William Connolly (1983:97), has observed that 'those who exercise power over others typically seek to deny it or to hide it'. They seek to limit the degree to which they are morally responsible for interfering in the lives of others. Similarly, those who submit to power have ethical and psychological interests in denying their subordination and concealing the extent to which they have either voluntarily surrendered to forces they might have resisted or involuntarily succumbed to structures they deem to be irresistible. Ongoing experiences of being subjected to meddling, curtailment, transgression, manipulation and coercion evoke feelings of shame, regret and anger. The feeling of having a less-than-absolute choice – of being compromised by the intractability of power structures – can unleash a torrent of unruly emotions. Easier, perhaps, to say nothing – to confine such decisions to the region of the unspeakable.

When Charlotte, a thirty-four-year-old dental nurse, told me that 'I asked me mum who she voted for once, just out of curiosity, and she went, "Oh, we don't discuss things like that"', one senses a tense sub-surface narrative of stealthy defensiveness and disappointed inquiry. That Charlotte's mother felt able to tell her daughter what 'we' discuss and what is proscribed suggests a well-established pattern of power within the family in which one actor felt bound to yield to the demands of the other. What else had Charlotte's mother led her to understand 'we don't discuss' and what implicit sense of the consequences of transgression would Charlotte have absorbed in the course

of growing up? In some families, the claim that 'we don't discuss things like that' might have triggered a power play; or
Charlotte might have decided that her mother's secrecy would
lead her to be much more open about her own voting behaviour with her own children. Her mother's statement proved to
be perlocutionary.

Herman, a postman in his late forties, explained how he would
never discuss voting with his wife's family:

> Everything gets too heated. You know, they're not … they won't
> take on people's opinions. They don't like it if you don't share
> their opinion. Which I don't mind at all, because I love winding
> them up.

For Herman, this habit of keeping quiet about voting was
acquired as a teenager:

> I think it was just the secrecy round it when I was brought up.
> You know, it was all a bit cloak and dagger. A bit 'shoosh', you
> know. I mean, I knew who my parents were voting for. But you
> didn't talk about it … and that stuck with me. And so, it's like,
> you keep it going.

Keeping it going is hard work. The abiding fortifications of the
family pecking order can subdue outspoken reflexivity; where
power relationships are both tacit and vexatious, stealthy silence
is often the easiest response.

Habits of political disappearance extend beyond the family.
Raji, a twenty-six-year-old bank worker, explained:

> I don't know if my friends vote, to be honest. It's not something
> that's talked about. I've never spoken about it with my friends …
> I suppose it's a bit of a taboo, isn't it?

Asked whether she would talk to anyone at all about how she
votes, Joan (who never discloses her voting preference to her
husband) responded mantra-like, 'You stay away from money
and politics, don't you? And religion. They're the only no-nos,
aren't they?' Likewise, Ella, a secretary in her early thirties,
responded instantly to my question by citing 'that old saying:
"You don't discuss politics or religion when you're out"'. Hugh,

a sixty-four-year-old pub entertainer, struggled for a moment to remember the standard response:

> What is it that people say? 'You shouldn't talk about religion and politics'. I wouldn't do it because I don't think it's worth it in the long run.

This all sounds rather perilous. No-nos; not worth it in the long run; not something that's talked about. Beneath such glib refusals and inhibitions, other feelings are surely at work. For several interviewees, the rationale for secrecy was ascribed to imagined external threats and predicaments that could only be avoided by playing dumb. Unlike Sana's real experience of being tormented, these projections were rarely based on anything that had actually happened to the interviewees or to anyone that they knew. They were phantom provocations, rooted in a counterfactual democracy in which safety was incompatible with transparency. In speaking of these projected risks and threats surrounding political discourse, interviewees spoke of how public disagreement between friends and neighbours might trigger violent disorder.

Edward, a retired lawyer, explained how the secret ballot ensured that he was 'not subject to any harassment or questioning by anybody else'. He offered no examples of where or when such harassment or interrogation had been suffered by others, but seemed to assume that the danger would be understood. Likewise, Robert, a fifty-year-old surveyor, explained that if voting were not secret, 'I feel that it would be open to some sort of misuse'. He paused and moved a little towards me: 'And you think of the possible brick through your window or something like that'. This fear was reinforced by retired textile manufacturer, Teddy:

> The great thing about a secret ballot is that that is your view. You're not being persuaded by your next door neighbour who is saying 'Hoorah hoorah, we're gonna do that' and everyone puts their hand up and you sort of feel, 'Well, this is going to the common vote. I don't really agree with it, but I don't want to be seen as not one of the herd, so I'd better put my hand up'. So I think I'm in favour of the secret ballot and continuing with that.

Such references to the dark consequences of open democracy were consistent with findings from social psychology showing that most people become nervous when faced with situations in which they are expected to express their views publicly. In their study of political self-censorship, Hayes et al. (2006) observe:

> The public expression of one's opinions entails the real likelihood of being scrutinized, criticized, put on the defensive, or ostracized by others who disagree.... It is not uncommon to hear of reports of people with different political beliefs clashing in public, sometimes to the point of physical violence.... Given these risks, it is hard to fault people for keeping their political opinions hidden from the views of others.

While fear of such embarrassing clashes and hostile responses might reasonably deter people in particularly divided societies from speaking openly about their political preferences, why should this apply to relatively stable and tranquil political cultures? Noelle-Neumann's (1993) work on the 'spiral of silence' shows how most people prefer to conform to perceived common opinion than to face the social consequences of unpopular dissent. Eliasoph's (1998:230) account of the strategies adopted by Americans to avoid explicit reference to politics in everyday conversation suggests that 'civic etiquette' has 'made imaginative, open-minded, thoughtful conversation rare in public, front-stage settings'. These theories of political reticence build on Goffman's (1968) dramaturgical account of how the performed self is committed to the ends of role maintenance and impression management. As a means of protecting 'face', citizens retreat into a backstage world in which political talk is euphemised as 'common sense' or 'localised action': the 'hidden transcripts' (Scott, 1990 by which the weak seek to evade and appease unvanquishable power-holders. While political discourse does indeed frequently vanish into strategic silence and sham indifference, the complex operation of voter secrecy amounts to more than a matter of where and before whom political self-presentation takes place.

The problem with Goffman's, Noelle-Neumann's and Eliasoph's accounts of political disappearance is that they all assume the political self to be a singular, integrated and stable entity, split between public coyness and private candour. But what if political identities are layered and internally inconsistent rather than settled and coherent? What if, rather than meanly refusing to reveal their political preferences, voters are driven to stealthiness by the impossible burden of condensing their multilayered selves into a political act that can never do justice to the plurality of their values? What if voting turns out to be less an expression of political identity than a painful reminder of the irreconcilability of the divergent subjective claims that inexorably fracture the political self? Interviewees alluded again and again to fears that political talk might somehow unmask voters' self-representations, exposing incongruities and shams that they would prefer to remain hidden. Tina, a woman in her early thirties, explained that non-secret voting would be a cause of discomfort to her:

> I think it would put a lot of people off. I think … you know … you may say one thing, but you may choose to do something else. And, you know, we're all … you know … complex characters. And I think it's just something that should be individual to you.

Lara, a housing worker in her mid-forties, alluded to the risk of being exposed to public shame:

> Say somebody who had political views that they were ashamed of, but they still held them … that could be that their friends are all massive Conservatives and they actually want to vote for the Green Party. But, you know, they're a bit ashamed because their mates are a bunch of lads, or anything like that. So I think it is important maybe to encourage people to … keep it secret.

I asked Lara to say more about what might cause people to feel ashamed of the way they vote. 'I think it could be if you're voting for a party that is uncool', she explained. Rose, a woman in her early fifties, seemed very conscious of this potential for shame when she spoke about her experience of voting:

> It's a very isolating action. I think it is. When you go to a polling booth everything is kind of, er … secret. You hide behind a booth. You hide.

I asked Rose whether she felt that she was actually hiding from anyone:

> Well, there are some people who might be feeling rather ashamed ... or, you know, wouldn't want other people to see what they were putting their cross for. Whatever reason that might be ... there would be some people who are in that position, I'm sure.

The reason for this discomfort, according to Rose, was that

> most people who vote ... the vast majority of people who vote ... are not really sure of their convictions ... at all. They vote because they've had peer pressure ... or whatever kind of pressure. They're not really sure of their convictions. And therefore, if people could see their vote they'd feel more exposed. It gives them some kind of protection from what others might say or might think.

Rose's account of people feeling compelled to encapsulate their diverse and uncertain personal convictions within a momentary expression of political preference resonated with what many other interviewees had said. Shame reflected deep-felt uncertainty rather than well-closeted convictions. Disappearance was less about withholding a formed political identity from public judgement than needing time and space to nurture a convincingly coherent sense of political self to put on show for public recognition.

The secret space of voting is not just the polling station, but what Archer (2003:130) calls 'the inner conversation ... by which agents reflexively deliberate upon the social circumstances that they confront'. Rejecting Goffman's behaviourist analysis, which assumes that intentions are revealed through external interaction, Archer argues that the emergence of preferences through internal dialogue is inherently invulnerable to extrospection:

> Because they possess personal identity, as defined by their individual configuration of concerns, they know what they care about most and what they seek to realise in society. Because they are capable of internally deliberating about themselves in relation to their social circumstances, they are the authors of projects that they (fallibly) believe will achieve something of what they want from and in society. Because pursuit of a social project generally spells an encounter with social power, in the form of constraints

and enablements, then the ongoing 'internal conversation' will mediate agents' receptions of these structural and cultural influences.

In this space of mediatory self-reflection, political identities are devised, rationalised, revised and rehearsed. Values are weighed against values and converted into opinions and prejudices, sometimes resolved into expressible preferences, but often remaining too raw to the touch for public exposure. Of course, the process that Archer so ably describes is invariably messy, with vast overlaps between thought and feeling, dream and consciousness, experience and projection, commitment and aspiration. Cutting across all of this, however, is a search for subjective sincerity: a need to give substance and integrity to the pronoun 'I' before it melds into the aggregative mix of the counted 'we'. Secrecy in this context guards the border between personal reflection and public performance. Before seeking recognition, people need to feel certain of their own sincerity: the integrating connection between experience, feeling and action. Without such self-assurance, voters risk being misunderstood as mere adventurers whose values are wholly opportunistic or fraudulent. When retired solicitor Theo worried aloud that 'you might appear to have been a life-long socialist and in actual fact you might have been a closeted Tory' and Anne, a council administrator in her early thirties, explained that 'people might think, you know, you got ideas above your station if you vote for one party', they were alluding to the shame of misrecognition. Convincing self-recognition has to precede recognition by others.

Esther, a retired nursing sister, explained that 'I think I did tell my friend who I voted for, and I think that she told me who she voted for. But not before the event'. Esther was happy to be sociable, exchanging information with her friend, but needed time before voting to reflect on her political identity. I asked her whether it would have been different had she spoken to her friend before casting her vote:

No ... after. There is no way that she tried to persuade me to vote in any way. She wouldn't be a friend if she did.

Angus, a retired research scientist, explained how he was a member of a golf club which he jokingly described as 'a bastion of fascism', but 'I'm not going to let politics ruin a good game of golf', so 'I don't talk about voting intentions'. He managed to separate his political identity from his everyday sociability. The layer of Angus's identity that could happily fraternise with people he wryly referred to as fascists co-existed with his commitment to the political values that he invests in his vote. The process of working through these conflicting layers of self-identity is for most people a highly sensitive and guarded project.

Political scientists have tended to focus mainly on preference outcomes rather than the individual struggles of conscience that underlie preference formation. In recent years, however, some political theorists have started to pay attention to how political preferences are the product of dramas of internal deliberation (Goodin, 2000). As Ankersmit (2002:106) has put it, referring to morally charged policy issues, 'conflict between citizens is exchanged for a conflict within the mind of the individual citizen'. This perspective is most cogently developed in Dryzek's (2010:323–4) critique of the liberal 'image of a well-organized and unitary self' that knows what 'it' wants and needs. Arguing that the political self is always a fractured entity, Dryzek argues that 'it is always some aspect of the self in its entirety that gets represented'. Following Castiglione and Warren's (2006) observation that what gets represented in democracies 'are not persons as such, but some of the interests, identities and values that persons have or hold', Dryzek invites us to abandon the simplistic conception of elections as aggregations of fixed interests emanating from bounded and stable individuals. It is much more complicated than that. Each voter is a site of competing internalised norms and scripts from which a silent vocabulary of moral reasoning is derived. Using this vocabulary to work through their experiences, feelings and actions, voters must come to terms with the frequently inconsistent clusters of perceived interests and values that shape their political subjectivity (Markus, 1977; Tajfel, 1981; Elster, 1987; Melucci, 1989; Brewer, 2001; Kristjansson, 2009). Goodin (2003:55) observes that, despite the emphasis placed by democratic theorists on external-collective deliberation, 'the weighing of reasons for or against a course of action … can and ultimately must take place within the head of each individual'. At its most basic level, such private reflexivity is a necessary means of sorting and ordering personal interests and values; at its best, it is a form of 'empathetic imagining' (Goodin, 2003:62) whereby the needs and feelings of others enter into the balance of personal preference formation. What Goodin calls 'inner deliberation' and Archer calls 'the internal conversation' amount to neither artful concealment nor a wish to hide from public appearance. They constitute a form of internalised aggregation, not unlike the external aggregation that turns individual votes into a public mandate.

Taking this conception of two aggregations a little further, we might say that each one comprises both a stage that cannot be conducted in public and a stage that must enter an Arendtian 'space of appearance' if it is to carry a democratic warrant. Internalised aggregation entails a first stage (Ii) in which the individual political self is put together. This is commonly referred to as making up one's mind. The second stage (Iii) entails discussion with others – and perhaps even more formal deliberation – so that one is exposed to the real (rather than imagined) voices of others. External-collective aggregation entails a secret first stage (Ei): the act of casting a vote without interference from anyone else. This is followed by a public second stage (Eii): the declaration of the combined public will. The problem of democratic disappearance occurs when there is no clear connection between Ii and Ei; when internalised aggregation feeds directly into external-collective aggregation, with no space in between for Ii thoughts to pass through public discourse into shared meaning.

When I asked interviewees whether they would consider engaging in discussion with their fellow citizens before casting their votes (a practice that Ackerman and Fishkin [2004] have suggested should be institutionalised), there were two common responses. The first was an anxiety that such discussion would lead to disagreement, mutual distrust and personal animosity. As Ella, a secretary in her early thirties, put it,

> I think it's such an emotive subject. People either feeling nothing
> for it or feel very strongly for it ... and it can become quite ...
> quite edgy, quite provo, – you know, to sit there and have that
> opinion, if you've got somebody else whose strong-minded. It can
> turn into an argument as opposed to a discussion.

Sana expressed concern that 'everyone's got a different opinion
and it would cause more trouble than it's worth', and Nyasia, a
builder in his late twenties, said that 'as much it can be good ...
it could become a big disadvantage because people might just get
a bit too personal'.

The second common response was a vaguely expressed recollection of a bygone age when politicians and voters had been
in much closer communication with each other, at least at election time. People would speak nostalgically about 'the hustings';
some were old enough to remember such moments of rhetorical
drama; others spoke of them as if drawing on a trace memory,
reminding themselves of a time when elections were public occasions and the mass visibility of the citizenry, enfranchised and
excluded alike, had not yet given way to the secretiveness of the
atomised voter. (See 2 for an account of this history). But even
when it was recalled, this trace was little more than a flicker followed by a sigh:

> Unfortunately neighbourhoods aren't like that anymore. It's a
> shame, but if they were they could get together and say: 'Well,
> you know, this is going to affect us, so let's say what we want out
> of out councillor'. I think things would work. But the world's just
> not like that anymore, is it? (Tracey, a forty-one-year-old single
> mother)

Distanced from the trace memory of public politics, few interviewees could even comprehend that there might be any alternative
to voter inscrutability. As Lara, a housing worker in her late thirties, explained when asked whether voting should be in secret,

> I've never thought about it because it always is in secret. I've never
> considered what it would be like if it weren't secret.

Like much else that is 'never considered' because it 'always is',
few interviewees could say for sure why voting was surrounded

by secrecy, but most felt quite sure that it had to be. From a rational-instrumentalist perspective, a case could be made for open voting as a guard against the free-riding and duplicity made possible by secret ballots. But such a remedy applies only to preference outcomes. From the perspective of preference formation and input, disappearance from public observation may well be crucial to the affective choreography through which voters move between the internalised construction of their political selves and their socially articulated demands to be counted.

'Not Accepted in the Community'

If democracy depends on making citizens appear, its counterpart is a form of bullying exclusion which makes them disappear. The violence inflicted upon Sana, whose family believed that, having dared to escape their grasp, she should be denied any consequential presence beyond it, well illustrates the way in which citizens can come to be discounted; hidden away and made politically invisible. Lakyta, a former deputy headmistress and community leader, explained how she too had been deterred from voting by racist threats from neighbours who objected to an Afro-Carribean family moving into their area:

> I didn't vote for years because they wouldn't let me. The community ... they would bar us from most of the clubs and the voting things so we didn't vote. We were told quite clearly, 'Just do not come. You're not ... you won't be allowed in'. They said we're not accepted in the community. We should keep ourselves to ourselves. Well, I'm saying it politely, but, more or less, you don't have a ... you shouldn't be here ...

It is not only self-selecting bullies from dysfunctional families and bigoted neighbourhoods that enforce such exclusions. As Arendt (1958:267) noted when writing about displaced people after the Second World War, 'once they had left their state they became stateless; once they had been deprived of their human rights they were rightless, the scum of the earth'. States have long endeavoured to ensure that those they regard as morally unfit for inclusion are made to disappear, leaving them to represent nothing but their 'own absolutely unique individuality which, deprived of expression within and action upon a common world, loses all significance' (Arendt, 1958:302). The notion of 'civil death', whereby the troublesome are cast out of the politico-judicial community, captures the sense in which states have claimed the power to sanction disappearance. As Ewald (2002:1059) points out:

> In ancient Greece, those criminals 'pronounced infamous' were unable to appear in court or vote in the assembly, to make public speeches, or serve in the army. In Rome, the ability to hold office and to vote in the public assembly could be denied to those tagged with *infamia*. During the Renaissance, peoples across Europe used the condition of 'outlawry' to punish some criminals; 'outlaws' could be killed with impunity, since they were literally considered to be outside the law. European lawmakers later developed the concept of 'civil death, which put an end to the person by destroying the basis of legal capacity, as did natural death by destroying physical existence.' In England, 'a person pronounced attainted after conviction for a felony or ... treason [faced] forfeiture corruption of the blood [meaning that land owned by the criminal would pass not to heirs but to king or lord], and loss of civil rights.' As on the continent, these practices were known in England as 'civil death,' and the attainted criminal was said to be 'dead in law' because he could not perform any legal function including, of course, voting.

Prisons are the contemporary repositories of the rightless. They are places of involuntary disappearance and compulsory appearance; the former an attempt by society to render invisible its least controllable subjects; the latter a surveillance strategy, intended to prevent the escape of miscreants from public scrutiny. Disenfranchising the incarcerated strikes at two of the most powerful human aspirations: to be recognised as an autonomous member of society, while possessing an identity over which one has control. To vote is to demand a certain kind of recognition, to make a mark and be counted as a member of the public. To be denied such recognition is a painful experience, made worse if one is reduced to being spoken for: represented without self-representation. In this sense, the disenfranchised prisoner is the other of the sovereign voter.

I was eager to understand more about this political 'other'. Might those who had been stripped of their right to vote articulate something important about what it is that they have lost? (By interrogating pathology, norms become apparent). Even though, as one prisoner candidly put it to me, voting was 'not going to be the first thing on my mind' when her release day came, the fact that it was on her mind at all suggests that there is some kind of an affective relationship between the frustration of enforced disappearance and the promise of civic appearance.

Thirty-three-year-old Tracey was an inmate on the lifer's wing of a women's prison in the north of England. 'Feeling free to me is just being able to make my own decisions on a day to day basis', she told me. 'Freedom's become a different thing to me since I've come into prison. I don't think I appreciated it before I came ... it's just about being able to make your own choices really, I think'. Once in prison, she explained, decisions are made for you by other people. And the right to contest those decisions disappears:

> Most [prison] officers, I can say to them, you know, 'I don't agree with that there and this is the reason why' and they will take time to explain to me why they've made that decision. There are a few that you couldn't possibly say that to because they would just say, 'I'm big, you're small. I'm right, you're wrong', you know?

Tracey experienced this denial of agency as truly dehumanising: 'you feel almost as if you're not a human being really'. Twenty-nine-year-old Veronica was also serving a long sentence in the same prison. Like Tracey, she spoke as if prison had robbed her of her self: 'When I first came in I were just stripped of me individuality ... you belong to somebody else'. Removed from the sphere of political interaction, Veronica felt as if she was in a solipsistic void where the action open to her was self-referential:

> You can't make decisions in here. You can try and make a change only to yourself. You can't make a change to others.

In this sense, far from being a place of socialisation and rehabilitation, prison is a space of desocialisation and radical atomisation. Anxiety-driven attempts to exclude the unworthy from society (Young, 1999), as if their presence might contaminate the moral air, are symbolically reinforced by adding disenfranchisement to incarceration. For if voters are citizens in a process of fusion with the social body, prisoners constitute a toxic threat from which the social body must be immunised.

As I have been writing this chapter, the issue has become a matter of intense debate in Britain, following a ruling by the European Court of Human Rights firmly rejecting the view that denying the vote is an appropriate element of prisoners' punishment and criticising the imposition of a sanction which bears no relation to the original crime. A government minister appeared before the House of Commons on 2 November 2010 to explain that

> the UK's blanket ban on sentenced prisoners voting was declared unlawful by the grand chamber of the European Court of Human Rights in October 2005, as a result of a successful challenge by a prisoner, John Hirst. The Government accept, as did the previous Government, that as a result of the judgment of the Strasbourg Court in the Hirst case, there is a need to change the law. This is not a choice; it is a legal obligation. (Hansard, 2 November 2010)

The following day Prime Minister David Cameron, responded to this acceptance of European law by his own government in somewhat visceral terms:

> It makes me physically ill even to contemplate having to give the vote to anyone who is in prison. It makes me physically ill to hear an elected official say such a thing…. Frankly, when people commit a crime and go to prison, they should lose their rights, including the right to vote. (Hansard, 3 November 2010)

The root of Cameron's queasiness can be traced to a fear that the body politic will be vitiated by base elements. Constructed through the aggregation of bodies worthy of being counted, the body politic must be shielded from the dross of the prodigal. The prime minister's feeling of illness at the very thought of the rightless being allowed to vote signifies a commitment to disappearance as a solution to abjection. Quite simply, those who are morally beyond the pale are best not seen or heard or counted. They cannot be trusted to perform the inner deliberation that is the hallmark of the citizen-voter. Even to 'contemplate' the idea that such worthless people might be permitted to arrive at values that could feed into the collective ethos fills him with horror, manifested in a proclaimed sickness. This was later echoed by the former government minister, Jonathan Aitken, who was convicted of perjury in 1999, receiving an eighteen-month prison sentence. 'One of the terms for criminal', writes Aitken, 'is an outlaw, someone who puts themselves outside the law. You might say people who commit crimes serious enough to go to put themselves outside the law-making process. The small-c conservative in me says don't change it' (*Guardian*, 'A Stretch too Far?' 23 April 2011).

But, returning to the multiple selves that cohere within the vote, one might wonder whether Cameron's disquiet and Aitken's predilection stem from a deeper anxiety. As figures of abjection, prisoners invoke disgust because 'they were a part of "us" yesterday, but are expelled from among us as the unnecessary and the redundant, the leftover from humanity's feast that is instinctively thrown aside' (Hyde, 1997:192). Seeming at first 'to emanate from an exorbitant outside', the most profound threat presented by the abject is that they in fact emanated from an 'inside, ejected' (Kristeva, 1982:1); that is to say, they bear worrying similarities to the social values, practices, contradictions, deceptions and self-delusions that characterise popular political judgement. They are disconcertingly like us.

The prisoners I interviewed were indeed remarkably like everyone else I interviewed: they argued that voting should be a secret act; that the most evil wrongdoers (never themselves) should be disenfranchised; and that voting was something of importance to them now that they were not allowed to do it. When released, they will once more become components and guardians of the body politic. The prime minister's disgust at the very thought of their being allowed to vote will turn into respect for them as potential electors. Their hitherto abject selves will remain a secret to their fellow voters, as will their expressed political preferences. They will be welcomed into a democracy in which nobody need ever know who they are, what they think or why they think it: from panoptic confinement to liberal invisibility.

7

Becoming Us

The good citizens meet on the last Thursday of every month in the restaurant of a hotel in a small market town in the north of England. They do not look conspicuously like good citizens – but, then, what exactly does a good citizen look like? They are all men aged forty-plus. Most are or were 'in business'. They wear blazers and ties and well-polished shoes. They move and speak with restraint.

At 7 PM they assemble in the bar and talk, over gin-and-tonics and, occasionally, glasses of mid-range wine, about their businesses, families and the latest news headlines. After a period of mingling, they take their seats in the restaurant, where the menu is never surprising. Between the main course and dessert, the chairman announces how much money they have raised in the previous month. This declaration is neither pompous nor self-congratulatory, but a modest sharing of positive news. The good citizens applaud their charitable accomplishment, and in doing so pay tribute to a way of being in the world that suits them well. By 9.30 PM the restaurant is empty.

But this month's gathering has an unusual mood about it. The air is pregnant with eventfulness. The pre-dinner mingling is somehow animated; men cast their eyes furtively across the room before exchanging comments with their own circle of trusted fraternisers. They choose their seats in the restaurant strategically, like men lining up for a battle. On this occasion, the chairman's announcement of the monthly charity collection is not the focus of the good citizens' attention. They are waiting for something else to happen. There is serious business to be done here. That is why I have come along.

I had been contacted by a man describing himself as a friend of one of my interviewees. He had heard about my interest in 'voting and that sort of thing'. The organisation of which he had been a member for more than twenty years was about to hold a contested election – the first one he could recall ever having taken place. Perhaps I would like to come and observe it? He had left a landline number on my answering machine: 'I don't do emails or text messages and that sort of thing' he explained, 'but if you'd like to come and see what happens, I'd be happy to take you along'. I called back, saying that I'd very much like to come along.

The terms of the electoral contest turned out to be perplexingly opaque, involving a major falling-out between two committee members over the interpretation of by-laws, the proposed price of lottery tickets for the Christmas party and an incident involving a parking space for the disabled. To this outsider, it seemed plainly to be a personality dispute between men of basically similar types holding essentially similar ideas. In this sense, it was depressingly reminiscent of too many elections I had witnessed in other contexts. But it was not the lustreless claims of the contestants that grabbed my attention. It was the fervour of the voters that I found intriguing. Their sense of being part of a social performance cast important light on how the aura of voting is generated.

Social performances are not naturally occurring situations, but purposefully devised events which depend for their success on a subtle combination of existing action repertoires and symbolic improvisation. When a social performance has not been enacted before (as in the case of the good citizens' contested election), it has first to be imagined, then shared as an ideal and then realised performatively in ways that maintain its credibility. That the good citizens decided to hold a contested election – in which disagreements were aired before all of their members – and not a duel, a bidding war or an appeal to the gods was because one particular action repertoire had come to dominate their collective imagination (Tilly, 2008). Before the event happened, it existed as a mental montage of fragmented memories, reveries and customs. Connolly (2002:28) has described how

> virtual memories are pervaded by affective charges, ranging from a surge of panic through a radiant feeling of joy to myriad other possibilities. As they are quickly mobilized to meet an encounter – that is, to translate a sensory encounter into experience – the affective charges help to move thinking and judgement in some directions rather than others. ... It is not ... that you first represent things and then add subjective feelings. Perception is set in action contexts and organized through complex mixtures of sensory encounter, virtual memory, and bodily affect.

Thrift (2008:35) refers to this affective evocation as 'the mobilisation of forethought'; a process of event-making that draws equally upon the inertia of habit, the limits of contingency and the vitality of the instant. Watching the good citizens as they sat listening to the speeches of the contending committee members, it was clear that they were more than mere consumers of a spectacle. Their task was to co-produce the performance in which they were acting. Their mood set the electoral scene, drawing on previous scenes that were spectrally present through their ambient effects. Like congregants at a funeral service or board members gathering to make a far-reaching decision, the scene had to accord with an appropriate affective register. While the gavel-wielding chairman's somewhat pompous introduction to the electoral contest contributed to the theatricality of the moment, it was the collective readiness of the good citizens to set the tone that modulated the drama and endowed it with eventfulness.

On the surface, the social performance of voting appeared to be a solemn political ritual, characterised by a rhetorical commitment to the sublimity of the occasion – an intensity of focused attention and a collective effort to display respect to the process. Upon closer observation, however, this apparently simple electoral event proved to be a stratified performance, comprising

membranous layers of affect. Closely beneath the sacerdotal surface was a layer of pronounced irony: muttered jokes about how
the candidates were 'playing at politics'; how the voters seated
at their tables would only be able to keep awake during the
speeches by putting matchsticks in their eyes; and, as one wry
ironist put it, how he would 'prefer not to vote for anyone who
actually wants to be a member of the committee'. This whimsi-
cality undermined the august character of the event by pointing
to the contrast between its foundation as a source of institutional
stability and endurance and its shabby instrumentalism. These
were the two most obvious features of the social performance.
Beyond them, something metaphysical appeared to be happening: the good citizens were forming themselves into a single, representable body; a moment of political metamorphosis through
which the estrangement of individual agency is fused into an
aggregated whole. While the contrapuntal mood music of solemnity and drollery sets the scene for the voting performance, this
third layer serves to make the scene possible. It engenders the
assemblage of the body politic.

To be represented as one body, hitherto dispersed and atomised bodies must come together in ways that allow others to
speak of them by one name. Without such a commitment to
being represented, any attempt to speak in their name would
lack legitimacy. The act of becoming representable entails a willingness to abandon oneself to the indivisible force of a collectivity. This resembles what Victor Turner (1969:177) refers to as
communitas: a liminal moment wherein the social order becomes
'an undifferentiated, homogeneous whole, in which individuals
confront one another integrally and not as "segmentalized" into
statuses and roles'. The more coordinated the fusion, the more
successful is representation likely to be. Conversely, weak integration tends to produce enfeebled forms of representation.

To the end of fusing affectively, and therefore effectively, the
good citizens worked hard to co-produce a common feeling:
a semblance of unbounded fellowship. How much depth lay
beneath that appearance and whether it was sustained after the
election is beyond the scope of this study. The relevance of the

good citizens' aspirational *communitas* was its sharp resonance with what my interviewees had spoken about when asked to tell me what they wanted voting to feel like. Listening to these accounts of counterfactual democracy, I was struck by how important mundane yearnings of democratic sociability were in creating the conditions for an 'us' that could be represented. As I re-heard and re-read the interviews, I began to detect a pervasive desire for social performances of voting to be rooted in something more than fleeting moments of civic estrangement. The aim of this chapter is to recognise and understand that desire and to explore the affective conditions for meaningful representability.

'Flying Around the Housing Estates Picking Up People'

When Anne spoke about her memories of voting, her face lit up. She recalled the 'big red bus' that symbolised her feeling of civic solidarity:

> I do remember. I have memories of things that have gone off in the past. I remember one of our local MPs having like a big red bus and sort of going around where we live with like a megaphone, encouraging people to go along ... and I thought that was quite cool. I didn't understand what it was all about because I was a child, but I know I have that memory in my mind: the red bus going around with music playing and people and balloons and you know ... So it was fun as well as something that they needed to get done.

As she spoke about how she wanted to feel as a voter, Anne kept returning to the image of the big red bus:

> I'd have me bus, me red bus that would go around with the balloons. And it would just pick people up and it just wouldn't ... you wouldn't have to pay. It would just, you know, be catchy music. It would be balloons. It would be banners. It would be everything. It would be just like a London open-top bus, just flying around the housing estates picking up people and saying 'Come on over to go and vote. Off you go' and they'd say 'I cant do it because of the kids' and you'd say 'Right, bring the kids as well'. Kids come on the bus ... you get some colouring pens; you get your the bag of stuff that they get, mum's been in, voted and

come back out. It's as simple as that. You've just got to know how to sell it really, I think. And if you can do that, then I think you might be on to a winner.

Why is this image of voting so powerfully evocative? The memory originates in what had most likely been a purely strategic manoeuvre: a group of politicians in an office deciding to hire a bus and travel round the constituency playing jolly music interspersed with megaphone-delivered slogans. To Anne and her fellow children, who 'didn't understand what it was all about' but knew instinctively that they were in the midst of something eventful, the red bus aroused an array of feelings that both exceeded and shaped the simple act of voting. Now in her mid-thirties, Anne imagined the big red bus as an aesthetic symbol, infusing the social performance of voting with sociability and *jouissance*. How does such symbolism work?

Consider two contrasting metaphors: Anne's 'big red bus' of electoral democracy and Plato's 'ship of state'. The latter has been much discussed by political theorists seeking to understand how this symbolic reference encapsulated Plato's conception of statehood (Walzer, 1983:284–7; Ankersmit, 1996:254–294). In contrast to the civic simplicity of a bus, the ship of state evokes purposeful grandiosity. According to Ankersmit, it implies that states must be goal-driven, following a course like a ship heading for land; that this course is determined by a captain whose perspective is beyond that of the ship or its crew; and that the function of the state is to integrate a range of elements – boards, ropes, sails, telescopes, crew – into a single entity. As these components of the metaphor come to seem like natural descriptions of statehood, reality comes to be constructed in the terms in which it was first only imagined. As Ankersmit (1996:261) puts it, 'Metaphor ... is the missing link between the "is" and the "ought"'. In the case of the big red bus, the metaphor brings together three powerful images: the evanescent and quotidian character of a public vehicle; the colourful spectacularity of the carnivalesque; and the promise of a journey, with its inherent linkage between intended destination and anticipated arrival.

As a banal symbol of everyday sociability, the bus is literally for everyone who wants to get on, especially when 'you wouldn't have to pay'. As Allyson Noble (2008:18) observes in her superb sociological study of Edinburgh buses, the bus is 'an important public space ... a place of potential equality where everyone has to make a small sacrifice for the greater good of the bus as an entity'. She argues that the bus is 'much more than a mode of transport that moves people from one location to another', for the bus passes through the city, while the city passes through the bus. (ibid:4; see also Jungnickel, 2003) While the conventional image of the static, silent polling station refers to citizens going to a place to complete a routine task, the metaphor of the big red bus captures the idea of democracy passing through the electorate. The social performance of voting takes in a motile, peripatetic form, circulating rather than frozen *in situ*.

For most interviewees, however, this notion of democratic mobility was absent from even their accounts of voter sociability. The relationship between the act of voting and a fixed place remained important to them. But not the voting places that we have come to know. The polling stations of interviewees' imaginations were characterised by an atmosphere of congeniality, represented by a symbol even more modest and mundane than the public bus: the cup of tea. Rita, a housewife, suggested that it 'would be nice to be able to get a cup of tea, even if you had to pay for it. And then you could have a chat. Yeah, that's right, have a chat. Even if it's only about weather'. It was as if the symbolic presence of the cup of tea gave permission for everyday talk to occur. Becca, a teenage mother, suggested:

> Drinks'd be good! I know that me dad's always mentioning drinks. Not like *drink* – just even a cup of tea. Yeah, he just mentioned a cup of tea. He says 'I can sit there waiting ages sometimes, depending how long it is. I want me cup of tea'.

Rose, a college administrator, was quite precise about what she wanted:

> I think that some refreshments would be a very good idea actually, especially for older people. I think, you know, it would ... get

more of a community feeling. And have a section of the polling booth, a room, a section of the room where they have tables and chairs. I think that would be quite useful. But I think they should go after they've voted. Not to go and have their tea beforehand. I think they should do the voting first and then a separate room, somewhere they can go and discuss things.

Denise, who works as a cook, expressed a similar desire:

All it would take would be that you could get a hot drink and have a newspaper and, you know, a designated area where people could just chill a little bit before you go and vote ... I used to walk. I used to make a point of walking to where I was voting. It's probably about ten, fifteen minutes from where I live and it would just be nice ... it's like, all the kerfuffle when you get there and all the dowerness of it. It's all a bit intense ... and I'm sure the volunteers that do it think it would lighten it a little bit.

The one polling clerk that I interviewed – Joan – told me how she had made a unilateral decision to brighten up her polling station. 'I always have music on', she told me:

I take me radio down. Background, yeah. It's not head banging stuff. I don't know whether it's allowed or not. I've never even looked into that.

I asked her whether anyone has ever complained about having music playing while they're voting. 'Absolutely not ... it's usually Radio Two', she says. 'They say it's a nice change to come in'. Joan tells me that she's 'wanted to put cups of tea on for years ... some of the old dears that come, they'd sit and have a chat and other people would come if there was something there for 'em'.

While some yearned for – and Joan offers – a cheery cup of tea to somehow normalise and hearten the dull routine of voting, others wanted the act itself to become more of an event. Twenty-two-year-old Imran wanted voting to feel as if the population were coming together:

You know, getting people together, it's like a ... you know, an event kind of thing. It's good to get people together in an event like this. You're actually going to vote. It's actually ... you know ... gonna, kind of change the government, isn't it? So it's good to get people together.

Nineteen-year-old Cass, who was sceptical about the value of voting, was suddenly enthusiastic when asked how elections could be made more meaningful:

> Bring people together. Instead of pushing them apart, which is what's being done now. You've got everybody in their own little communities. I'm not sure exactly what you can do, but you need to bring more communities together.

Sara, an eighteen-year-old single mother, was not quite sure what a polling station was, but felt that making democracy inviting entailed something more than the subdued rituals of the polling station:

> I'd make it more exciting. More like a party kind of thing really … Yeah, bar, dancing, some'at for kids to play on … bouncy castle … just nice, big like street party or some'at, yeah. Music, yeah. I'd have a lot of things actually. Make a day of it, like a big voting day.

Several people wanted there to be music while they voted, but only one (Rita, a housewife in her mid-fifties) was specific about what she wanted to hear:

> Just put a bit of background music on. Well, I like all sorts, me. I like Queen. I like Neil Diamond. … Just some, some background music, that's all. You don't want it blaring out, because I can't do with that. It was boring, last time I went. You know, I walked in, got my name ticked off and my piece of paper given and … nobody spoke.

Ali, a community worker, wanted there to be a voting carnival:

> Maybe, like, have a carnival kind of thing. Yeah, definitely, I mean, then you'd definitely get kids coming. Whether or not, you know, they'd actually go and vote, they'd definitely come along and they'd be one step closer … to voting. So, you know, since they're already there, they might, you know, say 'OK, if we're already here we might as well vote'.

Read superficially, such enthusiasm for more exciting, eventful moments of democratic expression might be interpreted as an appeal to 'dumb down' the political process. But such a reading does not take into account the values of social solidarity and self-realisation that proponents of eventful voting were expressing. Rather than dismissing bouncy castles, catchy background music and carnivalesque longings as diversions from the serious business of expressing a political preference, these counterfactual images of voting might more generously be read as symbolic articulations of an unfulfilled need. To become representable (as opposed to being merely represented), a sense of collective solidarity has to be generated that is capable of bridging the gap between situated experience and aggregated re-presentation. For this to happen, a common experience of being 'us' must be felt. Becoming an 'us' that can be represented as if it has one voice and a collective interest is an aesthetic project. Political campaigners, public relations experts and scholars of history have spent decades refining and deciphering aesthetic strategies designed to stimulate or simulate feelings of indivisible solidarity. In their own words, utilising metaphors of fellowship and conviviality rather than the constrained language of electoral administration, Imran, Cass, Sara, Ali and others whose counterfactual visions of voting I listened to were searching for more authentic ways of becoming representable as a collective political subject.

The performance of voting is an attempt to give empirical meaning to the figurative presence of the sovereign public. In pre-modern societies, symbolic meaning was communicated through well-established rituals; hence the long history of carnivalesque electoral performances discussed in Chapter 2. But, as Alexander (2006:31) has rightly argued, modern societies, far from having banished ritual, 'continue to depend on the simplifying structures of symbolic communications and on cultural interactions that rely on, and to some degree can generate, intuitive and unreflective trust'. Such 'ritual-like activities', as Alexander calls them, may differ from the culturally entrenched customs of the less socially fragmented past, but they nonetheless possess a rhetorically binding force. Through the imagined body politic, the democratic public is performed, in the Austinian-Searlian sense of speech acts bringing into being what did not exist before they were spoken. The most celebrated example of this in democratic theory was the American Declaration of Independence, which, by speaking as 'We the people', somehow gave political substance to the existence of the political entity in whose name it was uttered (Arendt, 1963; Honig, 1991).

In imagining voting as an incarnation of civic fellowship, the people I interviewed were not describing their experiences of democracy, but rather imagining a counterfactual performance of democratic sociability. Their hope was to bring about a situation in which being represented would amount to more than a crude cobbling together of discrete interests. The red bus, the cups of tea, the background music, the kids' entertainment were performative gestures towards the integrity of the pronoun 'us'. In themselves, these aesthetic props were probably no more than metaphorical pointers to what is missing from people's experience of voting. Not so much the cup of tea as the shared warmth of its piping steam; not so much the red bus as its mobile hospitality; not so much the bouncy castle as its acknowledgement of improvisational pleasure in contrast to the municipal cheerlessness of the official polling station.

The problem with these accounts of voting is not the richness of their imagery, but their micro-situational scale. The task of reconciling what Berlant (in Castronovo and Nelson, 2002:144) refers to as the 'antinomy between abstract universality and embodied particularity' within 'the indefinite mass' of the body politic depends on more than the kind of empathetic gestures that might encourage face-to-face sociability. Mass democracy entails mass mediation, but feeling counted within the circulatory orbit of mediated publicness is all too often a chimerical sensation.

'It Just Looked Fake'

Interviewees were all shown a visual prompt with images of ballot boxes, voting booths and election counts to see how they would describe them without the words being put into their mouths. In many cases, people spoke of knowing what these were because they recognised them from television. This did not make their knowledge of what they were talking about any less solid in their eyes; on the contrary, to be seen on TV was to be affirmed as socially real, significant and shared. If it was on the TV, it could be talked about by and to anyone.

Again, when I asked interviewees how they knew the result of the elections in which they had participated, this question was generally interpreted as being about whether it was their habit to stay up to watch the results on TV. 'I don't sit up all night, but I guess I … on General Election anyway … I'll sit up till 2 or 3 in the morning', explained George, a retired businessman, who seemed almost apologetic to be failing in his duty of nocturnal vigilance. Others, such as Daisy, a schoolteacher, explained politely that 'I don't watch the results; like, people stay up all night – I don't … I don't do that'. As the alchemy of aggregation moves from ballot box to the box in the corner and from polling station to TV station, its legitimacy comes to depend on the consumption of spectacle rather than the enactment of performance. The election is an event that is merely witnessed.

For some interviewees, the notion of television as a representation of social reality, and political democracy as the representation of real people, came to be seen as mutually unreliable. Lee, an eighteen-year-old single father, stared at the visual prompt for some time, somehow sensing a semiotic trick that was about to be played on him:

> These campaigns, you know … sometimes, when I see them on TV, I think, sometimes they look … they look a bit … they look a bit fake and that. Do you know what I mean? I've seen a few things on TV, when Tony Blair were like kicking football around and that, and it just looked fake.

The images I had shown Lee were of the voting process itself rather than election campaigning, but in his mind they raised questions about what sort of representations can be trusted. And he was right to make this connection, for there is no meaningful sense in which the mechanics of preference expression can be separated from the authenticity of the claims upon which selection must be based. Had Tony Blair been caught by a camera as he was casually kicking a ball around, or was the ball kicked to the cue of an image-producer who had spent days contemplating whether kicking a football or wielding a table-tennis bat would be most likely to produce the desired impression? Lee's anxiety about the veracity of the televised election campaign reflects a long-standing concern about the extent to which television has become less a mediating gaze, reporting on a reality external to and independent from itself, and more a stage on which political roles must be played out in accordance with its own peculiar logic. To the extent that the mass media now regulate the terms of publicness that allow would-be representatives to reach the represented, and political actors become increasingly aware of the rules of the media game, one might say that the performance of electoral democracy is now more about winning the attention of the media than entering into a direct relationship with those who are to be represented.

When television started to cover election campaigns in the mid-1950s, there was optimism that this would help to make the run-up to voting more meaningful and inclusive by conveying information about the parties and their positions to groups that had not been reached hitherto, and by diminishing the scope for selective, partisan exposure, as citizens who might previously have read only one party-supporting newspaper or attended their own party's public meetings were confronted by appeals from and reports about a range of parties. It was not long, however, before concerns were expressed about television's trivialisation of election issues, its focus on leading personalities rather than local candidates or party manifestos and its tendency to represent the campaign as a horse race and voters as punters to be polled regularly with a view to discovering the likely winners or losers. The story of electoral democracy in the late twentieth century was one of increasingly orchestrated performances in which favoured politicians and celebrity media pundits appeared to be locked into a suffocating embrace, to the exclusion of the voting public (Blumler and Gurevitch, 1995). The mass media's coverage of elections seemed to adhere to a formulaic script in which a civically enervating mixture of repetition, banality and populism prevailed. The evolution of

the televised campaign over half a century has been well summarised by Blumler (2010:8):

> In 1964, at a time when news and current affairs programming
> was just starting to play some, albeit modest, part in campaign
> provision, commentators described its role through the metaphor
> of 'platforms and windows' (Blumler and Katz, 1964; Blumler
> and McQuail, 1968). The idea was that, through their election
> broadcasts, the parties had a platform from which to address
> the voting public, while through its news and current affairs
> programmes, television was becoming a window through which
> the elector could observe the activities of the politicians and the
> independent reactions of informed individuals to the policies and
> claims of party spokesmen. In contrast, today's political journalist
> does far more than open a few windows. He or she helps to deter-
> mine what the elector can see through that window. He or she
> chooses what issues and opinions about them will be presented
> to viewers, sometimes `amplifying' them. He or she 'frames' the
> material in definitive ways; occasionally interviews leading politi-
> cians, deciding in advance what questions to pose; and regularly
> interprets what the election is about.

How does all of this fare for the mass electorate in search of
ways of making conspicuous its own representability as a body
politic? As the public comes to encounter itself mainly as a mediated entity, with studio audiences, callers to phone-ins and post-
ers to online fora serving as proxies for the represented millions,
where are opportunities to be found for the kind of embodied
co-presence that gives affective charge to solidarity?

The BBC's *Question Time* programme, in which a panel of
leading political figures answers questions posed by a selected
audience of 'ordinary people', has become one of the most celebrated 'public-sphere' moments' in contemporary British politics.
At election time, the programme's audience increases, as party
leaders are forced to confront crowds of potential voters whose
energy and even aggression veers between forensic scrutiny and
cathartic assailment. Edward, a retired lawyer, told me how he
watches the programme in exasperation at what he regards as a
travesty of public deliberation:

> I sometimes look at that *Question Time* programme with
> Dimbleby. I could throw my shoe at the television set. Because

nothing is achieved. It's all a blather and it's a show and it's meaningless because it doesn't achieve anything.

For Edward, the television spectacle illuminates what has been lost in the democratic culture of his memory and imagination:

I think that [politicians'] non-appearance in the street is a bad sign. I mean, nobody has been anywhere near us here for years ... they never appear. There is no communication of any substance between potential candidates and the voting population. That used to happen. They would put themselves up as Aunt Sallys to be questioned about what their views are and what they would like to do. ... But now they are frightened of ... of being subject to that sort of cross examination. They've got a mantra which you hear time and time again on television.

And he is not mistaken in observing a precipitous decline in physical encounters between politicians and citizens over the course of his adult life. In 1959, around one in three British people attended a public meeting during the course of the general election campaign. This fell by more than half, to 12 per cent in 1964 and to 3 per cent by 1979 (Lawrence, 2009). Over the same period, political parties all but gave up on local public meetings, preferring to devote their energies and resources to made-for-TV set pieces, such as leader walkabouts and member-only rallies. Writing about the 2000 U.S. presidential election campaign, Marvin and Simonson (2004:144) observed that physically embodied citizens seem to have become 'superfluous to collective gatherings that once lay at the heart of campaign ritual':

The embodied electoral crowd has largely ceased to be visible to itself or anyone else. ... An expert array of journalists, pollsters, media buyers, telemarketers, ad agencies, and political consultants deployed arsenals of computer databases, directmail, websites, and media outlets to assault demographic clusters reconstructed as a 'public' in numerical form. (Ibid:145)

At the same time, Edward is bothered by a belief that programmes such as *Question Time* constrain public agency: 'it doesn't achieve anything'. By reducing democracy to a game of posing and dodging tricky questions, the audience, both at home and in the studio, is left in the position of a Greek chorus, endlessly responding to the seduction, folly, duplicity and logic of the principal actors but never quite commanding centre stage. Rather than watching a studio audience playing its peripheral role within a professionally orchestrated simulation of an accessible public sphere, Edward yearns for the relatively unmediated liveness of direct encounter:

> Open it up to public debate ... the candidates presenting themselves in the local public hall to be subjected to questions and answers by the constituents. That would liven things up.

In this appeal to the efficacy of the live event, Edward joins ranks with a host of theorists who have cast doubt on the possibility of meaningful connections being generated across the disembodied distance inherent to mediated communication. The mass media, such theorists argue, trivialise issues, pacify audiences and discount moral efficacy (Mander, 1978; Postman, 1985; Winn, 1987; Kellner, 2003; Novak, 2006). As Habermas (1989:171) has put it, 'the world fashioned by the mass media is a public sphere in appearance only'. It follows from this perspective that, if citizens' democratic agency is to be sustained, direct experience must be salvaged from appropriation by the forces of simulated reality.

In contrast to such yearnings for a return to a pre-mediated public sphere, other theorists advance the bald claim that the mass media have already triumphed; that we are now a 'media democracy' (Manin, 1997) in which democratic appeal is no longer to ideology or interest, but to audience sensibility. According to this perspective, the hegemony of mass mediation is simply irresistible:

> One cannot now imagine how the public can be constituted, can express itself, can be seen to participate, can have an effect, without the mediation of various forms of mass communication. Making something public today means representing it in the media ... keeping something out of the media spotlight is to symbolically annihilate it. (Livingstone, 2005:18)

In thinking about voting as a social performance, neither of these extreme perspectives is particularly helpful, for they imply that there is an antithetical tension between mediated and non-mediated contexts. In reality, voters move seamlessly and imperceptibly from face-to-face to mediated forms of interaction, not only from one situation to another, but from second to second within particular situations. Consider, for example, the much-studied question of how voters make up their minds during an election campaign. The earliest election studies, conducted by Paul Lazarsfeld and his colleagues from Columbia University (Lazarsfeld et al., 1944; Berelson et al., 1954), studied voters in the context of their personal networks and discovered that the values and preferences they acquired from direct contact with their families, friends and neighbours mattered more than from the flow of information coming at them from the mass media. Media messages had most effect on people who were least informed about the issues on which they were being asked to vote, and who had fewer personal contacts to influence them, but for most voters, exposure to press, radio and campaign literature merely activated existing predispositions. These early election studies were not pursued for several decades. Instead, political scientists focused their attention on the socio-psychological factors leading to individual voting decisions (Campbell et al., 1960) and the limitations placed on voter choice by the paradoxes of rational calculation (Arrow, 1950; Ferejohn and Fiorina, 1974). It was not until the 1980s that a new wave of voting scholars, led by Huckfeldt and Sprague (1987; 1995), returned to an exploration of the interpersonal foundations of political judgement. They argued that

> political information is processed and integrated not by isolated individuals but rather by interdependent individuals who conduct their day-to-day activities in socially structured ways and who send and receive distinctive interpretations of political events in a repetitive process of social interaction. Thus, political behavior may be understood in terms of individuals tied together by, and located within, networks, groups and other social formations that largely determine their opportunities for the exchange of meaningful political information. (1987:1197)

Applying this theoretical approach to data on voter behaviour
during the 1992 U.S. presidential campaign, Beck et al. (2000:68)
concluded:

> If voters look for party cues in their environments, they will find
> no shortage of such cues. The primary source of these cues are
> personal networks and groups, not the modern mass media,
> which has often been ceded greater electoral significance.

Accounts focusing on the social context of voting decisions are
now widely regarded as being both more conceptually sophisticated and empirically telling than previous studies based
upon the stimulus-effect model of media effects (McLeod et al.,
1994, 1999; Eveland, 2001; Shah et al., 2001). Far from facing symbolic annihilation, publics do form, express themselves,
participate and act effectively without being represented in the
media. Political reality does exist beyond its mediated representation. Who voters think they are, and who they think best
able to represent them, is not in the gift of the mass media, even
though these questions are sometimes influenced by mediated
narratives.

The work of creating an electorate comprising citizens who
feel themselves to be collectively representable oscillates similarly between direct and mediated arenas of interaction. Whether
or not citizens come to think of themselves as an integral public
is contingent upon strategies of emotional coordination that can
sustain identification. Some of the emotional work of nurturing civic attachments is performed by media institutions, which
persist in reminding their audiences of their ties to a range of
local, regional and national communities (Anderson, 1983), but
these messages are always interpreted and acted upon by people
from the perspective of their own local and personal experience.
And, contrary to some postmodernist fantasies, experientially
generated feelings are rarely confounded by the force of mediated imagery. People use mediated representations to help them
to make sense of their identities as citizens, but do so in general with a view to supporting affective dispositions at which
they have already arrived. So, Edward's intense frustration when

watching *Question Time* arises from civic memories (however romanticised) of vivacious, local deliberation and a sense that his autonomy as a citizen is somehow being undermined by constraining the public's representation to that of an audience of extras. On the other hand, Jo, a young single mother, was eager to tell me that watching *Question Time* provided her with a much-appreciated connection to the political world:

> I love that on the TV. God, that is something I absolutely adore. I just like … I like the debates, you know, and the … the issues that are raised … I like stuff like that cos it's people from the public, you know, speaking out and it is good. It's good. Really good.

Despite this stark contrast in their reaction to *Question Time* – with Jo witnessing it as an entry point to an inclusive public sphere, whereas for Edward it is a reminder of a lost public sphere that he once knew – both of them were driven by a common normative concern: that the represented public should be in a position to set the terms on which others may speak for them; that by 'speaking out', the question of who 'we' are might be addressed.

The persistent criticism of mass-mediated politics has been its sidelining of the public – its aesthetic construction of a political democracy in which spectacle displaces participation. Hugo Young's observation that 'politicians do not want the public, ragged and random, near them', but prefer them to be 'walk-on extras at the walkabouts' (*Guardian*, 25 March 1992, quoted in Lawrence, 2009:231), accords with a popular contemporary sentiment that the demos has been banished from democracy (Entman, 1989; Marquand, 2004; Coleman and Ross, 2010). In his excellent study of the rise and the demise of the hustings in British election campaigns, Jon Lawrence (ibid:247) suggests that 'we should be careful not to overstate the recent reaction against public participation in Britain's mediated politics'. Cataloguing a number of examples of politicians being ambushed by citizens within the mediaspace from which they were meant to be excluded, Lawrence (ibid:242) suggests that by the end of the twentieth century, 'many of the most memorable moments of British electioneering were not just media moments … they were moments when the public crashed through the Westminster bubble to impose itself on the campaign'. These include such episodes as the BBC television phone-in in May 1982 when housewife Diana Gould interrogated Margaret Thatcher about the sinking of the *Belgrano*, and the 2001 general election campaign when thirty-eight-year-old Sharon Storer challenged Tony Blair about his government's record on supporting the National Health Service during a set-piece visit to a Birmingham hospital, explaining that there was no bed for her partner, a cancer patient in need of a bone marrow transplant. During the 2008 U.S. presidential election campaign, a plumber in Ohio took on Barack Obama in a hostile face-to-face street encounter. 'Joe the Plumber', as the media dubbed him, became an iconic presence in the campaign, referred to no less than nineteen times during the subsequent televised presidential debate by the Republican candidate, John McCain – as well as four times by Obama. It was almost as if a symbol had been discovered through which all the ambivalent complexities of the elusive 'public' could be finally embodied.

Making the public representable, however, entails rather more than the creation of a media caricature exhibiting the crude features of the imagined multitude. The question of how the public is to be imagined and then re-presented is both aesthetic and political. It is aesthetic because, as Ankersmit (1996:47) rightly puts it, 'political reality is not first given to us and subsequently represented; political reality only comes into being after and due to representation'. This does not imply that there is no material world to be represented, but that the ways in which complex social phenomena such as voters, communities and publics are constructed is by appealing to them as if they were real and seeing whether such appeals resonate with their subjectively apprehended identities. This suggests that we would do best to think of representations as claims rather than facts (Saward, 2003) – claims that are absorbed, revised, rejected or celebrated through plausible social performances.

An election campaign is just such a social performance, for any appeal to voters must be based on at least three claims being acted out and then taken seriously:

1) You, to whom my appeal is addressed, are the voters – the sovereign power, the decision makers, the great public – and not someone or something else.
2) You, as voters, are willing to become a collective entity wherein the whole carries more weight than its parts.
3) You, as voters, have sufficiently common values and interests to allow you to be spoken and acted for as if you were one body.

Performing these moves entails aesthetic sensibility. These claims have to look and feel right; they must be so rhetorically structured that they induce plausibility rather than dismissal or ridicule; they must appeal to broad sensations of pleasure rather than pain; and their expression is often most effective when it exceeds the constraints of linear speech, unadorned reason or plain text. At the same time, making the public representable is political because different interests have radically dissonant conceptions of what the public comprises, wills and deserves, as well as possessing quite unequal resources with which to affirm their impressions. The representative claims made by well-financed presidential candidates, political parties or media organisations are likely to have more influence than those made by any of the people to whom such claims are generally addressed. But the political can be undermined by the aesthetic. If the represented feel that they have no capacity to affect the claims being made to and about them, they are likely to distrust the ensuing representation and, at worst, disengage from it. If they feel that the social performance of voting adheres to a script to which they are significant contributors, representative claims are more likely to be acknowledged and accepted.

For representative claims to be credible, then, they must resonate meaningfully with the background culture in which subjectivities are formed, disputed, shared and, occasionally, metamorphosed into feelings of solidarity. As we have seen in this and the previous three chapters, the political is always embedded in the cultural. A culturally disembedded democracy is like a musical score without instruments on which to perform it – or a queue of people waiting for a big red bus that never arrives.

8

Who Feels What, When and How

People need to become democracies within themselves. They must recognise that there are different possible selves within themselves; they must become convinced that they can grow stronger by sorting and mustering these different selves, for self-defined ends. They must feel that they can put a stop to bossing, that they are the equals of others, that they have it within themselves to change things, or to keep things as they are.

(Keane, 2009:709)

What does it mean to speak of a democratic sensibility? And what becomes of civic life in the absence of such sensibility? To raise these questions is to suggest that the performance of political democracy cannot be evaluated in purely instrumental terms; that what democracy *does* and how democracy *feels* are not separable considerations. As a mode of experiencing, perceiving and valuing the world, sensibility focuses on 'nothing less than our sensate life together – the business of affections and aversions, of how the world strikes the body on its sensory surfaces, of what takes root in the guts and the gaze and all that arises from our most banal, biological insertion into the world' (Eagleton, 1990:13). In the main, political scientists have treated these conative, affective and aesthetic dimensions of democratic citizenship with profound suspicion, as if they were secondary matters of private experience, irrelevant to the procedural efficiency of democracy. But democratic legitimacy is just as much rooted in popular feeling as in constitutional principle. No political system that is dependent on the willing consent and active participation of millions of people can afford to take subjective dispositions, competencies and feelings for granted. For, without the conditions in which intersubjective public consciousness can be formed, expressed and shared, democracy amounts to little more than an administrative regime. Democratic sensibility opens up space for fusion between the subjective grammar of affective experience and the objective procedures of the democratic polity. Where this sensibility is strongly present, democracy has deep roots in popular culture; where it is weak and atrophying, it is as if the rhetorical call of the democratic state is transmitted at full blast, but at a frequency that is beyond the public register.

Democratic sensibility refers, then, to ways of being attuned to the world, intellectually, emotionally and physiologically. In contrast to procedural democracy, which is (theoretically) measurable against a checklist of principles and practices, democratic sensibility flows through the sinuous streams of public consciousness, bridging private and public experience. While procedural democracy seems to be erected upon the hard, material surfaces of political interest and constitutional structure, sensibility apprehends democracy in a range of embodied, kinaesthetic, paratextual ways that give feeling to meaning. It is not, of course, a question of one or the other – procedure or sensibility – as if democracy must wager its sources of strength by entering into a strange Cartesian pact. Democratic legitimacy depends on a combination of manifest procedural fairness and deep subjective attachment.

How does citizenship feel when the most common form of democratic practice – voting – is so dominated by a discourse of arid proceduralism that it seems almost absurd to speak of it in terms of affective satisfaction? When the voter, as civic actor, is motivated by the range of sensibilities we have witnessed in the last four chapters, while the act of voting remains mechanically and stubbornly insentient, the contrast between the affective force of the agent and the listless routine of the act casts doubt upon the lofty claims made for democratic citizenship.

In uncritically idealised accounts of democracy, the image of the voter assumes an almost utopian status. To be a voter is to have come of age as a trusted and competent member of a community; to have a voice that can make a difference; to be recognised as a public person, while at the same time remaining entitled to the discretion of private self-reflection and judgement; to be a necessary component in the making of a sovereign public. At least, that is the promise – the utopian legacy of emergent democracy. Too often, however, this invitation to civic power is stifled by cultural constraints. The much-celebrated coming of age as a citizen is blighted by an array of confused signals which leave many first-time voters uncertain about their position and value within the political world. The ubiquitous metaphor of voice, supposedly amplified by plebiscitary power, turns out for many to be little more than an indistinct and inefficacious noise, degraded over time into the monotonous whine of offended neglect. The recognition and respect that is supposed to come with being a public person is too often experienced as a sense of being a manipulated target within a hyper-mediated polity. And, for many voters, to be part of a sovereign 'us' is most vividly experienced through the hurt of its absence. The utopia of democratic agency degenerates into the dystopia of thwarted sensibility.

How might these disappointments be avoided? How might the social performance of voting build upon the foundations of democratic sensibility? These are the questions to be addressed in this final chapter. It is not a question of turning voting into an act of sublime pleasure or of giving less attention to the important demands of procedural fairness. It is a question of trying to make the most common act of democratic participation a little less like it has become and a little more like it could be, were we to take seriously the aesthetic and affective dimensions of citizenship.

The aim of this final chapter, then, is to consider how the act of voting could be made worthier of the intense emotions

that are invested in it. The argument that is developed here dif-
fers significantly from previously aired proposals to make voting fairer (Bogdanor and Butler, 1983; Gallagher and Mitchell,
2005; Carey and Hix, 2011), more convenient (Coleman, 2002;
Gronke et al., 2008; Stein et al., 2008), more deliberative (Gastil,
2000; Ackerman and Fishkin, 2004; Setala, 2011) or more efficacious (Clarke and Acock, 1989; Bowler and Donovan, 2002;
Anderson et al., 2005; Banducci and Karp, 2009). All of these
aspects of voting are important, but none of them addresses
directly the particular democratic deficit that is the central
theme of this book. The argument that follows proceeds from
the basic understanding that voting is a cultural act – a performance through which something called the public makes itself
known. The extent to which this performance resembles an
act of expressive improvisation or a routinised citational reflex
determines its democratic character. Performative improvisation is interruptive: it opens up space for what was never in the
script or the stage directions. It has scope, however fleetingly,
for the stable order of sense-making to be unsettled. Citational
performances of voting replay known dramatic scripts, avoiding
interruption in the manner that an actor endeavours to follow
his or her prompt. While most citizens have grown used to the
latter, joking amongst themselves that 'whoever you vote for, the
government always wins', they harbour a lingering belief in the
interruptive potential of their power as a voting *demos*. Though
rarely articulated in these terms, this power is intimately related
to the potency of voices and bodies that cannot be reduced to
the silent rituals of the ballot box. Democracy depends on forms
of interruptive speaking, movement and place-taking that defy
the almost all-encompassing image of the public as extras on
the stage of history. Whether from the perspective of right-wing
populism, left-wing romanticism or liberal notions of the right to
make a difference, this interruptive potentiality simmers beneath
the seemingly solid ground of undemocratic democracy, with
seismic potential to destabilise the order of civic inertia.

Responding to some of the most vivid anxieties and aspirations
expressed in the interviews reported in the previous chapters, this

chapter explores three moments of potential interruption in the cultural production of voters and voting. First is the constitution of people as voters. In the hours and years leading up to their first encounter with the ballot box, citizens-to-be are presented with an array of instructions, invocations and images relating to their role as future voters. How might this period of preparation for civic maturity be revitalised with a view to unleashing actualising energies rather than only dutiful reflexes? Second is the experience of exercising the franchise. In and around the few, fleeting moments of voting that most citizens ever experience – cumulatively, perhaps no more than a single hour in a life of countless hours – what can be done to enrich the eventfulness of democratic engagement? Third is the experience of having voted and awaiting the consequences of the performance. In the long days and months after votes have been cast, how might the feeling of having been counted come to resemble a sense of counting for something in the political world?

What follows is far from being a programme or blueprint for the future of voting; it is intended, rather, as a stimulus to democratic imagination. An atrophying faculty in contemporary political regimes, imagination has historically served as a creative incubator of dreams and schemes for autonomy. Diggers, Levellers and, later, Chartists were prolific in their accounts of how votes for all would prepare the ground for a kingdom of mutual recognition and respect; Spanish anarchists and republicans would pause during their bloody war against fascists to hold heated debates about how fair and just decisions would be made in a future of human equality; as they fought to dislodge dictatorships, the street protesters who made the Arab Spring were preoccupied by the need to devise democratic arrangements that would never again regard the voices of the people as mere noise to be ignored, distorted or suppressed. Never is the democratic vision as vibrant and vivid as when the right to vote remains a tantalising aspiration. But need the journey to democracy always be so much more exciting than the arrival? Might we conceive of ways of thinking of the arrival as something more like an ongoing journey? The thoughts that follow comprise faint and tentative outlines of a strategy for the enhancement of democratic sensibility.

The Constitution of Voters

The experience of the political begins in infancy, long before there is any awareness of politics. To be a child is to be somehow incomplete; a slow-cooking adult. Referred to by one wry theorist as less human beings than 'human becomings' (Qvortrup, 1990), children are always a work in progress; an object of constitution. The process of socialisation (as this constituting work is commonly known) is undertaken both strategically and unwittingly by a variety of actors, foremost amongst which are the family, from which formative values and dispositions are picked up, and schools, which exist to shape children into normatively acceptable adults. As Rose (1989:123) argues, 'the modern child has become the focus of innumerable projects that purport to safeguard it from physical, sexual or moral danger, to ensure its "normal development", to actively promote certain capacities of attributes such as intelligence, educability and emotional stability'. The socialisation of children entails the nurturing of three kinds of capacity: cognitive, moral and psychological.

First is the cognitive ability to make sense of the world. Language, literacy and numeracy are key cognitive tools, but effective socialisation also depends on other pedagogically shaped competencies, including an awareness of what it means to be a member of a political community. Scholars of socialisation disagree about which cognitive abilities deserve highest status, the extent to which they can be inculcated, tested and measured, and how best to nurture different competencies in the cognitively less able. Until recently, however, few have questioned the assumption that successful cognitive socialisation is mainly dependent on deliberate operations of reasoning. This view has been challenged in recent years by the development of the dual-process model of cognition, the proponents of which distinguish between two modes of cognitive function: intuition, which 'generates *impressions* of the attributes of objects of perception and thought' involuntarily and not necessarily verbally explicitly; and rational judgments which 'are always explicit and intentional, whether or not they are overtly expressed' (Kahneman, 2002:101). According to dual-process theorists, the acquisition of intuitive, impressionistic, spontaneous knowledge plays a key role in sense-making, once thought to be the exclusive domain of effortful and rule-governed reason (Tversky and Khaneman, 1983; Jacoby, 1991; Stanovich and West, 2000). A key strength of this approach to socialisation is its holistic acknowledgement of children as more than sponge-like absorbers of factual knowledge.

From a cognitive-transmission perspective, the success of civic education has tended to be measured in terms of the degree to which students are able to give 'correct' answers to standard political questions. For example, a major study conducted by the International Association for the Evaluation of Educational Achievement (IEA) invited 90,000 14-year-olds in 28 countries to respond to a series of questions 'about democratic institutions, principles, processes and related topics'. The report on findings from this study claimed it to have been 'a meaningful, reliable and valid international test of student knowledge' (Torney-Purta, 2002:44). This begs the question of what kind of knowledge young people need to acquire in order to become effective citizens. As with the United Kingdom government's *Life in the UK Test*, discussed in Chapter 3, civic competence is reduced to the assimilation of prescribed knowledge. The transmission model of teaching (Tishman, Jay and Perkins, 1993:149) is predicated upon the assumption that there is a seamless progression from learning the rules to enacting them. The more young people know, the more likely they will be to behave in culturally desirable ways. Contrary to this assumption, evidence from the 2001 IEA study showed quite the opposite to be the case: while most fourteen-year-olds declared that 'voting in national elections' was 'the most preferred future political activity' (followed by 'collecting money for charity'), the students most likely to declare an intention to vote had the poorest skills in understanding political material, but the highest levels of trust in government

(Torney-Purta et al., 2001). In short, far from civic knowledge being a spur to informed participation, young people's intention to vote is quite often founded upon political ignorance combined with blind faith. This suggests that, contrary to rationalist assumptions, young people's orientations towards civic life are as much, if not more, shaped by how they feel than by what they know.

Second, during the long process of socialisation, children are sensitised to a range of moral cues intended to help them to interact appropriately with the established social order. This moral capacity attunes children to the rules of the game that they will be expected to adhere to as adults. Whether in the street, the workplace, the cinema, the home or the political sphere, these rules of the game comprise a collection of hints about what it means to be a good member of society – and, by implication, how to identify and sanction cultural rule-breakers. A child who has acquired cognitive skills but is unable to navigate the moral universe is likely to be just as disadvantaged as one who can present herself well in social situations, but is short on knowledge. The socialisation of children entails a fine balance between teaching them to understand their surroundings and instructing them to fit in with the ways of the world.

If a predominantly cognitivist approach to citizenship education might be accused of being too formulaic, instrumental and utilitarian, the conspicuous moral inflection of much civic learning is open to the criticism of being little more than psychological manipulation. For much of political history, children were regarded as politically invisible and insignificant. While attention was paid to shaping them as future workers, consumers and householders, their emergence as political subjects or voters was barely registered. From Aristotle (1948:1310a) onwards, however, the moral conditioning of children was regarded as a means of securing cultural stability:

> The greatest ... of all means for ensuring the stability of constitutions ... is the education of citizens in the spirit of their constitution. There is no profit in the best of laws, even when they are sanctioned by general civic consent, if the citizens themselves have

not been attuned by the force of habit and the influence of teaching, to the right constitutional temper – which will be the temper
of democracy where the laws are democratic, and where they are
oligarchical will be that of oligarchy.

In this way, the civically educated child *becomes* the constitution, absorbing the spirit of its laws and values in their most
intimate dispositions. Educating the citizen, in this deeply visceral and intuitive sense, entails the cultivation of a particular
kind of political sensibility, while warning them against the
undesirability of 'uncivic' propensities. Indeed, it was the fear of
such indoctrination that led critics to resist the introduction of
civic education as part of the school curriculum. From the left,
concerns have long been expressed that this would amount to
little more than an exercise in patriotic propaganda and the cultivation of conformity; from the right have come anxieties that
liberal-minded teachers could not be trusted to transmit politically correct maxims and interpretations of good citizenship. For
these reasons, in most countries, it took many years for formal
civic education to become embedded within the school curriculum (Heater, 2004:65–151) and arguments still rage as to the
impartiality and democratic efficacy of such instruction (Hahn,
1998; Westheimer and Kahne, 2004; Biesta, 2006; Bennett and
Wells, 2009; Zembylas, 2007 and 2009; Lawy et al., 2010).

In her study of compulsory classroom recitation of the Pledge
of Allegiance in the United States, Bennett (2004:57) explains
how, in the aftermath of the 9/11 attacks, half of all states of
the Union passed laws requiring schools to ensure that children
chant the Pledge at least once a day. In Colorado, a legal challenge to this edict was mounted and the court ruled that 'pure
rote recitation of a pledge … cannot be said to be reasonable or
legitimate in a pedagogical sense', and that 'there is no legitimate
or reasonable educational value to it' (ibid:60). (This ruling was
overturned a year later). In defence of this daily patriotic ritual,
Bennett (ibid:64) quotes McKinney's claim that 'it is impera-
tive today that we take action and focus on the importance of
reproducing our shared democratic and political life' in order
to 'protect those traditions and values, like the Pledge, that lead

to a sense of collective membership and attachment in this society'. But, as Bennett astutely recognises, the forced recitation of a pledge intended to defend the right to personal liberty and freedom of speech is something of an irony. Recitation of the Pledge is not, of course, supposed to be an act of reflection, less still contestation; rather, it is a performative cue intended to reinforce and make visible collective belonging, regardless of individual commitments.

While few democratic polities beyond the United States compel children to recite such crude daily mantras in their schoolrooms, it is still the case that much of what constitutes civic education is oriented towards forms of pre-scripted moral performance. Whether in the form of voluntary service in the community or participatory decision making in school councils, there is a sense in which appropriate norms of citizenship are passed on to young people as an imposed legacy, and the scope for them to determine their own script is extremely limited. How one should behave as a good citizen, the language one should use, the range of issues one should take seriously, and the parameters of tolerable dissent are received as a set of culturally inflexible conditions, in some ways no less restrictive than the doctrinaire rhythm of the Pledge of Allegiance.

Third, socialisation has increasingly come to be associated with the therapeutic cultivation of the self. In this context, childhood is seen as not only a process of cognitive and moral development, but also the first stage of an individually directed project for the accomplishment of emotional stability through the shaping and governance of subjectivity. As Rose (1989:231) has put it:

> The self is not merely enabled to choose, but obliged to construe a life in terms of its choices, its powers and its values. Individuals are expected to construe the course of their life as the outcome of such choices, and to account for their lives in terms of the reasons for those choices. Each of the attributes of the person is to be realized through decisions, justified in terms of motives, needs and aspirations, made intelligible to the self and others in terms of the unique but universal search to find meaning and satisfaction through the construction of a life for oneself.

To the socialisers and educators of the nineteenth and early twentieth centuries, this kind of self-actualising reflexivity would have seemed quite alien. For them, the determinism of social structure appeared to be an inviolable force and attention to psychic moulding only relevant to treatment of the manifestly deranged. The cultivation of therapeutic subjectivity is part of 'a new way of thinking about the relationship of self to others and imagining its potentialities' (Illouz, 2007:7). This therapeutic emotional style describes

> the ways in which twentieth-century culture became 'preoccuppied' with emotional life – its etiology and morphology – and devised specific 'techniques' – linguistic, scientific, interactional – to apprehend and manage these emotions. (Ibid:6)

So, while socialisation was once conceived as a natural developmental process of cognitive and moral acquisition, the emphasis is now upon helping children to realise and feel positive about themselves and their futures. A consequence of this reflexive preoccupation is the conspicuous presence of an affective thread running through contemporary theories of socialisation, so that the child who knows much and behaves well is deemed to be incomplete unless he or she is also comfortable living in his or her own skin.

If democratic citizenship is understood in essentialist terms, as a set of values and practices that are fully constituted and passed down from generation to generation, then cognitive and moral approaches to civic education might be sufficient. But if, as I would argue, what makes citizenship democratic is the fact that it is open to ever-expansive definition, informed by the contingencies of diverse experience and the reflexivity of autonomous practice, cognitive and moral approaches to the transmission of 'correct' civic behaviour would seem to be at best thin and insufficient, and at worst dogmatic and constraining. For, thinking about socialisation as a form of transmission is predicated upon an image of children as empty vessels to be filled with civic virtue. In reality, however, long before the first lesson is taught, children will have absorbed a range of behavioural and dispositional characteristics that define and constrain their worldview. Children are neither mere products of social structure, destined to reflect their environments, nor free agents, driven by innate personalities. Young people's preparedness for the performance of citizenship is determined by the complexity of their lives as embodied beings who are both active subjects in the world and receptive objects of the world. Bourdieu (1998:81), whose notion of 'habitus' invites sensitivity to the embodied foundations of personal biography, suggests that children, like adults, inhabit 'a body which has incorporated the immanent structures of a world ... and which structures the perception of that world as well as the action of that world'. Through the first forgotten skins of their socialised and structured bodies, children internalise the range of possibilities open to them in life; a feel for the game that they must play, a sense of the bounded nature of choices before them, at the same time as a glimmer of what might be at stake if they were to transcend those boundaries. As children grow up, they acquire almost imperceptibly durable ways 'of standing, speaking, walking, and thereby of feeling and thinking' (Bourdieu, 1990:70). These are the physical and mental manifestations of their habitus. When proponents of the therapeutic cultivation of the self speak of the need to make children feel comfortable in their own skin, they are probably referring to one of two things: that children need to be helped to come to terms with the parameters of their own habitus, or that they should be encouraged to move beyond the contours of habitus. The former is reinforcing and conservative, the latter interruptive and potentially liberating.

Civic education syllabi and textbooks remain remarkably silent about the situated dispositions of their target audience. Most of them proceed as if classrooms were filled with equally positioned young people, any one just as able as any other to pursue the rights and duties offered to them. An emphasis upon personal rights rather than collective obligations within civic education can give rise to the misleading impression that citizenship is a matter of instrumental self-interest. (The belief, for example, that voting is all about satisfying personal interests rather than realising social ends). In their examination of U.S. syllabi and textbooks, Riedel et al. (2001) and Gonzales et al. (2004) found that there was a much greater emphasis upon individual rights than collective participation, and Bos et al. (2007:1276), on the basis of a study of the effects of civics textbooks upon school students, arrived at the devastating finding that

> the agenda-setting focus on rights, to the exclusion of obligations in civic texts, may diminish the democratic involvement of students. Not only do authors' focus on rights spell less attention to devoted to obligations and civic and political participation in civics textbooks ... but an individual-rights focus also might directly contribute to diminished civic and political involvement among young people.

If children are addressed as if they are primarily rights-bearers, they are much more likely to think and act in terms of entitlements rather than responsibilities to others or society as a whole. Just as important as their observations about textual bias is the recognition by these researchers that how young people are imagined and then addressed at close range will determine how they learn. Conceived as a bundle of rights to be enacted, children will respond to knowledge likely to strengthen their self-interest, but might not comprehend or see the point of more collective civic pursuits.

It is as sentient, vocalised bodies that children emerge as citizens and voters. The corporeal and affective dimensions of this emergence should be central to civic education. In conducting a research project in schools and youth groups in and around the city of Leeds in the United Kingdom in 2011, exploring how young people express themselves about civic issues in public contexts, I became acutely aware that even the most mundane performances of public speech presented a challenge to most young people.[1] The very act of enunciating statements about the world

---

[1] This was the Youth Amplified project, set up to explore the barriers experienced by young people when speaking in public and to produce a range of educational resources that might help them to find and use their civic voices. The research findings from this study are in press. The educational resources can be accessed via www.youthamplified.com

around them became a struggle fraught with embarrassment and fear. Habitus was manifested through micro-behavioural articulations, such as the avoidance of certain words and phrases; millisecond-long movements of the eye or facial muscles indicating an awareness of being judged; physically awkward ways of standing; adaptations of dialect with a view to fitting in with expected performances; and radical misalignments between words and gestures. What seemed like intangible barriers to dauntless self-expression stood between these young people and the events, decisions and institutions of the world around them. Where in the school curriculum are these internalised obstacles to the emergence of confident citizenship addressed? If children are lucky, some of these traits are worked on through drama or the 'oracy' strands of English language education, but it is revealing that civic education – the one school subject that is inescapably linked to the use of public voice – pays hardly any attention to the training of the voice as a political instrument.

The idea of voice as a metaphor of voting was discussed in Chapter 1, but its relevance here is at a far-from-symbolic level. The human voice is a key instrument of embodied citizenship. While much has been written about the political voice as a metaphor (Schlozman et al., 2005; Couldry, 2010), too little attention has been paid to the fully vibrating, subjectively invested voice through which citizens first announce their presence and articulate their claims upon the world. The subtle fashion in which, from the earliest age, schoolchildren are culturally differentiated in terms of the ways they use (and leave unused) their voices has for too long been confined to studies of socio-linguistics and child psychology. The political sociology of voice was systematically explored by Bernstein (1971), but it is only recently that culturally-generated disparities of civic vocality have been subjected to critical attention (Reay, 2006; Baxter, 2002; Zembylas and Michaelides, 2004; Cremin et al., 2011). In one of the few studies to address directly inequalities of speech between school students, Baxter (2000:26) observes:

> Many students find the business of speaking in a public context, whether participating in a whole class discussion or performing

in front of the class, intimidating and nerve-wracking. The more quiet and hesitant students are likely to resist such opportunities, allowing the more confident and dominant to take over. This clearly can become a 'self-fulfilling prophecy' during a school career; the more a student is used to evading or opting out from public or large group oral activities, the more they reinforce their position as a non-speaker.

In arguing that teaching students to speak in public contexts should be regarded as an ongoing educational challenge, Baxter (2000:36) suggests:

> Students need to learn that becoming an effective speaker isn't just about self-confidence or acquiring a bag of skills. It is also about understanding the politics of discourse and about how certain people in their class (as mirrored in the outside world) are more powerfully positioned than others within different speech contexts.

A good example of such effective inequality would be the fourteen-year-olds in Torney-Porta's international study, who saw voting as the civic activity they would most likely undertake in the future, while knowing very little about the political issues they would be voting upon. This profile of dutiful, but inert and unforthcoming, future voters is congruent with the embarrassed silence that pervades vast regions of contemporary political democracy. If the status of the democratic citizen is taken to extend beyond the dumb and sullen expression of secret preferences and incorporate elements of position-taking, confidence and outspokenness, then Torney-Porta's civically educated children do not fit the bill. An explicit objective of schools, if they are to prepare children for vocally confident citizenship, must be to level the affective resources that people bring to democratic engagement. The outcome of such education – democratically socialised citizens, capable of speaking confidently in public about affairs that matter to them in terms and tones of hope rather than despair or indifference – would be less vulnerable to the disappointments facing contemporary voters, for whom political participation is all too often a weak and isolated act of devocalised expression.

Acknowledging the injuries and insults that underlie the default inhibitions of habitus is crucial if civic education is to go beyond the transmission of constitutional erudition by attending to the cultivation of self-assured expression. Perhaps that is what Bernard Crick's (1998:7) Advisory Group on Citizenship education meant when it called for 'no less than a change in the political culture of this country'. But there are few signs of such change having been accomplished at even the most elementary level. Its realisation calls for an educational strategy designed to ensure that all future citizens, regardless of their backgrounds, stand an equal chance of developing robust civic capacities. This could only be achieved by radically disrupting the current order of stratification and insisting that second-rate democratic sensibilities are not acceptable for children just because they were born into social disadvantage. Democracy depends on the participation of people who feel motivated to engage in civic life, even when such participation goes against the grain of frustrated experience. To simply cast a vote is to commit to a hope that affective aspiration can trump thwarted expectation. At stake here is what Abensour referred to as 'the education of desire': an attempt to 'teach desire to desire, to desire better, to desire more, and, above all to desire in a different way' (cited in Thompson, 1977:791). If schools are to perform a useful role in preparing young people to play their part in democracy, this must entail conferring resources of hope upon those who have been routinely and systematically persuaded to think of themselves as naturally or inevitably lacking voice or efficacy.

The relationship of hope to democratic sensibility has tended to be under-theorised. Indeed, the very construct of 'hope' by psychologists such as Erikson (1964), Bandura (1977) and Snyder (1994) has been mainly confined to the context of goal-directed cognition and rational instrumentality. To be hopeful in this sense is to experience an above-zero expectation of attaining a goal. The danger inherent to this calculus of hope is that, given the unequal status and resources of different individuals, it is easy to conclude that only those who possess the means of satisfying their wills have reason to be hopeful – a rather circular and self-perpetuating rationale for the optimism of the already fortunate. Instead of seeing hope as a well-calculated acknowledgement of existing probabilities, a rather more radical approach is to see hope as a rationale for working upon what is probable; of acting to upset the odds and shake up the future in surprising ways. According to Lazarus (1999:653), to hope 'is to believe that something positive, which does not presently apply to one's life, could still materialize'. Thus understood, hope is rather more than a positive calculation or a sanguine disposition; it is a conviction in the possibility of action leading to a desired outcome, regardless of past or present conditions. Without such hope, argues Lazarus, 'there would be little to sustain us' (ibid:654) – especially those with the fewest resources upon which to draw.

Hope is most conspicuous in its absence – in the muttered semi-articulation of seasoned despondency. In the absence of hope, vocal utterances become aggressive or pathetic, perfunctory or obsessive, irresolute or over-performed. The voice filters personal credibility, betraying the weakness of the weakened before they have had a chance to finish a single sentence. The body betrays the unconfident in the way it holds itself, moves and hesitates. In my interviews with voters, sighs, pauses, evasive gestures, cryptic snorts and cynical chuckles would often punctuate responses to my questions, betokening feelings that could not be put into words. My interviewees were rarely inarticulate or indisposed to talk, but there was something about political expression that often eluded them. Confidence in speaking about social power was the elusive, unnerving factor. It was as if the distribution of social power either had nothing to do with them or could only be approached in terms of deep ethical suspicion. The political had come to be associated with a script in which voters, as opposed to the voted-for, could expect to have no meaningful part. The political socialisation of citizens-to-be is all too often a desocialising process through which voices are trained to the limits of the sayable, rote words and their inflections conspire against the energy of self-actualisation, and impassioned speech is tamed. If civic education is to provide a way out of this rut, it must attend as a matter of priority to the cultivation of voices that can transcend the ossification of habitus.

Whether the vapid routines of contemporary democratic participation would be found sufficient by a generation taught to regard acts of citizenship as expressions of personal hope is quite another question. People have turned to other sites – of consumption, mobility, entertainment, intimacy – as loci of self-expression and efficacy. The idea of voting as a creative and spirited act, performed within a vivacious cultural sphere, is difficult to conceive and harder still to realise. It is to this challenge of radical democratic redesign that we now turn.

The Mediation of Democratic Feeling

How might the experience of voting be infused by democratic sensibility? How might the expression of public preferences and sentiments recover the vibrancy of those grand, rambunctious electoral ceremonies of the eighteenth and nineteenth centuries? Some scholars are pessimistic about the scope for civic reinvigoration. Writing about the public's fear of self-exposure and the *migration intérieure* that has come to characterise secular modernity, Sennett (1992:xi) suggests that 'were modern architects asked to design places that better promote democracy, they would lay down their pens'.

When they have felt motivated to pick up their pens, it has been upon spectacular edifices of representation, such as parliaments, congresses and city halls, that contemporary architects have focused their aesthetic attention. Rather than seeking to replicate or reimagine anything resembling the Greek *agora*, they have proceeded on the assumption that the gathering together of citizens with a view to finding a collective voice has been rendered superfluous by the institutionalisation of representation. The place of citizens within the performance of democracy is no longer at all clear.

As symbolic embodiments of democratic meaning, parliamentary buildings purport to be nerve centres of national feeling. The most publicised moments of parliamentary performance are neither deliberative nor instrumental, but comprise expressive responses to moments of crisis, accomplishment and anxiety in which a collective mood calls out to be articulated and acted upon. For parliaments to be recognised as democratic spaces, the echo of public affect must always be in the air; an ambience that can only be realised performatively. In seeking to re-present the voices of others as if they were somehow present, the tonal quality of such ventriloquism is no less significant than its polemical content. (Tone without content amounts to empty populism, but content without tone is blatantly inauthentic). As elected politicians feel increasingly compelled to speak to and for the affective states of their constituents, as well as their material interests (and are judged increasingly in terms of their empathetic skills), it is vital for their credibility that the settings in which they perform seem to be congruent with public sensibilities.

A key function of parliamentary architecture, then, is to evoke a sense of relationship between present and absent voices, to make it seem as if what is beyond the outer walls of the edifice is somehow reflected within. For example, Norman Foster's glass dome above the rebuilt Reichstag building in Berlin (now home of the German Bundestag) both invites citizens to see into the parliamentary chamber, thereby emphasising the inescapable transparency of the elected, while allowing them to see outwards across the city, somehow reflecting back upon the parliament the complex scenes and sentiments it claims to represent. While such design is intended to invoke an image of outsiders as being virtually present, its play on the relationship between those within and without serves to underline and reinforce the relational terms of the political order. The role of a parliament is to speak in place of those who cannot speak for themselves; if these mute constituents were to speak for themselves, the exclusionary architecture of institutional representation would become redundant. In this sense, however much parliamentary architecture encourages the perception of transparent inclusion, this gesture is always bound to be secondary to its primary function of making visible those entitled to speak while at the same time depreciating the significance of the spoken-for. Parliaments are monuments to those who cannot speak.

There is an important link here to the thought of Jacques Rancière, who, more than any other theorist in recent times, has contributed to an understanding of the relationship between aesthetics and the political order. Rancière argues for a distinction between politics, which he equates with dissensus, and what he calls the *police*: the framing powers that reinforce notions of who can speak about what, the proper place of passion in public expression, and the extent to which topics are appropriate or out of bounds for common discourse. Rather than seeing it as a physical organisation, the police, for Rancière (1998:29 *Disagreement*), comprises 'an order of the visible and the sayable that sees that a particular activity is visible and another is not, that this speech is understood as discourse and another as noise'. The function of this regime of sensibility is to disclose the inevitability of the social order, while at the same time pointing to the delimitations of the roles, parts and positions that lie within it. In the context of political architecture, for example, the police task of architects is to make apparent the inevitability of a spoken-for citizenry, while circumscribing the scope for any other sensible perception of democratic arrangements. In contrast, politics, for Rancière, entails a reconfiguration of permissible sensibility, a rupture between the terms and tones of those competent to speak about, and in the name of, power and those hitherto regarded as having no part in sensible discussion. As Rancière (1994:24) puts it in one of his most eloquent moments, 'The scene of the dead or silent king allows another scene to appear ... that of a living person who speaks too much, who speaks incorrectly, out of place, and outside the truth'. To experience politics, in this sense, people must do or say something that transcends the boundaries of regulated propriety. In so doing, they 'make visible that which is not perceivable; that which, under the optics of a given perceptible field, did not possess a *raison d'etre*; that which did not have a name' (Rancière and Panagia, 2000:123).

Perhaps, before picking up their pens, Sennett's architects should pause to reflect on what democratic performance consists of for those who, in Rancière's terms, have 'no part': voters as well as non-voters whose role is to not exceed an approved repertoire of actions and not to upset a taken-for-granted distribution of sensibilities. In so reflecting, architects as well as other designers, planners, constitutional reformers and information mediators may wish to enlarge their sense of what it means to be democratically engaged in the complex conditions of late modernity.

The most significant feature of contemporary culture is that experience has come to eclipse the local. No longer tuned to the key of the vernacular, the primary sites for the generation of social meaning lie beyond the familiar landmarks of market squares, high streets and town halls. Public life is now conducted increasingly within the metaphorical space of mediated connection. What Isaiah Berlin (1960:10) called 'the general texture of experience' increasingly encompasses trends and events that might once have been considered exotic and irrelevant. The 'news' provides an ongoing narrative of interdependence and unexpected impacts. The terms and content of interpersonal communication have become inextricably linked to the rhythms and stories of the mass media, so that the immediate and parochial appear to mimic the remote and universal. As Silverstone (1999:6) has put it:

> It is in the mundane world that the media operate most significantly. They filter and frame everyday realities, through their singular and multiple representations, providing touchstones, references, for the conduct of everyday life, for the production and maintenance of common sense.

In watching, listening in and logging on, people are not just accessing the experiences of others, but being in the world themselves, in virtual interaction with an array of characters, communities, events, ideas and emotions that now constitute common experience. Whereas in pre-modern society rituals of cultural legitimation were enacted 'at one time or place, after which the participants scatter[ed] to engage in activities of a more individual and instrumental kind' (Alexander, 2006:77), it is now much more common through the mediated circulation of cultural symbols that reality comes to be apprehended, norms come to be established and cultural positions are made legible. As Silverstone (2007:5) argues:

> The media are becoming environmental. Not in the Baudrillardian sense of the media as generating a distinct sphere, a separation of the symbolic from the realities of everyday life, a kind of more or less escapist excursion into the realm of fantasy and simulation. More a sense of the media as tightly and dialectically intertwined with everyday life. ... They have become the new *sine qua non* of the quotidian.

So, while the citizens of late modernity are still rooted within physically delineated, historically inflected space, thinking as they go about their business of the immediacy and specificity of their lifeworlds, they are at the same time subjected to a torrent of voices from the distance, competing for their attention, offering them reports about what they do and do not want to know about, bombarding them with conflicting statistics, jargon and analyses, and inviting them to 'have their say', make their thoughts and feelings public, become 'interactive'. They are both here and there, embodied in the parochial and familiar and embedded in the national and global.

Where does all of this leave voters, in their search for a meaningful relationship with the forces that govern and affect their lives? The most common criticism of mediated citizenship is that it turns citizens into spectators rather than actors. Dependent upon distant others to help them to make sense of the situations and choices they encounter, they experience a disjuncture between the meaningfulness of their own, relatively isolated activities and the significance of such action within the complex and extensive chain of events that constitutes the political narrative. In short, whereas the self is experienced individually, the political self only seems to make sense through a mediated lens. Consequently, citizens rely on the media to read back to them the meaning of their votes, thereby incorporating them into a narrative of which they were not fully aware before acting. This may be what Victor Turner (1974:37) had in mind when he suggested that what we perceive as formal social structures 'only become visible through this flow which energises them, heats them to the point of visibility'. In mediated polities, it falls to television, radio and the press to make visible and meaningful the fragmented local experiences and distant forces that constitute political culture.

Voting has become a mediated performance, not only insofar as it is dependent on the mass circulation of information upon which rational-cognitive choices are based, but because it has come to depend on a series of claims made by the media about what the political world is and how citizens are positioned within it. These claims are rarely explicit. They are tacit, oft-repeated declarations of 'common sense' that anchor experience within the cultural order. Firstly, the media delineate the space of collective experience. They set the terms and boundaries of communicative reach, thereby marking off an immediate 'us' from a remote 'them'. Anderson's (1983) work on nation states as 'imagined communities', assembled through the medium of print, pointed to the ways in which 'publics' – including electorates – assume a common consciousness, despite having no direct interaction with one another. The electronic media, such as broadcasting and the Internet, take this further by rearticulating the scale of community and embedding the spatially and temporally remote in the sphere of immediacy. In this way, they open up potential space for vast, sometimes supranational communities, to attempt to regulate their own visibility. Most importantly, however, technologies of mediation are deeply implicated in the symbolic metamorphosis of independent preferences into collective will. In the electoral context, the media make possible not only the physical casting and counting of votes, but the attachments that surrounds these seemingly mechanical activities and confer cultural meaning upon them.

Secondly, the media contribute to the shaping of civic identities. Through both direct and implicit modes of address, they remind audiences of their bonds of integration, while devalorising the experience of blurrily depicted outsiders. An experiential hierarchy, comprising dichotomies of experts and laypeople, moderates and fanatics, metropolitans and provincials, occidentals and orientals, the responsible and the irresponsible is tacitly advanced, reinforcing the idea that certain utterances are of value while others deserve to be dismissed or disparaged. In this sense, the media tell people not only what to think about, but what is appropriately sayable by whom. Political journalism is increasingly a meta-commentary on the skills of would-be leaders in relating to the audiences they imagine themselves to be addressing. By contrast, voters tend to be spoken about as if they were a passive, responsive audience, silently weighing up competing appeals for their ephemeral attention. The folly of the opinionated 'man in the street', the indifference of the apathetic dupe and the spectre of the mob animated by inchoate commitments stand as common media caricatures of civic identity gone wrong. Through these pathologies of the sensible, the sayable is affirmed.

Thirdly, the media organise public attention. By making certain experiences, feelings and relationships seem natural and significant, they configure political subjectivities around officially acclaimed moments and events. In the context of voting, this means telling people what elections are: explaining the basic rules of the game and reminding citizens that both the sanctity of the rules and participation in the game provide protection against anarchy and disorder. The media tell people when it is 'election time', just as the Breakfast Show points to getting up time and the Christmas Special to family relaxation time. Media audiences are offered a road map from the declaration to the conclusion of the election, marking out critical moments for attention and action, identifying the 'key issues' that they should be thinking about and stressing the virtue of acknowledging that some problems are beyond resolution. The media will hint at the irresponsibility of the non-voter, while celebrating the absolute freedom of all citizens to withdraw from the political drama. And after the votes have been counted, it is through the media that a consensual resolution to the electoral contest is realised. Having reported the winners, losers and overall fair play of the contest, the media will move seamlessly back into 'politics as usual', conferring legitimacy upon the victors while serving as a permanent reminder that the next electoral drama is never far away. In naturalising a particular repertoire of political actions, the media denaturalise others; the more widely the vote is regarded as *the* (rather than *an*) expression of political voice, the more threatening, eccentric and irresponsible other modes of political claim-making come to seem.

Finally, the media work on experience, turning sensations into sense. They are implicated in a form of secular re-enchantment, devising ever-more creative and sophisticated ways of shaping sensibility: of making the standardised feel special, the distant intimate, the inevitable demanded, the superficial penetrating and the populist popular. Fashioning sensibilities entails persuading people that, while being disembodied and remote, the media remain in touch with the situated realities of their diverse audiences. The mass media specialise in the generation of personalised relationships at a distance – what Horton and Wohl (1956) called 'parasocial interaction' and Thompson (1995) called 'mediated quasi-interaction'. In their earliest days, broadcasters addressed audiences as if they were a homogeneous public who would eventually adjust their sensibilities to the lofty tones of their masters' voices. But this mode of address came to be experienced by people as condescending and alienating (Coleman and Ross, 2010). The trick of contemporary mediation is to produce an aura of intimate sociability that acknowledges distance while simulating closeness. This has entailed the adoption of what Scannell (2000:9) refers to as the 'for everyone as someone' mode of communication, by which audiences are addressed as if each member were the sole recipient of the transmitted utterance. From Roosevelt's 'fireside chats' to the smooth 'talking just to you' disc jockey, the aim is to make affective connection count for more than physical co-presence. Election campaign strategies are increasingly built upon such parasocial foundations. Communications are directed towards 'you', the voter, as a singular bundle of experiences, rather than a previously imagined mass electorate, addressable via the industrial transmission of messages 'to everyone'. Ever-more sophisticated technologies of mediated narrowcasting enable nuanced politico-demographic targeting, geared towards constituencies of one person. Mediated ties of sensibility supersede physical propinquity as a basis for effective and affective communication. The irony is that, as techniques of simulation have been refined and ever-more intense levels of authenticity-at-a-distance manufactured, media audiences have become more conspicuously sceptical. The benign communicative tones of political persuasion are increasingly vulnerable to public incredulity, irritation and mockery. As crude attempts to appropriate democratic sensibility have come unstuck, the plausibility of mediated communicative performance – the so-called quest for trust – has become the most fervent aspiration of late-modern culture. Where once value was primarily a reflection of productive energy, it has now become a symbol of circulatory credibility (Coleman, 2012).

Critics of the current political communication system lament the tendency of governments, politicians and parties to appeal to citizens as if they were spectators upon a drama not of their own making. Thinking of the public as a mere audience, they argue, degrades democratic citizenship, substituting habits of docile consumption for norms of active engagement (Postman, 1985; Habermas, 1989; Blumler and Gurevitch, 1995; Iyengar and Reeves, 1997; Luhmann, 2000; Bennett and Entman, 2001; Lewis et al., 2005; Dahlgren, 2009; Stromback, 2010; Coleman in Brants and Voltmer, 2011). The public as audience cannot be a *demos*.

Other scholars are less certain about the audience-public dichotomy. Livingstone (2005:18–19), for example, acknowledges that 'audiences are denigrated as trivial, passive, individualised, while publics are valued as active, critically engaged and politically significant', but suggests that such sweeping definitions construct a 'reductive polarisation' which misses the empirical intersections between the conduct of audiences and publics. Indeed, engaged publics are often less than rational and efficacious, and active audience are often more than frivolous and inconsequential. As both entities comprise the same people, it is hardly surprising that there is no radical contrast in their collective personalities. The French political theorist Bernard Manin

(1997) takes the argument one step further, claiming that we now inhabit an 'audience-democracy' in which media consumption is so integral to civic experience that it is almost inconceivable to imagine mass democratic judgements originating in experiences exclusive to media performance. While Manin can be accused of failing to recognise the many ways in which political experience and judgement are organised by counter-publics in opposition to prevailing media narratives, he is astute in observing the extent to which the media no longer report on the political drama, but constitute it. As the mass media grew as a pervasive force over the years of the twentieth century, the public sphere came to be represented within a single 'regime of intelligibility' (Rancière, 2009:74) that blurred distinctions between the mundane immediacy of political culture and the media logic (Altheide and Snow, 1979) through which events became publically perceptible.

In recent years, however, emergent technologies and practices of mediation have led to radical changes in the circulation of political symbols, messages and memes (Bennett and Iyengar, 2008; Gurevitch et al., 2009; Bennett and Segerberg, 2011). This has led to a reconfiguration of the order of perceptibility, affording a new kind of presence to the hitherto spectatorial audience-public. Blumler and Kavanagh (1999) have referred to this change as 'the third age of political communication'. In the first stage, they argue, the media saw themselves as reporters, agenda-setters and interpreters of action conducted within the independent public sphere. In the second stage the media took it upon themselves to create their own quasi-public sphere in which a range of political performances, such as the expression of public angst, the organisation of civic debate and even voting, were staged for consumption by mass audiences.

Now, in the third stage, control of messages and their reception by audiences is slipping from the grasp of media producers. Technologies of interactive communication have not only altered the power relationship between producers and audiences, but made it much more difficult for the former to guard the cultural portals of the sayable and sensible. More than any previous media technology, the Internet, with its routinised feedback

path between senders and receivers, has destabilised the pro-
duction-reception relationship and problematised the notion
of the unspeaking audience. Even before the emergence of the
Internet, mass-media formats such as phone-ins, user-generated
content and content-shaping tele-votes expanded interactivity
across time and distance, bringing the audience 'in' to the space
of mediated expression. Now, as audiences have become able to
state and share their feelings with one another through such plat-
forms as Twitter and Facebook, at exactly the same time as they
are being subjected to the affective prompting of media output,
it has become much harder for producers to tell people what
they are feeling or how others in the media audience might be
expected to be feeling. Horizontally connected audience-publics,
generating networks of common sensibility, become part of the
media content to which they were once subjected. These new
techno-cultural entanglements between message and response
make it impossible to imagine the audience-public as a mere
recipient of or accessory to mediated experience. As an active –
or interactive – force, the audience-public, far from yielding to
or colluding with media-made events, have become integral to
the affective construction of eventfulness (Ampofo et al., 2011;
Anstead and O'Loughlin, 2011). Reflecting on this phenomenon,
Lucy Mangan (*Guardian*, 18 January 2012) has argued that

> social networking sites – especially Twitter, because it is designed
> to exchange real-time responses among a loose group of people –
> are restoring a sense of excitement to television. ... This reflexive
> element – further strengthened by the fact that many of the people
> you are seeing on screen are also present online – has revitalised
> television for the viewer.

The emergence of the interactive audience-public has prompted
diametrically opposed responses, with populists celebrating
the empowerment of media consumers, on the basis that any
opportunity for feedback constitutes a democratic development
(Bazalgette, 2005), while Foucault-inspired governmentalists
insist that persuading people to watch each other on television
or online amounts to little more than a sinister surveillance project – a cunning 'ruse of economic rationalization' (Andrejevic,

2004:7). Both of these simplistic analyses take for granted the pre-existing political subjectivity of the audience-public, as if technologies and strategies of media interactivity work upon an already formed public sensibility. Following Rancière's understanding of politics as an act of violation against the order of perception and intelligibility, I want to suggest that media interactivity is neither inherently democratic nor undemocratic, but that it has potential to enable those who were previously locked out of meaningful discourse to refuse their given role and assert their political significance as people with something to say.

When audience-publics claim the right to perform a speaking part, capable of interrupting what had hitherto seemed to be an impregnable cultural order, two things happen: first, the hitherto settled question of who counts as a speaker is up for reconsideration; second, the question of what constitutes a sensible contribution to public thought is complicated by the introduction of modes of expression that could once have been dismissed as merely vacuous. Consider, for example, the pervasive use of voting within broadcast and online formats, widely disparaged as an empty, trivialising degradation of 'proper' voting. What starts as a form of judgemental muscle-flexing and a demand to be counted in relatively trivial contexts such as *Big Brother* or *American Idol* might lead to habits and expectations that do not simply dissolve in the more politically consequential contexts of televised leaders' debates or political interviews (van Zoonen, 2005). Once the audience-public begins to conceive itself as an entity that can speak as well as vote, and whose words as well as preferences might count, it becomes extremely difficult to confine such democratic aspirations to the domain of inconsequential playfulness. To be sure, interactive audience-publics will often be disappointed by the weak relationship between their input and otherwise determined outcomes (as can happen in political elections, when, for example, professional politicians form coalition governments in defiance of the voters' mandate), but the key point here is that a mode of response once dismissible as mere ranting and babble (the living-room mutterings of the domestic audience) can now assert itself as a right to be heard.

Just as in the early days of media research audiences per se were frequently denigrated as being mindless, distracted and gullible dupes, so it has now become fashionable to claim that voters seeking to affect the outcomes of mass-media productions, or people using social media networks to express ideas and sentiments, are engaged in senseless collective prattle. But, as Panagia (2009:61) rightly notes,

> this senselessness is not synonymous with an absence of intention or meaning, nor is it reducible to unintelligibility. Rather it refers to a field of iteration that operates on registers other than the ones available for sense-making. There is, then, a category of speech … identifiable as democratic non-sense (or babble); such a category does not refer to the content of that speech but rather to its status within the common language of deliberation.

Similarly, Rancière (1998:50) argues that the snooty dismissal of the cacophonous public is not a critique of the linguistic or semantic sophistication of their utterances, but a cultural repulse – a refusal to accept that those with no speaking part in the political drama might indeed have something to say:

> The problem is knowing whether the subjects who count in the interlocution 'are' or 'are not', whether they are speaking or just making a noise. The quarrel has nothing to do with more or less transparent or opaque linguistic contents; it has to do with consideration of speaking beings as such.

Democratic sensibility is intimately bound up with the 'consideration of speaking beings as such'. In pre-modern societies, elections were characterised by the unleashing of saturnalian freedom to invert cultural positions and transcend the barriers of oligarchic order. As we saw in Chapter 2, the traces of this narrative have never quite disappeared; a relationship between moments of voting and interruptions in power status permeates even the tightly managed campaigns of the twenty-first century, in which members of the voting public occasionally get the better of would-be leaders. With the rise of the mass media, great emphasis came to be placed on the special qualities of 'speaking beings'. Politicians, and the political journalists who had direct access to them, were seen as a particular product of the cultural division of labour, capable of projecting their voices and views in ways that would defeat and/or embarrass ordinary citizens. The politically literate were those who could follow these coded texts and subtexts. Democratic sensibility came to be understood as an attunement to the voices and messages of politicians as legitimate 'speaking beings'. Counter-publics did their best to insist upon the validity of their own alternative modes of discourse, but what mattered most occurred within a sphere of managed mass-mediation.

As the hegemony of the mass media has been weakened (though far from broken) by the new conditions of what Blumler and Kavanagh (1999) call 'the third age of political communication', it has become much more difficult than it once was for elites to frame the terms of discursive propriety or for those once denigrated as 'the masses' to be described as 'just making a noise'. Questions about who might qualify as 'speaking beings as such' are now central to interpretations of political performance. Voters, whose role once seemed limited and settled, are now in a position to reflect publically not only on who should represent them, but who they, the represented, imagine themselves to be. The balance within election campaigns between the crafted oratory of the stage and the noisy buzz of the audience has shifted, especially online, where politicians are finding the stage surfaces increasingly slippery.

In these new circumstances, the experience of voting has less to do with architectural constructions of appropriate spaces for democracy to 'take place' than the cultivation of mediated relationships across time and space in which the represented can practise speaking as themselves. Panagia (2009:48) puts this very well:

> Democratic politics ... is first and foremost a politics of noise. Though a political utterance may be retroactively tuned to sound like a reasonable expression of interests, its first pitch is an interruptive noise.

Those who seek to infuse the experience of voting with a more acute democratic sensibility would be well advised to develop an aural sympathy for the 'interruptive noise' that augurs and runs through political performance. This does not imply a preference for randomly disruptive cacophony, but rather a recognition that what might at first seem like mere noise may well constitute meaningful communication. In this sense, democratic sensibility entails an ontological and epistemological openness: a willingness to be persuaded that people one had discounted do in fact count, and that the sounds which they are emitting may in fact constitute statements of truth, even if the means by which they have come to be enunciated do not conform to certain standards of knowingness.

The scope for democratic sensibility is enlarged when those who constitute the *demos* experience an intensified sense of inhabiting a communicative universe within which they possess a capacity to make a difference by making themselves heard. This was probably the most conspicuous distinction that I found between people in my interviews with voters: there were those who, however limited their faith in the political system, considered themselves to be voluble actors within the electoral drama, while others felt themselves to be sidelined and silent spectators.

Insofar as the new interactive and networked media ecology opens up potential space for voters to move psychically from the muted margins to the clamour of the stage, there are grounds for expecting the act of voting to become more meaningfully connected to (or less blatantly severed from) the normative expectations, vernacular discourses and affective reflections of the everyday lifeworld. It is impossible to imagine future elections in which the instantaneous interactions made possible by digital technologies will not interrupt and reconfigure the cycle and tempo of elite campaigning. Performances on televised leaders' debates or high-profile interviews are already judged and rated by audiences long before the political pundits have had time to tell them what they ought to think. There is no online equivalent to the imposed hush of the polling station, no online presenter empowered to disparage the comments of the off-message critic, no online agenda from which all else can be made to appear as fatuous deviation. We are in an era of mediated interruption.

The Feeling of Recognition

Democratic representation may not depend on a mimetic reproduction of the features, thoughts and feelings of the represented,
but neither can it succeed when these are routinely misrecognised. As Pitkin (1967) has famously argued:

> Despite the resulting potential for conflict between representative
> and represented about what is to be done, the conflict must not
> normally take place. The representative must act in such a way
> that there is no conflict, or if it occurs an explanation is called
> for. He must not be found persistently at odds with the wishes
> of the represented without good reason in terms of their interest,
> without a good explanation of why their wishes are not in accord
> with their interest.

The credibility of voting depends, therefore, on its objective
and subjective consequences. The objective conditions of recognition have been widely studied by political scientists who
ask questions such as: Do all members of society participate
as voters or is active voting skewed towards certain social
strata? Do elected governments represent voters equally? To
what extent do voting majorities constitute a democratic mandate? From the perspective of normative democratic theory,
the findings of political science research in relation to the first
and second of these questions have been strikingly disappointing, while those relating to the third question remain at best
equivocal.

Who participates in the political performance of voting? The
short answer is that richer and more educated people are significantly more likely to vote than those who are poorer and less
educated. As Schlozman and Burch (2009) have put it:

> Students of civic involvement in America are unanimous in
> characterizing political input through the medium of political
> participation as being extremely unequal. The exercise of politi-
> cal voice is stratified most fundamentally by social class. Those
> who enjoy high levels of income, occupational status and, espe-
> cially, education are much more likely to take part politically
> than are those who are less well endowed with socio-economic
> resources.

In their study of unequal voting in the United Kingdom, Keaney and Rogers (2006:7) refer to polling data from MORI showing that in the previous two general elections there was

> a 15–16 percentage point difference between the rates at which the top class (ABs) and the bottom class (DEs) turned out. MORI estimates that 70 per cent of ABs voted in the 2005 election, compared to 54 per cent of DEs.

Indeed, in virtually all political democracies, while the right to vote is almost universal, voting is exercised unequally, largely as a result of structural factors over which voters have little control. (Whether one is rich or well educated is largely a matter of natal luck rather than personal choice). Ironically, citizens who are most likely to be dependent on the state for welfare protection are the least likely to participate in determining who will run the state and how.

Given these inequalities surrounding the act of voting, is it the case that elected representatives and the governments that they form are equally responsive to the policy preferences of all voters? The objective findings from political science suggest that they are not. In their seminal study of 'American Democracy in an Era of Rising Inequality', Jacobs and Skopcol (2005:1) observe:

> Public officials, in turn, are much more responsive to the privileged than to average citizens and the less affluent. The voices of citizens with lower or moderate incomes are lost on the ears of inattentive government officials, while the advantaged roar with a clarity and consistency that policymakers readily hear and routinely follow.

In his study of U.S. senators' responsiveness to voters' policy preferences, Bartels (2005:29–30) concludes that 'senators are vastly more responsive to the views of affluent constituents than to constituents of modest means' and notes in passing that 'the fact that senators are themselves affluent, and in many cases extremely wealthy, hardly seems irrelevant to understanding the strong empirical connection between their voting behavior and the preferences of their affluent constituents'. In another widely cited study, Gilens (2004:23) concludes that

> the link between preferences and policy is substantially stronger for high income than for middle or low income Americans. Moreover, when the policy preferences of these latter groups diverge from the preferences of those with high incomes, the association between preference and policy for middle and low income Americans virtually disappears.

This is not a case of American exceptionalism. In their study of government responsiveness to voter preferences in twelve western European democracies between 1973 and 2002, Adams and Ezrow (2009:218) conclude:

> Parties display no tendency to respond positively to the vast majority of the public, namely the constituency of rank-and-file citizens who do not engage regularly in political discussion and persuasion. By contrast parties appear highly responsive to the viewpoints of opinion leaders, i.e., the relatively small subconstituency of citizens that habitually discuss politics and who attempt to persuade others on political issues.

Similar conclusions have emerged from studies of Swiss (Rosset, 2010), British (Soroka and Wlezien, 2005) and Latin American (Zechmeister and Luna, 2005) policymaking. Weakliem et al. (2005) provide global evidence for the same conclusion.

If participation in voting tends to be unequal, and responsiveness to those who do vote skewed towards the richer and more formally educated, can democratically elected governments at least meet the challenge of reflecting the broad policy preferences of the majorities that elect them? (Let us leave aside for this moment the awkward fact that governments elected on the basis of non-proportional voting systems are usually dependent on support from a minority of their national electorates). Although there is some evidence to suggest that citizens' aggregate policy preferences are reflected by policy outputs (Manza and Cook, 2002; Soroka and Wlezien, 2005; Hobolt and Klemmensen, 2005; Enns and Wlezien, 2011), this is not quite the same as saying that how citizens vote in elections determines policy outcomes.

There are three reasons for this. First, as Downs (1957) and others (Brunner and Ross, 2010; Ezrow et al., 2011; Imbeau and Foucault, 2011) have shown, politicians tend to respond less to voters at either end of a range of preferences than to the preferences of median voters. Even if one end of the preference spectrum comprises the most popular position, governments seeking election or re-election tend to be more interested in the variation between preferences and the median point between them than in the most publically favoured policy position. For this reason, increased dispersion of preference distribution will have little effect on policy unless it is matched by a corresponding shift in the median position.

Second, governments seeking to follow aggregate policy preferences are more likely to turn to opinion polls, which offer them a more granular, issue-based picture of public preferences, than electoral voting, in which citizens commit themselves to vast, disparate bundles of policy positions and values. In most of the political science literature on government responsiveness, data from opinion polling rather than election voting are used as evidence of citizens' policy preferences. In exceptional circumstances, a government or individual candidate might be elected or thrown out because of a highly salient policy divergence with voters, but it is generally the case that electoral mandates are expressions of complex packages of support for policies of varying public salience, political values, social identities and image impressions and should not be confused with aggregate preferences for specific policies.

A third reason for not expecting there to be a correlation between preferences expressed through the ballot box and policy outcomes is that many of the policy decisions that governments need to make are neither discussed nor contested during election campaigns. For example, in the 2010 British general election, when for the first time ever the main party leaders confronted one another in three televised debates, there was hardly any reference to specific cuts in public expenditure that the parties would make to reduce the deficit, even though all three leaders were of the view that drastic cuts would need to be made. Some of the most controversial policies of the subsequently elected coalition government – a significant increase in tuition fees and a major reorganisation of a marketised National Health Service – were never presented in the manifestoes or debate speeches of any of the parties.

It would be wrong to conclude from this analysis that voters do not influence policymaking. They do so in two critical ways: by removing from office broadly unpopular leaders and by conferring electoral legitimacy upon leaders who, once in office, are expected to demonstrate a commitment to the popular values which won them the election. In referenda, voters can achieve even more clearly demonstrable policy outcomes, although often at the cost of diminishing the capacity of governments to pursue electoral mandates that are undermined by conflicting, often populist signals arising from one-issue campaigns. When political theorists such as Dahl (1971:1) argue that 'a key characteristic of democracy is a continued responsiveness of the government to the preferences of the people', one might say that this is more of an ideal than an empirical reality; that, in fact, most political democracies are characterised by government responsiveness to (1) the socially unrepresentative section of the population who vote; (2) the richer and more educated amongst those who vote; (3) those whose policy preferences veer towards median positions; (4) discrete preferences, as expressed in opinion polls, rather than comprehensive electoral mandates; and (5) those issues upon which citizens have been invited to form an opinion, rather than many others upon which there is a marked absence of public awareness or debate. These objective deficits in 'actually existing' political democracy have led some theorists to argue for its normative incompleteness as a form of popular sovereignty and for radical changes in its modus operandi (Barber, 1984; Fishkin, 1991; Beetham, 1994; Gastil, 2000; Fung, 2003; Coleman and Blumler, 2009; Fischer and Gottweiss, 2012).

Rarely do political scientists stray beyond accounts of the objective limitations of existing democracy. It is as if normative shortcomings can be measured and reformed, but subjective frustrations are too close to the borders of the non-rational to be of 'scientific' interest. There is, however, one important context in which political science has drifted into deeply subjective territory. The concept of *political efficacy*, introduced into the literature by Campbell et al. in 1954, refers to 'the feeling that political and social change is possible, and that the individual citizen can play a part in bringing about this change' (Campbell et al., 1954:187). Unlike most other variables measured by political scientists, efficacy is wholly subjective. Feeling politically efficacious need have no empirical relationship to one's objective influence on the world. Political scientists are interested in this subjective feeling because of its strong correlation with regime support (governing democratically depends on citizens believing that they can play a meaningful part in the process) and civic participation (people are unlikely to participate in a system that they feel regularly ignores them). Over the years, the concept of political efficacy has been broken down into two dimensions: internal efficacy, which reflects 'a belief in one's own competence to understand, and to participate effectively in, politics' (Niemi et al., 1991:1407), and external efficacy, which reflects 'beliefs about the responsiveness of government authorities and institutions to citizen demands' (Niemi et al., 1991:1408). Once again, both of these dimensions of political efficacy refer to entirely subjective perceptions. Empirically, an individual or group can have relatively high internal efficacy (they trust their own capacities to wield influence competently) and low external efficacy (they do not trust politicians and governments to listen to people like them), or the other way round. In most contemporary political democracies, both dimensions of political efficacy are at a low level across the entire population, with significant gaps between the more affluent and educated, who feel more politically efficacious, and poorer, less formally educated citizens, who have markedly less confidence in their own democratic capacities and in the responsiveness of governments.

Given the strong and undisputed evidence of unequal patterns of political efficacy, it would seem reasonable to conclude that these subjective feelings are rooted in objective conditions of

structural inequality. When citizens express a consciousness of
lacking the means required to exercise political power – effectively, money and education, or economic and cultural capital – they are merely sensing in a visceral fashion what scholarly
volumes on political science have confirmed. Even though people might believe that their votes count as much as any other in
the formal process of electoral aggregation, they are unlikely to
assume that either before or after the moment of voting their
interests, thoughts and voices matter as much as those who possess the conventional means of exercising social influence.

While all votes counted in fairly conducted elections may be
equal, not all voters count equally and many experience a sense
of being discounted and discarded. Voters living in 'safe' constituencies are often ignored – either because they are bound to
vote the 'right' way and do not require any attention, or because
they are bound to vote the 'wrong' way and are considered
unworthy of persuasion. Voters living in marginal constituencies
are bombarded with catch-all messages, intended to reach the
abstraction of the median floater rather than the reflective intelligence of the undecided. Voters whose support can be relied on
by a particular party or candidate tend to be taken for granted,
neglected and expected to put up with uncomfortable distortions
in the expression of the values that made them loyalists in the
first place. In-between elections, voters often feel forgotten by
their elected representatives. And, all too often, when ventriloquising on behalf of the public dummy, politicians ascribe the
most simplistic and unreflective viewpoints to 'most people'. Such
experiences of misrecognition are bruising. They feel like casual
disrespect. They are shaming. And, as Eliasoph (1998:154) has
suggested, a common response to them is for citizens to strike
a 'cynical chic' pose, feigning political disinterest as a way of
pre-empting the humiliation of political exclusion. These are the
conspicuous affective deficits of voting, which lead so many people either to vote without any hope of making a difference or to
not vote at all (see Chapter 5). Add to these the less conspicuous,
faintly felt, but oft-repeated experiences of being spoken about

by politicians without due acknowledgement; of finding the language and rules and customs of politics confusing and distancing; of feeling ethically compromised between the materiality of immediate needs and the aspiration towards enduring ideals; of encountering the frustrating vacuity of much that passes for political journalism; and of the discrepancies between promise and delivery, even when one has voted for the winning side. And it is hardly surprising that the right to vote, so pervasively celebrated as a civilised accomplishment, is commonly spoken about in terms of profound disappointment.

It might be said that it was always thus: that the very act of compression and substitution entailed by political representation has long tended to engender elite actors who are competitively driven to make cynical appeals and engage in manipulative tactics; that voters have never been much more than a wooable mass, to be first seduced and later disappointed; that inequalities embedded deep within the social structure have forever been replicated in the political sphere; and that it has always been rather more important for citizens to trust their leaders than to imagine themselves to be efficacious actors. But, in fact, for most of the first century of the mass franchise – from the 1880s to the 1980s – there was always an explicit tension between the systemic foundations of structural inequality and the political scope of democratically elected governments to overcome their most unjust consequences. Terms such as liberal democracy, social democracy and Butskellism captured the prevailing conviction of most twentieth-century governments, be they of the left, right or centre, that they could – and, moreover, should – implement policies designed to tame the most unjust excesses of market forces. From schemes for full employment and income control to redistributive taxation and educational policies intended to stimulate social mobility, governing was seen to entail a degree of independence from, and control over, the otherwise anarchic impulses of the market.

Since the late 1970s (with the rise of Thatcherism in the United Kingdom, developing later in other countries), this assumption that the political state should play an interventionist economic role has been widely abandoned. The current ethos of neoliberalism has been defined by Harvey (2007) as the belief that

> individual liberty and freedom are the high point of civilization and … individual liberty and freedom can best be protected and achieved by an institutional structure made up of strong private property rights, free markets, and free trade: a world in which individual initiative can flourish. The implication of that is that the state should not be involved in the economy too much, but it should use its power to preserve private property rights and the institutions of the market and promote those on the global stage if necessary

According to Leys (2001:68), 'politics is no longer about managing the economy to satisfy the demands of voters, they [sic] are increasingly about getting voters to endorse policies that meet the demands of capital'. Couldry (2010:10) points to the inherent conflict between rationalities of neoliberalism and the democratic ethos of what he calls 'voice':

> Neoliberalism insists that there is no other valid principle of human organization than market functioning. The tension between neoliberal doctrine and the value of voice becomes clear when we consider how markets work. Markets match inputs and outputs in regular ways at the level of individual transactions … it is no part of market functioning that a particular individual's sequence of inputs and outputs match in a particular way, let alone a way that matches with that individual's reflections on that sequence. Markets do not therefore function to provide voice. … Market functioning does not require the exchange of narratives between reflexive, embodied agents; but voice does.

Governments before the 1980s – and the opposition parties competing with them for power – tended to operate on the basis that the market could and should be subjected to legislative regulation, and indeed that there was a close relationship between the democratic distribution of political values and the administrative allocation of public values. Neoliberalism has redefined the consequential scope of electing a government, impacting upon the efficacy of voters in three important ways. First, the choices facing voters are increasingly limited, as all mainstream parties cluster around a narrow policy agenda shaped by a fundamentalist acceptance of the inevitability of market rationality. Second, the extent to which neoliberalism operates on the level of transnational flows of capital rather than the sovereign borders of the nation state limits the significance of elected governments in relation to huge areas of deeply consequential policy. Having no votes in the election of officials running the International Monetary Fund or World Bank, let alone private transnational corporations that are increasingly allowed free reign, voters understandably feel estranged from many of the most important sources of power over their lives. Third, as the neoliberal principle of wholesale marketisation pervades the political sphere itself, parties and governments tend to address voters as if they were consumers, with votes to 'spend' on themselves rather than preferences to contribute to the common good. When, as Couldry (2010:55) notes, 'these various influences are non-negotiable, operating seemingly beyond the margins of national political deliberation', it is hardly surprising that voters have come to perceive a closing down of already limited political options: fewer policies to choose from, fewer differences between politicians as people, and, above all, fewer discernible effects of electing A rather than B or X rather than Z. It is too early to be sure how profoundly this abject surrender of governments before the inviolable supremacy of the unregulated global market will impinge upon long-term political efficacy, but it seems reasonable to assume that the less citizens believe they can depend on elected representatives to enact consequential changes, the less seriously they will attend to the process by which such constrained legitimacy is conferred upon them. A survey of 5,000 British adults conducted by YouGov in January 2012 found that only 20 per cent agreed with the statement that 'Parliament does a good job representing the interests and wishes of people like you', 16 per cent agreed that 'Parliament does a good job understanding the lives of people like you' and more than half (58 per cent) agreed with the statement that 'It doesn't make much difference to my daily life who wins general elections these days – there's very little difference between the main political parties'. Citizens continue to go through the motions of voting for candidates and parties and calling upon the elected to understand their lives and represent their interests and wishes, but their heart is clearly not in it.

Political representation may not be in full-blown crisis, but neither is it in ruddy health. One thing is clear: the fortunes of voting cannot be separated from the efficacy and affectivity of representative relationships. A central theme of this book has been that voting is a performative act which both brings into being and aggregates into one a representable *demos*. The social performance of voting is inextricably linked to experiences of being represented, misrepresented, acknowledged, ignored, spoken for and spoken to. Insofar as representation is an act of ventriloquism in which 'the representative contributes to the identity of what is represented' (Laclau, 1996:87), voting is a culturally creative act, both defining and reflecting the subject of democracy in a single manoeuvre. It may not be the only way for publics to make themselves known and representable, but the institutionalised nature of voting makes it the most obvious and common form of claim-making for contemporary citizens to access, comprehend and enact.

For more than half a century, Pitkin's (1972:209) famous definition of political representation as 'acting in the interest of the represented, in a manner responsive to them' has been widely accepted by democratic theorists. The explanatory value of Pitkin's definition lies in its acknowledgement that representation entails a mode of speaking or acting on behalf of others that depends on a two-way communicative relationship characterised by responsiveness. Quite recently, Pitkin's theory has been radically revised by Saward (2008:4), who argues that representation is less a settled relationship than a constitutive activity. 'Representation', he argues, 'is an ongoing process of making and receiving claims – in, between and outside of electoral cycles'. This is how Saward (2006:303) sees representative claim-making working:

> Makers of representative claims attempt to evoke an audience that will receive the claim, and (hopefully, from the maker's point of view) receive it in a certain desired way. Makers of representative claims suggest to the potential audience: (1) you are/are part

of this audience; (2) you should accept this view, this construction – this representation – of yourself; and (3) you should accept
me as speaking and acting for you. The aim of the maker of the
claim in such cases can be said to be to avoid disputatious 'reading back', or contestation of their claims, by would-be audience
members.

Saward's suggestion (2006:5) that 'representative claims only
work, or even exist, if "audiences" acknowledge them in some
way, and are able to absorb or reject or accept them *or otherwise engage with them*' (my emphasis) recasts the terms of representative legitimacy. Indeed, I would want to push Saward's
argument slightly further, focusing on the agentic power of the
represented to contribute to their own definition as a democratic
subject in ways only hinted at by the words 'otherwise engage'.
In short, this is a performative conception of representation: one
which sees the act of representing not as an effect of a political
relationship, but as the creative construction of such a relationship. For Saward, aesthetic and rhetorical resources are essential
determinants of representative legitimacy, for any claim to be a
person who can speak and act for others must always depend
on complex and subtle feelings of linked identity that cannot be
expressed in terms of arid reason.

Saward's theory of the representative claim 'is having a nearly
revolutionary effect on the way political theorists think and speak
about political representation' (Disch, 2012:118). It contributes
to an affective and aesthetic turn in democratic theory, initiated
before Saward's work by cultural theorists such as Ankersmit
(1996), Street (2001), Marcus (2002), Corner and Pels (2003),
Hajer (2005), Hall (2005) and Dahlgren (2010).

The arguments and evidence presented throughout this book
suggest that a cultural reading of the act of voting is helpful
in casting light upon not just *how* people vote, but why they
bother to do so and what they think they are doing during these
moments of mysterious engagement. I have attempted to suggest
that when people vote, they are doing more than engage with
an institutional technology intended to make them seem to be
present; they are taking a view about who they think they are,

how they are prepared to be addressed and the potential risks of being spoken for but misrecognised. Like any other act of cultural communication, voting is always a gamble: some will lose – perhaps, the would-representative whose claims lack the ring of credibility; perhaps the represented, beguiled by the allure of an enchanting but specious political performance; others will win – not only in terms of political power or economic interests, but feelings of social recognition.

As a performed demand for recognition, voting is dependent on a mode of democratic sensibility that is attuned to the possibility of improvisation and interruption, and conversely, that is not obsessively preoccupied by citational ritual and disembodied action. Both Arendt's 'space where I appear to others as others appear to me' and Rancière's interruptive citizens who demand to be understood as doing more than 'just making a noise' must be at the centre of any democracy in which the recognition of the represented is a serious objective. Resources for the assertion of democratic recognition would include the skills of speaking in public and the interactive technologies of political mediation that I have outlined in this chapter. The very least that this book might achieve is a wider understanding of the constructed nature of democratic practices such as voting, which have come to mean different things to different people, and nothing at all to some. A rather more ambitious outcome would be the instigation of a debate in which hitherto unarticulated accounts and feelings can be rehearsed in public.

References

ACE Project, 1999. *The user's guide to the ACE project electronic resources*. New York: United Nations International Foundation for Electoral Systems (IFES), International IDEA.

Ackerman, B. and Fishkin, J. S., 2004. *Deliberation day*. New Haven, CT: Yale University Press.

Adams, J. and Ezrow, L., 2009. Who do European parties represent? How Western European parties represent the policy preferences of opinion leaders. *Journal of Politics*, 71(1), pp. 206–223.

Adams, J. Q., 1776. *Thoughts on government*. Boston: Hayes Barton Press.

Adorno, T., Frenkel, B., Levinson, D. and Sanford, N., 1950. *The authoritarian personality*. New York: Norton.

Aguilar, F., 2007. Betting on democracy: Electoral ritual in Philippine presidential campaign. In Huat, C-B, ed., *Elections as Popular Culture in Asia*, London: Routledge, pp. 72–93.

Aitken, J., 2011. A stretch too far? *The Guardian*, 27(April), pp. 28–29.

Alexander, J. C., 1989. *Structure and meaning: Relinking classical sociology*. New York: Columbia University Press.

    1992. Citizen and enemy as symbolic classification: On the polarizing discourse of civil society. In M. Lamont and M. Fournier, eds., *Where culture talks: Exclusion and the making of society*. Chicago: University of Chicago Press, pp. 289–308.

    2006. Cultural pragmatics: Social performance between ritual and strategy. In J. Alexander, B. Giesen and J. Mast, eds., *Social Performance: Symbolic action, cultural pragmatics, and ritual*. Cambridge: Cambridge University Press, pp. 29–90.

Allen, J., 2003. *Lost geographies of power*. Oxford: Blackwell.

Althaus, S., 1998. Information effects in collective preferences. *American Political Science Review*, 92(3), pp. 545–558.

Altheide, D. and Snow, P., 1979. *Media logic*. Beverly Hills, CA: Sage.

Ampofo, L., O'Loughlin, B. and Anstead, N., 2011. Trust, confidence, credibility: Citizen responses on Twitter to opinion polls during the 2010 UK general election. *Information, Communication and Society*, 14(6), pp. 850–871.

Anderson, B., 1983. *Imagined communities: Reflections on the origin and spread of nationalism*. London: Verso.

Anderson, C. J., Blais, A., Bowler, S., Donovan, T. and Listhaug, O., 2005. *Losers' consent: Elections and democratic legitimacy*. Oxford: Oxford University Press.

Andrejevic, M., 2004. *Reality TV: The work of being watched*. Lanham, MD: Rowman and Littlefield.

Ankersmit, F. R., 1996. *Aesthetic politics*. Stanford, CA: Stanford University Press.

2002. *Political representation*. Stanford, CA: Stanford University Press.

Anstead, N. and O'Loughlin, B., 2011. The emerging viewertariat and BBC Question Time: Television debate and real-time commenting online. *The International Journal of Press/Politics*, 16(4), pp. 440–462.

Appelbaum, P. S., Bonnie, R. and Karlawish, J. (2005). The capacity to vote of persons with Alzheimer's disease. *American Journal of Psychiatry*, 162, pp. 2094–2100.

Archer, M. S., 2003. *Structure, agency and the internal conversation*. Cambridge: Cambridge University Press.

Arendt, H., 1958. *The human condition*. Chicago: University of Chicago Press.

1963. *On revolution*. New York: Viking.

Aristotle, 1948. *Politics*. Translated from the Greek by E. Barker. Oxford: Clarendon.

Arnold, M., 1867. *Culture and anarchy: An essay in political and social criticism*. London: Smith, Elder & Co.

Arrow, K. J., 1950. A difficulty in the concept of social welfare. *The Journal of Political Economy*, 58(4), pp. 328–346.

1963. *Social choice and individual values*, 2nd ed. New Haven, CT: Yale University Press.

Austin, J. L., 1962. *How to do things with words: The William James Lectures delivered at Harvard University in 1955*. Oxford: Clarendon.

Avis, J., 2003. Re-thinking trust in a performative culture: The case of education. *Journal of Education Policy*, 18(3), pp. 315–332.

Back, L., 2007. *The art of listening*. Oxford: Berg.

Bakhtin, M., 1981. *The dialogic imagination*. Translated from the Russian by C. Emerson and M. Holquist. Austin: University of Texas Press.

1986. *Speech genres and other late essays*. Translated from the Russian by V. W. McGee. Austin: University of Texas Press.

Ball, S. J., 2003. The teacher's soul and the terrors of performativity. *Journal of Education Policy*, 18(2), pp. 215–228.

Banducci, S. A. and Karp, J. A., 2009. Electoral systems, efficacy, and voter turnout. In H. Klingemann, ed., *The comparative study of electoral systems*. New York: Oxford University Press.

Bandura, A., 1977. Self-efficacy: Toward a unifying theory of behavioral change. *Psychological Review*, 84, pp. 191–215.

Barber, B. R., 1984. *Strong democracy*. Berkeley: University of California Press.

Bartels, L. M., 1996. Uninformed votes: Information effects in presidential elections. *American Journal of Political Science*, 40, pp. 194–230.

2005. *Economic inequality and political representation*. Princeton University online. Available at: http://www.princeton.edu/~bartels/economic.pdf (accessed 18 June 2012).

Barthes, R., 2000. *Mythologies*. Translated from the French by A. Lavers. London: Vintage.

Bauman, Z., 1999. *In search of politics*. Stanford, CA: Stanford University Press.

Baxter, J., 2000. Going public: Teaching students to speak out in public contexts. *English in Education*, 34, pp. 26–34.

2002. Competing discourses in the classroom: A post-structuralist analysis of girls' and boys' speech in public contexts. *Discourse and Society*, 13(6), pp. 827–842.

Bazalgette, P., 2005. *Billion dollar game. How three men risked it all and changed the face of television*. London: Time Warner Books.

Beck, D. and Fisch, R., 2000. Argumentation and emotional processes in group decision-making: Illustration of a multi-level interaction process analysis approach. *Group Process Intergroup Relations*, 3(2), pp. 183–201.

Beck, P. A, Dalton, R. J. and Huckfeldt, R., 2000. *Cross-national election studies: United States study, 1992*. ICPSR Study No. 6541. Available at: www.icpsr.org (accessed 18 June 2012).

Beetham, D., ed., 1994. *Defining and measuring democracy*. London: Sage.

Bell, V., ed., 1999. *Performativity and belonging*. London: Sage.

Belli, R. F., Traugott, M. W., Young, M. and McGonagle, K. A., 1999. Reducing vote overreporting in surveys. Social desirability, memory failure, and source monitoring. *Public Opinion Quarterly*, 63, pp. 90–108.

Bennett, L. J., 2004. Classroom recitation of the pledge of allegiance and its educational value: Analysis, review, and proposal. *Journal of Curriculum and Supervision*, 20(1), pp. 56–75.

Bennett, S. E., 1988. Know-nothings revisited: The meaning of political ignorance today. *Social Science Quarterly*, 69, 476–490.

  2003. Is the public's ignorance of politics trivial? *Critical Review*, 15(3–4), pp. 307–337.

Bennett, W. L. and Entman, R. M., eds., 2001. *Mediated politics: Communication in the future of democracy.* Cambridge: Cambridge University Press.

Bennett, W. L. and Iyengar, S., 2008. A new era of minimal effects? The changing foundations of political communication. *Journal of Communication*, 58, pp. 707–731.

Bennett, W. L. and Segerberg, A., 2011. Digital media and the person-alization of collective action. *Information, Communication, and Society*, 14, pp. 770–799.

Bennett, W. L., and Wells, C., 2009. Civic engagement: Bridging dif-ferences to build a field of civic learning. *International Journal of Learning and Media*, 1(3), pp. 1–10.

Bentham, J., 1819. *Radical reform bill: With extracts from the reasons.* London: E. Wilson.

Berelson, B. R., Lazarsfeld, P. F. and McPhee, W. N., 1954. *Voting: A study of opinion formation in a presidential campaign.* Chicago: University of Chicago Press.

Berger, P. and Luckmann, T., (1967) *The social construction of reality: A treatise in the sociology of knowledge.* Harmondsworth: Penguin Books.

Berlant, L., 1993. National brands/national body: Imitation of life. In B. Robbins, ed., *The phantom public sphere.* Minneapolis: University of Minnesota Press, pp. 173–208.

  2002. Uncle Sam needs a wife: Citizenship and denegation. In R. Castronovo and D. D. Nelson, eds., *Materializing democracy: Toward a revitalized cultural politics.* Durham, NC: Duke University Press, pp. 144–174.

Bernstein, N., 1971. *Class, codes and control.* Vol. I. Theoretical Studies towards a Sociology of Language, London: Routledge & Kegan Paul.

Berlin, I., 1960. History and theory: The concept of scientific history. In I. Berlin, ed., *Concepts and categories: Philosophical essays.* Princeton, NJ: Princeton University Press, p. 115.

Bevir, M. and Rhodes, R. A. W., 2006. Defending interpretation. *European Political Science*, 5, pp. 69–83.

Biesta, G. J. J., 2006. *Beyond learning: Democratic education for a human future*. Boulder, CO: Paradigm Publishers.

Billig, M., 1995. *Banal nationalism*. London: Sage.

Black, D., 1958. *The theory of committees and elections*. Cambridge: Cambridge University Press.

Blackshaw, T. and Crabbe, T., 2005. Leeds on trial: Soap opera, performativity and the racialization of sports-related violence. *Patterns of Prejudice*, 39, pp. 327–342.

Blair, T., 2006. *Our sovereign value: fairness*. Speech given to the Rowntree Foundation, York, 6 September. Available at http://www.number10.gov.uk/output/Page10037.asp (accessed 18 June 2012).

Blanchard, A., 2004. The birth of the law-court: putting ancient and modern forensic rhetoric in its place. In M. Edwards and C. Reid, eds., *Oratory in Action*. Manchester: Manchester University Press, pp. 11–32.

Block, J., and Block, J. H., 2006. Nursery school personality and political orientation two decades later. *Journal of Research in Personality*, 40, pp. 734–749.

Blumler, J. G., 2010. Innovation in political communication, innovation in research. In S. Coleman, ed., *Leaders in the living room-the prime ministerial debates of 2010: Evidence, evaluation and some recommendations*. Oxford: Reuters Institute for the Study of Journalism, pp. 7–13.

Blumler, J. G. and Gurevitch, M., 1995. *The crisis of public communication*. London: Routledge.

Blumler, J. G. and Kavanagh, D., 1999. The third age of political communication: Influences and features. *Political Communication*, 16, pp. 209–230.

Bogdanor, V. and Butler, D., eds., 1983. *Democracy and elections*. Cambridge: Cambridge University Press.

Bos, A. Williamson, I., Sullivan, J., Gonzales, M. H. and Avery, P. G., 2007. The price of rights: High school students' civic values and behaviors. *Journal of Applied Social Psychology*, 37, pp. 1265–1284.

Bottoms, S., 2006. Putting the document into documentary: An unwelcome corrective. *The Drama Review*, 50(3), pp. 56–68.

Boudreau, C., 2006. *Are citizens competent to perform their duties? How institutions substitute for political sophistication*. Research Paper 07–66, Legal Studies Research Paper Series online. Available at: http://ssrn.com/abstract=929580 (accessed 18 June 2012).

Bourdieu, P., 1973. Cultural reproduction and social reproduction. In R. Brown, ed., *Knowledge, education and cultural change: Papers in the sociology of education*. London: Tavistock, pp. 71–112.

 1990. *The logic of practice*. Translated from the French by R. Nice. Cambridge: Polity.

1998. *State nobility: Elite schools in the field of power*. Cambridge: Polity.

Bowler, S. and Donovan, T., 2002. Democracy, institutions and attitudes about citizen influence on government. *British Journal of Political Science*, 32, pp. 371–390.

Brants, K. and Voltmer, K., eds., 2011. *Political communication in postmodern democracy: Challenging the primacy of politics*. Basingstoke: Palgrave-Macmillan.

Breton, A., 1974. *The economic theory of representative government*. Chicago: Aldine Publishing Company.

Brewer, P. R., 2001. Value words and lizard brains: Do citizens deliberate about appeals to their core values? *Political Psychology*, 22, pp. 45–64.

Brown, C., 1982. The Nazi vote: A national ecological study. *The American Political Science Review*, 76(2), pp. 285–302.

Brown, R. and Kulik, J., 1977. Flashbulb memories. *Cognition*, 5(1), 73–99.

Brunner, E. J. and Ross, S., 2010. Is the median voter decisive? Evidence from referenda voting patterns. *Journal of Public Economics*, 94(11–12), pp. 898–910.

Buchanan, J. M., 1954. Individual choice in voting and the market. *Journal of Political Economy*, 62(4), pp. 334–343.

Burke, E., 1854–1856. *The Works of the Right Honourable Edmund Burke Vol. III*. London: Henry G. Bohn.

Butler, J., 1997. *Excitable speech: A politics of the performative*. New York & London: Routledge.

Callon, M., 2006. *What does it mean to say that economics is performative?* No 005, CSI Working Papers Series online. Available at: http://EconPapers.repec.org/RePEc:emn:wpaper:005 (accessed 18 June 2012).

Campbell, A., Converse, P. E., Miller, W. E. and Stokes, D. E., 1960. *The American voter*. New York: John Wiley & Sons.

Campbell, A., Gurin, G. and Miller, W. E., 1954. *The voter decides*. Evanston, IL: Row, Peterson.

Canovan, M., 1999. Trust the people: Populism and the two faces of democracy. *Political Studies*, 47(1), pp. 2–16.

Carey, J. M. and Hix, S., 2011. The electoral sweet spot: Low-magnitude proportional electoral systems. *American Journal of Political Science*, 55(2), pp. 383–397.

Carney, T. and Tait, D., 1998. Adult Guardianship: Narrative Readings in the "Shadow" of the Law? *International Journal of Law and Psychiatry*, 21, pp. 147–162.

Castiglione, D. and Warren, M., 2006. *Rethinking Representation: Nine Theoretical Issues*. In Midwest Political Science Association,

Midwest Political Science Association Annual Meeting, Chicago, IL, 6–10 April.

Cathcart, B., 1997. *Were you still up for Portillo?* London: Penguin.

Caunce, S., Mazierska, E., Sydney-Smith, S. and Walton, J. K., eds., 2004. *Relocating Britishness*. Manchester: Manchester University Press.

Central Advisory Council for Education (CACE). (1967). *Children and their primary schools (Plowden Report)*. London: HMSO.

Charman, M., 2009. *The observer*. London: Faber and Faber.

Chetham-Strode, W., 1946. *The guinea pig*. London: Sampson Low, Marston.

Childers, T., 1983. *The Nazi voter: The social foundations of fascism in Germany, 1919–1933*. Chapel Hill: The University of North Carolina Press.

Chirumbolo, A. and Leone, L., 2008. Individual differences in need for closure and voting behavior. *Personality and Individual Differences*, 44, pp. 1279–1288.

Clarke, H. D. and Acock, A. C., 1989. National elections and political attitudes: The case of political efficacy. *British Journal of Political Science*, 19(4), pp. 551–562.

Coleman, J. and Ferejohn, J., 1986. Democracy and social choice. *Ethics*, 97(1), pp. 6–25.

Coleman, S., 2002. *Elections in the 21st century: From paper ballot to e-voting*. London Electoral Reform Society online. Available at: http://www.electoral-reform.org.uk/oldsite20070123/publications/books/Report.pdf (accessed 18 June 2012).

2007. Doing IT for themselves: Management versus autonomy in youth e-citizenship. In W. L. Bennett, ed., *Civic life online*. Cambridge, MA: MIT Press, pp. 189–206.

2011. Representation and mediated politics: Representing representation in an age of irony. In Brants, K. and Voltmer, K., eds., 2011. *Political communication in postmodern democracy: challenging the primacy of politics*. Basingstoke: Palgrave-Macmillan, pp. 39–58.

2012. Believing in the news: From sinking trust to atrophied efficacy. *European Journal of Communication*, 27(1), pp. 35–45.

Coleman, S. and Blumler, J. G., 2009. *The internet and democratic citizenship: Theory, practice and policy*. New York: Cambridge University Press.

Coleman, S., Morrison, D. E. and Anthony, S., 2009. *Public trust in the news*. Oxford: Reuters Institute for the Study of Journalism.

Coleman, S. and Ross, K., 2010. *The media and the public: Them and us in media discourse*. Oxford: Wiley-Blackwell.

Connerton, P., 1989. *How societies remember*. Cambridge: Cambridge University Press.

Connolly, W., 1983 [1974]. *The terms of political discourse*, 2nd ed. Princeton, NJ: Princeton University Press.

Connolly, W. W., 2002. *Neuropolitics: Thinking, culture, speed.* Minneapolis: University of Minnesota Press.

Conrad, P. and Schneider, J., 1992. *Deviance and medicalization: From badness to sickness.* Philadelphia: Temple University Press.

Constable, L., 1999. Introduction: States of shame. *L'Esprit Créateur*, 39(4), pp. 3–12.

Converse, P. E., 2000. Assessing the capacity of mass electorates. *Annual Review of Political Science*, 3, pp. 331–353.

Cooks, L., 2009. You are what you (don't) eat? Food, identity, and resistance. *Text and Performance Quarterly*, 29(1), pp. 94–100.

Corner, J. and Pels, D., 2003. *Media and the restyling of politics.* London: Sage.

Couldry, N., 2000. *The place of media power: Pilgrims and witnesses of the media age.* London: Routledge.

2010. *Why voice matters: Culture and politics after neoliberalism.* London: Sage.

Coward, N., 1947. *This happy breed: A play in three acts.* New York: Doubleday.

Craig, S. C., Martinez, M. D., Gainous, J. and Kane, J. G., 2006. Winners, losers and election context: Voter responses to the 2000 presidential election. *Political Research Quarterly*, 59(4), pp. 579–592.

Cremin, H., Harrison, T., Mason, C. and Warwick, P., 2011. *Engaging practice.* University of Cambridge/University of Leicester online. Available at: http://engaged.educ.ac.uk (accessed 18 June 2012).

Crick, B., 1998. *Education for citizenship and the teaching of democracy in schools: Final report of the advisory group on citizenship.* London: Qualifications and Curriculum Authority.

Crook, M., 2002. *Elections in the French revolution: An apprenticeship in democracy, 1789–1799.* Cambridge: Cambridge University Press.

Crosby, A. W., 1997. *The measure of reality: Quantification and western society, 1250–1600.* Cambridge: Cambridge University Press.

Dahl, R., 1971. *Polyarchy: Participation and opposition.* New Haven, CT: Yale University Press.

1989. *Democracy and its critics.* New Haven, CT: Yale University Press.

Dahlgren, P., 2009. *Media and political engagement: Citizens, communication, and democracy.* New York: Cambridge University Press.

2010. Opportunities, resources and dispositions: Young citizens' participation and the Web environment. *International Journal of Learning and Media*, 2(1), pp. 1–13.

Dayan, D. and Katz, K., 1992. *Media events: The live broadcasting of history*. Cambridge, MA: Harvard University Press.

Delli Carpini, M. X. and Keeter, S., 1996. *What Americans know about politics and why it matters*. New Haven, CT: Yale University Press.

Deneen, P., 2008. A different kind of democratic citizenship: Citizenship and community. *Critical Review*, 20(1–2): pp. 57–74.

Denzin, N. K., 2001. The reflexive interview and a performative social science. *Qualitative Research*, 1(1), pp. 23–46.

Dickinson, H. T., 1977. *Liberty and property: Political ideology in eighteenth-century Britain*. London: Weidenfeld and Nicolson.

Disch, L., 2012. Critical Exchange on Michael Saward's The representative claim, *Contemporary Political Theory* 11: pp. 109–127.

Dowding, K., 2005. Is it rational to vote? Five types of answer and a suggestion. *British Journal of Politics and International Relations*, 7(3), pp. 442–459.

Downs, A., 1957. *An economic theory of democracy*. New York: Harper and Row.

Dryzek, J. S., 2010. *Foundations and frontiers of deliberative governance*. Oxford: Oxford University Press.

Duckitt, J., Wagner, C., du Plessis, I. and Birum, I., 2002. The psychological bases of ideology and prejudice: Testing a dual process model. *Journal of Personality and Social Psychology*, 83, pp. 75–93.

Durkheim, E., 1995 [1912]. *The elementary forms of the religious life*. Translated from the French by K. E. Fields. New York: Free Press.

Eagleton, T., 1990. *The ideology of aesthetic*. Oxford: Blackwell.

Easton, D. and Dennis, J., 1967. The child's acquisition of regime norms: Political efficacy. *American Political Science Review*, 61, pp. 25–38.

Edgar, D., 2008. Doc and dram. *The Guardian* online. Available at: http://www.guardian.co.uk/stage/2008/sep/27/theatre.davidedgar (accessed 18 June 2012).

Eliasoph, N., 1998. *Avoiding politics: How Americans produce apathy in everyday life*. Cambridge: Cambridge University Press.

Elster, J., 1987. *The Multiple Self*. Cambridge: Cambridge University Press.

Enns, P. and Wleizen, C., 2011. *Who gets represented?* New York: Russell Sage Foundation.

Enosh, G., Ben-Ari, A. and Buchbinder, E., 2008. Sense of differentness in the construction of knowledge. *Qualitative Inquiry*, 14(3), pp. 450–465.

Enosh, G. and Buchbinder, E., 2005. The interactive construction of narrative styles in sensitive interviews: The case of domestic violence research. *Qualitative Inquiry*, 11, pp. 588–617.

Entman, R. M., 1989. *Democracy without citizens: Media and the decay of American politics*. New York: Oxford University Press.

Erikson, E. H., 1964. *Insight and responsibility*. New York: Norton.

Eveland, W. P., 2001. The cognitive mediation model of learning from the news: Evidence from non-election, off-year election, and presidential election contexts. *Communication Research*, 28, pp. 571–601.

Ewald, A. C., 2002. Civil death: The ideological paradox of criminal disenfranchisement law in the United States. *University of Wisconsin Law Review*, pp. 1045–1137.

Ezrow, L., De Vries, C. E., Steenbergen, M. and Edwards, E. E., 2011. Mean voter representation versus partisan constituency representation: Do parties respond to the mean voter position or to their supporters? *Party Politics*, 17(3), pp. 275–301.

Federico, C. M., and Goren, P., 2009. Motivated social cognition and ideology: Is attention to elite discourse a prerequisite for epistemically motivated political affinities? In J. T. Jost, A. C. Kay and H. Thorisdottir, eds., *Social and psychological bases of ideology and system justification*. New York: Oxford University Press, pp. 267–291.

Fell, D., 2007. Putting on a show and electoral fortunes in Taiwan's multi-party elections. In J. C. Strauss and D. B. Cruise O'Brien, eds., *Staging politics. Power and performance in Asia and Africa*. Richmond: I. B. Tauris, pp. 133–150.

Ferejohn, J., 1990. Information and the electoral process. In J. Ferejohn and J. H. Kuklinski, eds., *Information and Democratic Process*. Chicago: University of Illinois Press, pp. 1–19.

Ferejohn, J. and Fiorina, M. P., 1974. The paradox of not voting: A decision theoretic analysis. *American Political Science Review*, 68, pp. 525–536.

Fernando, S. with Campling, J., 2002. *Mental health, race and culture*, 2nd ed. Basingstoke: Palgrave.

Finkenauer, C., Luminet, O., Gisle, L., el-Ahmadi, A., Van Der Linden, M. and Philippot, P., 1998. Flashbulb memories and the underlying mechanism of their formation: toward an emotional-integrative model. *Memory and Cognition*, 26, pp. 516–531.

Fischer, F. and Gottweis, H., eds., 2012. *The argumentative turn revisited: Public policy as communicative practice*. Durham, NC and London: Duke University Press.

Fishkin, J. S., 1991. *Democracy and deliberation: New directions for democratic reform*. New Haven, CT: Yale University Press.

Foucher, V., 2007. 'Blue Marches': Public performance and political turnover in Senegal. In J. Strauss and D. C. O'Brien, eds., *Staging politics: Power and performance in Asia and Africa*. New York. I. B. Tauris & Co, pp. 111–132.

Foucault, M., 1973. *The birth of the clinic: An archaeology of medical knowledge*. London: Tavistock.

Fung, A., 2003. Recipes for public spheres: Eight institutional design choices and their consequences. *Journal of Political Philosophy*, 11(3), pp. 338–367.

Gallagher, M. and Mitchell, P., eds., 2005. *The politics of electoral systems*. Oxford: Oxford University Press.

Gallup, G., 1938. *Public opinion in a democracy*. Princeton, NJ: The Stafford Little Lectures.

Galsworthy, J., 1911. *The patrician*. London: Heinemann.

Garfinkel, H., 1964. Studies in the routine grounds of everyday activities. *Social Problems*, 11, pp. 225–250.

Gastil, J. (2000). *By popular demand: Revitalizing representative democracy through deliberative elections*. Berkeley: University of California Press.

Gaw, A., ed., 1993. *Culture, ethnicity, and mental illness*. Washington, DC: American Psychiatric Press.

Gilens, M., 2004. *Public opinion and democratic responsiveness: Who gets what they want from government?* New York: Russell Sage Foundation.

2005. Inequality and democratic responsiveness. *Public Opinion Quarterly*, 69(5), pp. 778–896.

Goffman, E., 1968. *The presentation of self in everyday life*. New York: Penguin.

Gonzales, M. H., Riedel, E., Williamson, I., Avery, P., Sullivan, J. L. and Bos, A., 2004. Variations of citizenship education: A content analysis of rights, obligations, and participation in high school civic textbooks. *Theory and Research in Social Education*, 32(3), pp. 301–325.

Goodin, R., 2000. Democratic deliberation within. *Philosophy and Public Affairs*, 29(1), pp. 81–109.

2003. *Reflective democracy*. Oxford: Oxford University Press.

Goss, S., 1999. *Managing Working with the Public in Local Government*, London: Kogan Page.

Gronke, P., Galanes-Rosenbaum, E., Miller, P. A. and Toffey, D., 2008. Convenience voting. *Annual Review of Political Science*, 11, pp 437–455.

Gubrium, J. and Holstein, J., 1995. *The active interview*. Thousand Oaks, CA: Sage.

Gurevitch, M., Coleman, S. and Blumler, J. G., 2009. Political communication: Old and new media relationships. *Annals of the American Academy of Political and Social Science*, 625, pp. 164–181.

Habermas, J., 1989. *The structural transformation of the public sphere: An Inquiry into a category of bourgeois society*. Translated from the German by T. Burger. Cambridge, MA: MIT Press.

1996. *Between facts and norms: Contributions to a discourse theory of law and democracy.* Cambridge: Polity.

Hacking, I., 1999. *The social construction of what?* Cambridge, MA: Harvard University Press.

Hahn, C., 1998. *Becoming political: Comparative perspectives on citizenship education.* Albany: State University of New York Press.

Haidt, J., 2001. The emotional dog and its rational tail: A social intuitionist approach to moral judgment. *Psychological Review*, 108, pp. 814–834.

Hajer, M. A., 1996. *The politics of environmental discourse: Ecological modernization and the policy process.* Oxford: Clarendon.

Hajer, M., 2005. Rebuilding ground zero: The politics of performance. *Planning Theory and Practice*, 6(4), pp. 445–464.

Halbwachs, M., 1992. *On collective memory.* Chicago: University of Chicago Press.

Hall, C., 2005. *The trouble with passion: Political theory beyond the reign of reason.* New York: Routledge.

Hansen, M. H., 1991. *The Athenian democracy in the age of Demosthenes: Structure, principles, and ideology.* Translated by J. A. Crook. Oxford: Basil Blackwell.

Hardin, R., 1982. *Collective action.* Baltimore: The Johns Hopkins University Press.

Harvey, D., 2007. *A brief history of neoliberalism.* New York: Oxford University Press.

2009. *Cosmopolitanism and the geographies of freedom.* New York: Columbia University Press.

Hatemi, P. K., Alford, J. R., Hibbing, J. R., Martin, N. G. and Eaves, L. J., 2009. Is there a 'party' in your genes? *Political Research Quarterly*, 62(3), pp. 584–600.

Hayes, A. F., Scheufele, D. A. and Huge, M. E., 2006. Nonparticipation as self-censorship: Publicly observable political activity in a polarized opinion climate. *Political Behavior*, 28(3), pp. 259–283.

Heater, D., 2004. *Citizenship: The civic ideal in world history, politics and education*, 3rd ed. Manchester: Manchester University Press.

Heder, S., 2007. Political theatre in the 2003 Cambodian elections: State, democracy and conciliation in historical perspective. In J. C. Strauss and D. B. Cruise O'Brien, eds., *Staging politics. Power and performance in Asia and Africa*. Richmond: I. B. Tauris, pp. 151–172.

Heyes, C., 2009. *Self-transformations: Foucault, ethics, and normalized bodies.* New York: Oxford University Press.

Hirst v. the United Kingdom (2005) ECHR 651.

Hobolt, S. B. and Klemmensen, R., 2005. Responsive government? Public opinion and policy preferences in Britain and Denmark. *Political Studies*, 53, pp. 379–402.

Hobsbawm, E. and Ranger, T., 1992. *The invention of tradition*. Cambridge: Cambridge University Press.

Home, D. H., 1947. *The Chiltern hundreds*. London: Samuel French.

Home Office, 1999. *Final report of the working party on electoral procedures (Howarth report)*. London: Home Office.

Honig, B., 1991. Declarations of independence: Arendt and Derrida on the problem of founding a republic. *The American Political Science Review*, 85(1), pp. 97–113.

Honneth, A., 2007. *The normative foundations of disrespect*. Oxford: Polity.

Horton, D. and Wohl, R. R., 1956. Mass communication and parasocial interaction: Observations on intimacy at a distance. *Psychiatry*, 19, pp. 215–229.

Horwitz, A. V., 2002. *Creating mental illness*. Chicago: University of Chicago Press.

House of Commons Hansard Debates for 2 November 2010. *Prisoner's right to vote*. Available at: http://www.publications.parliament.uk/pa/cm201011/cmhansrd/cm101102/debtext/101102–0001.htm (accessed 18 June 2012).

House of Commons Hansard debates for 3 November 2010. http://www.publications.parliament.uk/pa/cm201011/cmhansrd/cm101103/debtext/101103–0001.htm (accessed 18 June 2012).

Huckfeldt, R. and Sprague, J., 1987. Networks in context: The social flow of political information. *American Political Science Review*, 81, pp. 1197–1216.

   1995. *Citizens, politics, and social communication: Information and influence in an election campaign*. New York: Cambridge University Press.

Huntington, S. P., 1993. *The third wave: Democratization in the late twentieth century*. Oklahoma City: University of Oklahoma Press.

Hurme, S. B. and Appelbaum, P. S., 2007. Defining and assessing capacity to vote: The effect of mental impairment on the rights of voters. *McGeorge Law Review*, 38, pp. 931–1014.

Hyde, A., 1997. *Bodies of law*. Princeton, NJ: Princeton University Press.

Hyman, H. H., and Sheatsley, P. B., 1947. Some reasons why information campaigns fail. *Public Opinion Quarterly*, 11, pp. 412–423.

Illouz, E., 2007. *Cold intimacies: The making of emotional capitalism*. London: Polity.

Imbeau, L., and Foucault, M., 2011. *Policy speech, fiscal rules, and budget deficit: A median voter model*. Rennes: European Public Choice Society.

Inglehart, R., 1977. *The silent revolution: Changing values and political styles in advanced industrial society*. Princeton, NJ: Princeton University Press.

1997. *Modernization and postmodernization: Cultural, economic, and political change in 43 societies*. Princeton, NJ: Princeton University Press.

Institute for Democracy and Electoral Assistance, 2006. *Electoral management design: The international IDEA handbook*. Stockholm: IDEA.

Isin, E. F., 2002. *Being political: Genealogies of citizenship*. Minneapolis: University of Minnesota Press.

2008. Theorizing acts of citizenship. In E. F. Isin and G. M. Nielsen, eds., *Acts of citizenship*. London: Zed Books, pp. 15–43.

Iyengar, S. and Reeves, R., eds., 1997. *Do the media govern? Reporters, politicians and the American people*. Thousand Oaks, CA: Sage.

Jacobs, L. R., and Skocpol, T., 2005. American democracy in an era of rising inequality. In L. R. Jacbos and T. Skocpol, eds., *Inequality and American democracy: What we know and what we need to learn*. New York: Russell Sage Foundation.

Jacoby, L. L., 1991. A process dissociation framework: Separating automatic from intentional uses of memory. *Journal of Memory and Language*, 30, pp. 513–541.

Jagodzinski, J., 2003. Women's bodies of performative excess: Miming, feigning, refusing, and rejecting the phallus. *Journal for the Psychoanalysis of Culture*, 8(1), pp. 23–41.

Jameson, F., 1981. *The political unconscious: Narrative as a socially symbolic act*. London: Methuen.

Johnson, M. K., Hashtroudi, S. and Lindsay, D. S., 1993. Source monitoring. *Psychological Bulletin*, 114, pp. 3–28.

Joseph, M., 1999. *Nomadic identities: The performance of citizenship*. Minneapolis: University of Minnesota Press.

Jost, J. T., Frederico, C. M. and Napier, J. L., 2009. Ideology: Its structure and functions. *Annual Review of Psychology*, 60, pp. 307–337.

Jost, J. T., Ledgerwood, A. and Hardin, C. D., 2008. Shared reality, system justification, and the relational basis of ideological beliefs. *Social and Personality Psychology Compass*, 2, pp. 171–186.

Jungnickel, K., 2003. *73urbanjourneys.com*. Available at http://www.73urbanjourneys.com (accessed 16 June 2012).

2002. Maps of bounded rationality: A perspective on intuitive judgment and choice. Nobel Prize Lecture, Oslo, Norway, 8 December.

Karp, J. and Brockington, D., 2005. Social desirability and response validity: A comparative analysis of over-reporting voter turnout in five countries. *Journal of Politics*, 67(3), pp. 825–840.

Katz, R., 1997. *Democracy and elections*. New York: Oxford University Press.

Keane, J., 2009. *The Life and Death of Democracy*. London: Simon and Schuster.

Keaney, E. and Rogers, B., 2006. *A citizen's duty: Voter inequality and the case for compulsory turnout*. Institute for Public Policy Research online. Available at: http://www.ippr.org.uk/ecomm/files/a_citizens_duty.pdf (accessed 18 June 2012).

Kelley, J., 2008. Assessing the complex evolution of norms: The rise of international election monitoring. *International Organization*, 62(2), pp. 221–255.

Kellner, D., 2003. *Media spectacle*. London: Routledge.

Kessler, O., 2007. Performativity or risk and the boundaries of economic sociology. *Current Sociology*, 55, pp. 110–125.

Keyssar, A., 2000. *The right to vote: A contested history of democracy in the United States*. New York: Basic Books.

King, G., Rosen, O., Tanner, M. and Wagner, A., 2008. Ordinary economic voting behavior in the extraordinary election of Adolf Hitler. *Journal of Economic History*, 68(4), pp. 951–996.

Kohn, M., 2003. *Radical space: Building the house of the people*. Ithaca, NY: Cornell University Press.

Konner, J., Risser J. and Wattenberg, B., 2001. *Television's performance on election night 2000: A report for CNN*. Atlanta, GA: CNN.

Kristeva, J., 1982. *Powers of horror: An essay on abjection*. New York: Columbia University Press.

Kristjansson, K., 2009. Realist versus anti-realist moral selves – and the irrelevance of narrativism. *Journal for the Theory of Social Behavior*, 39, pp. 165–187.

Kvale, S., 2006. Dominance through interviews and dialogues. *Qualitative Inquiry*, 12, pp. 480–500.

Laclau, E., 1996. *Emancipation(s)*. New York: Verso.

Lakoff, G., 1993. *The contemporary theory of metaphor*. In A. Ortony, ed., *Metaphor and thought*. Cambridge: Cambridge University Press, pp. 201–251.

Lau, R. R. and Redlawsk, D. P., 1997. Voting correctly. *American Political Science Review (American Political Science Association)*, 91(3), pp. 585–598.

Law, J. and Urry, J., 2004. Enacting the social. *Economy and society*, 33(3), pp. 390–410.

Lawrence, J., 2009. *Electing our masters: The Hustings in British politics from Hogarth to Blair*. Oxford: Oxford University Press.

Lawy, R., Biesta, G. J. J., McDonnell, J., Lawy, H. and Reeves, H., 2010. The art of democracy. *British Educational Research Journal*, 36(3), pp. 351–365.

Lazarsfeld, P. F., Berelson, B. and Gaudet, H., 1944. *The people's choice*. New York: Duell, Sloan and Pearce.

Lazarus, R. S., 1999. Hope: An emotion and a vital coping resource against despair. *Social Research*, 66, pp. 653–678.

Le Bon, G., 2008. *The crowd. A study of the popular mind*. Radford 2008 (first published 1895).

Lefort, C., 1986. *The political forms of modern society: Bureaucracy, democracy, totalitarianism*. Cambridge: Polity.

    1988. *Democracy and political theory*. Translated from the French by D. Macey. Cambridge: Polity.

Levinas, E., 1991. *Otherwise than being or beyond essence*. Translated from the French by A. Lingis. The Hague: Martinus Nijhoff.

Lewis, J., Inthorn, S. and Wahl-Jorgensen, K., 2005. *Citizens or consumers? What the media tell us about political participation*. Maidenhead: Open University Press.

Leys, C., 2001. *Market-driven politics: Neoliberal democracy and the public interest*. London: Verso.

Limerick, B., Burgess-Limerick, T. and de Grace, M., 1996. The politics of interviewing: Power relations and accepting the gift. *Qualitative Studies in Education*, 9(4), pp. 449–460.

Lippman, W., 1922. *Public opinion*. New York: Harcourt, Brace and Company.

Livingstone, S., 2005. On the relation between audiences and publics. In Livingstone, S., ed., *Audiences and publics: When cultural engagement matters for the public sphere*. Bristol: Intellect Books, pp. 17–41.

Lodge, M., McGraw, K. M. and Stroh, P. K., 1989. An impression-driven model of candidate evaluation. *American Political Science Review*, 83, pp. 399–419.

Lodge, M. and Taber, C. T., 2005. The automaticity of affect for political candidates, groups, and issues: An experimental test of the hot cognition hypothesis. *Political Psychology*, 26(3), pp. 455–482.

Luhmann, N., 2000. *The reality of the mass media*. Stanford, CA: Stanford University Press.

Lukes, S., 1975. *Power: A radical view*. London: Palgrave-Macmillan.

Lupia, A., 2006. *How elitism undermines the study of voter competence*. MPRA Paper No. 349. Available at: http://mpra.ub.uni-muenchen.de/349/ (accessed 18 June 2012).

MacKenzie, D., Muniesa, F. and Siu, L., eds., 2007. *Do economists make markets? On the performativity of economics*. Princeton, NJ and Oxford: Princeton University Press.

Maddux, J. E. and Winstead, B. A., 2007. *Psychopathology: Foundations for a contemporary understanding*. Mahwah, NJ: Lawrence Earlbaum Associates.

Mander, J., 1978. *Four arguments for the elimination of television*. New York: William Morrow.

Mangan, L., 2012. How Twitter saved event TV. *The Guardian* online. Available at: http://www.guardian.co.uk/technology/2012/jan/18/how-twitter-saved-event-tv (accessed 18 June 2012).

Manin, B., 1997. *The principles of representative government*. Cambridge: Cambridge University Press.

Mansbridge, J. J., 1976. Conflict in a New England town meeting. *The Massachusetts Review*, 17(4), pp. 631–663.

1983. *Beyond adversary democracy*. Chicago and London: University of Chicago Press.

Manza, J. and Cook, F. L., 2002. A democratic polity? Three views of policy responsiveness to public opinion in the United States. *American Political Research*, 30, pp. 630–667.

Markus, G. B., and Converse, P. E., 1979. A dynamic simultaneous equation model of electoral choice. *American Political Science Review*, 73, pp. 1055–1070.

Marcus, G. E., 2002. *The sentimental citizen: Emotion in democratic politics*. University Park: Pennsylvania State University Press.

Marcus, G. E., and MacKuen, M. B., 1993. Anxiety, enthusiasm, and the vote: The emotional underpinnings of learning and involvement during presidential campaigns. *American Political Science Review*, 87(3), pp. 672–685.

Markus, H., 1977. Self-schemata and processing information about the self. *Journal of Personality and Social Psychology*, 35, pp. 63–78.

Marquand, D., 2004. *Decline of the public*. Cambridge: Polity.

Marriott, S., 2000. Election night. *Media, Culture and Society*, 22(2), pp. 131–148.

Martin, C., 2006. Bodies of evidence. The *Drama Review*, 50(3), pp. 8–15.

Marvin, C. and Simonson P., 2004. Voting alone: The decline of bodily mass communication and public sensationalism in presidential elections. *Communication and Critical/Cultural Studies*, 1(2), pp. 127–150.

McComas, K. A., 2001. Theory and practice of public meetings. *Communication Theory*, 11(1), pp. 36–55.

McLaughlin, P., 1979. *Guardianship of the person*. Downsview: National Institute on Mental Retardation.

McLaughlin v. City of Canton (1995) 947 F. Supp. 954, 971.

Mclean, I., 1982. *Dealing in votes: Interactions between politicians and voters in Britain and the USA*. Oxford: Martin Robertson.

McLeod, J. M., Kosicki, G. and McLeod, D. M., 1994. The expand-
ing boundaries of political communication effects. In J. Bryant and
D. Zillman, eds., *Media effects: Advances in theory and research*.
Hillsdale, NJ: Lawrence Earlbaum Associates, pp. 123–162.

McLeod, J. M., Scheufele, D. A. and Moy, P., 1999. Community, communication, and participation: The role of mass media and
interpersonal discussion in local political participation. *Political
Communication*, 16, pp. 315–336.

Melucci, A., 1989. *Nomads of the present: Social movements and
individual needs in contemporary society*. Philadelphia: Temple
University Press.

Micheli, R., 2008. La construction argumentative des émotions: Pitié et
indignation dans le débat parlementaire de 1908 sur l'abolition de
la peine de mort. In M., Rinn, ed., *Emotions et discours: L'usage
des passions dans la langue*. Rennes: University of Rennes Press,
pp. 127–141.

Mill, J. S., 1830. The ballot. *Westminster Review*, 18, pp. 1–37.

   1960. *Autobiography of John Stuart Mill: Published from the original manuscript in the Columbia University Library*. New York:
Columbia University Press (originally published 1873).

Moore, S. F., 1978. *Law as process: An anthropological approach*.
London: Oxford University Press.

Morrison, T., 1984. Memory, creation, and writing. *Thought*, 59,
385–390.

Mouffe, C., 1999. Carl Schmitt and the paradox of liberal democracy. In
C. Mouffe, ed., *The challenge of Carl Schmitt*. London: Verso.

Mutz, D. C., 2002. The consequences of cross-cutting networks for
political participation. *American Journal of Political Science*, 46(4),
pp. 838–855.

Myers, P., Barnes, J. and Brodie, I., 2004. *Partnership working in Sure
Start local programmes: Synthesis of early findings from local programme evaluations*. London: Sure Start Unit.

Natali, C., 1987. Ἀδολεσχία, Λεπτολογία and the philosophers in Athens.
Phronesis, 32(2), pp. 232–241.

Negra, D., ed., 2007. *The Irish in us: Irishness, performativity, and popular culture*. Durham, NC and London: Duke University Press.

Neugebauer, R., 1978. Treatment of the mentally ill in medieval and
early modern England: A reappraisal. *Journal of the History of
Behavioural Science*, 14, pp. 158–169.

Niemi, R. G., Craig, S. C. and Mattei, F., 1991. Measuring internal political efficacy in the 1988 national election study. *American Political
Science Review*, 85(4), pp. 1407–1413.

Noble, A. F., 2008. *Quotidian bus journeys: City life reflections on Lothian buses*. PhD dissertation, Napier University.

Noelle-Neumann, E., 1993 [1984]. *The spiral of silence: Public opinion – our social skin*. Chicago: University of Chicago Press.

Nora, P., 1989. Between memory and history: Les lieux de mémoire. *Representations*, 26, 7–25.

Novak, T., 2006. *Shocked and awed: Propaganda and the cultural aesthetics of the 'televisual news spectacle'*. New York: New School for Social Research..

O'Gorman, F., 1992. Campaign rituals and ceremonies: The social meaning of elections in England 1780–1860. *Past and Present*, 135, pp. 79–113.

O'Loughlin, J., Flint, C. and Anslein, L., 1994. The political geography of the Nazi vote: Context, confession, and class in the Reichstag election of 1930. *Annals of the Association of American Geographers*, 84, pp. 351–380.

Ober, J., 1989. *Mass and elite in democratic Athens: Rhetoric, ideology, and the power of the people*. Princeton, NJ: Princeton University Press.

1993. Public speech and the power of the people in democratic Athens. *PS: Political Science and Politics*, 26(3), pp. 481–485.

Ormerod, P., 2005. The impact of Sure Start. *The Political Quarterly*, 76(4), pp. 565–567.

Page, B. I., and Shapiro, R. Y., 1993. The rational public and democracy. In G. E. Marcus and R. K. Hanson, eds., *Reconsidering the democratic public*. University Park: Pennsylvania State University Press.

Panagia, D., 2009. *The political life of sensation*. Durham, NC: Duke University Press.

Park, J. H., 1931. England's controversy over the secret ballot. *Political Science Quarterly*, 46(1), pp. 51–86.

Pattie, C. J. and Johnston, R. J. 2008. It's good to talk: Talk, disagreement and tolerance. *British Journal of Political Science*, 38(4), pp. 677–698.

Peters, J. D., 2001. 'The Only Proper Scale of Representation': The Politics of Statistics and Stories. *Political Communication*, 18(4), pp. 433–450.

Pitkin, H. F., 1967. *The concept of representation*. Berkeley: University of California Press.

Plantin, C., 2004. On the inseparability of reason and emotion in argumentation. In E. Weigand, ed., *Emotion in dialogic interaction*. London: Fellowes, pp. 269–281.

Poovey, M., 1995. *Making a social body: British cultural formation, 1830–1864*. Chicago: University of Chicago Press.

Popkin, S. L., 1991. *The reasoning voter: Communication and persuasion in presidential campaigns*. Chicago: University of Chicago Press.

Postman, N., 1985. *Amusing ourselves to death: Public discourse in the age of show business*. New York: Penguin.

Pourcher, Y., 1991. Passions d'urne: Réflexion sur l'histoire des formes, des pratiques et des rituels de l'élection dans la France rurale. *Politix*, 4(15), pp. 48–52.

Prasad, M. M., 2007. Fun with democracy: election coverage and the elusive subject of Indian politics. In Huat, C-B., ed., *Elections as popular culture in Asia*. London: Routledge, pp. 139–154.

Presser, S., 1990. Can changes in context reduce vote overreporting in surveys? *Public Opinion Quarterly*, 50, pp. 563–572.

Prior, M., 2007. *Post-broadcast democracy: How media choice increases inequality in political involvement and polarizes elections*. New York: Cambridge University Press.

Qvortrup, J. (1990) *Childhood as a social phenomenon: an introduction to a series of national reports*, Vienna: European Centre for Social Policy Welfare and Research.

Rancière, J., 1994. *The names of history: On the poetics of knowledge*. Minneapolis: University of Minnesota Press.

   1998. *Disagreement: Politics and philosophy*. Minneapolis and London: University of Minnesota Press.

   2009. *Aesthetics and its discontents*. Cambridge: Polity.

Rancière, J. and Panagia, D., 2000. Dissenting words: A conversation with Jacques. Ranciere. *Diacritics*, 30(2), pp. 113–126.

Reay, D., 2006. 'The Zombie Stalking English Schools: Social Class and Education Inequality', *British Journal of Educational Studies* 54(3), pp. 288–307.

Ree, J., 1999. *I see a voice: Deafness, language, and the senses*. New York: Metropolitan Books.

Renan, E., 1882. What is a nation? Translated from the French by M. Thom. In H. K. Bhabha, ed., *Nation and narration*. London: Routledge, pp. 8–22.

Rich, E. and Evans, J., 2009. Now I am NO-body, see me for who I am: The paradox of performativity. *Gender and Education*, 21(1), pp. 1–16.

Richter, D., 1971. The role of mob riot in Victorian elections, 1865–1885. *Victorian Studies*, 15(1), pp. 19–28.

Ricoeur P., 2003 *Memory, history, forgetting*. University of Chicago Press, Chicago.

Riedel, E., Gonzales, M. H., Avery, P. G. and Sullivan, J. L., 2001. Rights and obligations in civic education: A content analysis of the National Standards for Civics and Government. *Theory and Research in Social Education*, 29, pp. 109–128.

Riker, W. H., 1982. *Liberalism against populism: A confrontation between the theory of democracy and the theory of social choice.* San Francisco: WH Freeman.

Riker, W. H. and Ordeshook, P. C., 1968. A theory of the calculus of voting. *American Political Science Review*, 62, pp. 25–43.

Robinson, E. W., 1997. *The first democracies: Early popular government outside Athens.* Stuttgart: Steiner.

2008. *Democracy beyond Athens: Popular government in the Greek classical age.* Cambridge: Cambridge University Press.

Rogers, B., 2004. *Reinventing the town hall.* London: Institute for Public Policy Research.

Rokkan, S., 1970. *Citizens, elections, parties: Approaches to the comparative study of the processes of development.* Oslo: Universitetsforlaget.

Rorty, R., 1989. *Contingency, irony and solidarity.* Cambridge: Cambridge University Press.

Rose, N. (1989) *Governing the soul.* London: Routledge.

Ross, L., 1967. Two people in a room. *The New Yorker*, 25(February), p. 34.

Rosset, J., 2010. Citizens' income and the representations of their policy preferences in the Swiss Parliament. In ECPR graduate conference, Dublin, Ireland, 30 August–1 September.

Roth, A. L., 1995. Men wearing masks: Issues of description in the analysis of ritual. *Sociological Theory*, 13(3), pp. 302–327.

Rottinghaus, B., 2005. *Incarceration and enfranchisement: International practices, impact and recommendations for reform.* Washington, DC: International Foundation for Election Systems.

Samuel, R., 1994. *Theatres of memory, vol. 1.* London: Verso.

Saramago, J., 2004. *Seeing.* Translated from the Portuguese by M. J. Costa. Orlando, FL: Harcourt.

Saward, M., 2003. Enacting democracy. *Political Studies*, 51(1), pp. 161–179.

2006. The Representative Claim. *Contemporary Political Theory*, 5, pp 297–318.

2008. Making representations: Modes and strategies of political parties. *European Review*, 16, pp. 271–286.

Sayer, A., 2005. *The moral significance of class.* Cambridge: Cambridge University Press.

Scannell, P., 2000. For-anyone-as-someone structures. *Media, Culture, and Society*, 22(1), pp. 5–24.

Schattschneider, E. E., 1960. *The semisovereign people: A realist's view of democracy in America.* New York: Holt, Rinchart, and Winston.

Schechner, R., 1988. *Performance theory.* London: Routledge.

2002. *Performance studies: An introduction.* London: Routledge.

Schlozman, K. L., and Burch, T., 2009. Political voice in an age of inequality. In R. Faulkner and S. Shell, eds., *America at risk: Threats to liberal self-government in an age of uncertainty*. Ann Arbor: University of Michigan Press, pp. 140–173.

Schlozman, K. L., Page, B. I., Verba, S. and Fiorina, M., 2005. Inequalities of political voice. In L. Jacobs and T. Skocpol, eds., *Inequality and American democracy: What we know and what we need to learn*. New York: Russell Sage Foundation, pp. 18–87.

Schmitt, C., 1985. *Political theology: Four chapters on the concept of sovereignty*. Translated from the German by George Schwab. Cambridge, MA: MIT Press.

Schriner, K., 2002. Creating the disabled citizen: How Massachusetts disenfranchised people under guardianship. *Ohio State Law Journal*, 62(1), pp. 481–533.

Schudson, M., 2000. America's ignorant voters. *The Wilson Quarterly*, 24(2), pp. 16–25.

Schuessler, A. A., 2000. *A logic of expressive choice*. Princeton, NJ: Princeton University Press.

Scott, J. C., 1990. *Domination and the arts of resistance: Hidden transcripts*. New Haven, CT: Yale University Press.

Searle, J., 1995. *The construction of social reality*. New York: The Free Press.

Sen, A. K. and Pattaniak, P. K., 1969. Necessary and sufficient conditions for rational choice under majority decision. *Journal of Economic Theory*, 1(2), pp. 178–202.

Sennett, R., 1992. *The fall of public man*. New York: Norton.

Setala, M., 2011. The role of deliberative mini-publics in democratic systems: Lessons from the experience of referendums. *Representation*, 47(2), pp. 201–213.

Settle, J. E, Bond, R. and Levitt J., 2010. The social origins of adult political behavior. *American Politics Research* online. Available at: http://apr.sagepub.com/content/early/2010/09/08/1532673X1038 2195 (accessed 18 June 2012).

Shah, D. V., Domke, D. and Wackman, D. B., 2001. The effects of value-framing on political judgment and reasoning. In S. D. Reese, O. H. Gandy, Jr. and A. Grant, eds., *Framing public life*. Mahwah, NJ: Lawrence Erlbaum Associates, pp. 227–244.

Shelley, P. B., 1821. A Defence of Poetry. In M. Shelley, 1841. *Essays, letters from abroad: Translations and fragments*. London: Edward Moxon, p. 84.

Silverstone, R., 1999. *Why study the media?* London: Sage.
 2007. *Media and morality: On the rise of the mediapolis*. Cambridge: Polity.

Snyder, C. R., 1994. *The psychology of hope*. New York. Free Press.

Somin, I., 1998. Voter ignorance and the democratic ideal. *Critical Review*, 12, pp. 413–458.

2004. When ignorance isn't bliss: How political ignorance threatens democracy. *Cato Institute Policy Analysis No. 525*.

Soroka, S. N. and Wlezien, C., 2005. Opinion-policy dynamics: Public preferences and public expenditures in the United Kingdom. *British Journal of Political Science*, 35, pp. 665–689.

Stanovich, K. E., and West, R. F., 2000. Individual differences in reasoning: Implications for the rationality debate? *Behavioral and Brain Sciences*, 23, pp. 645–665.

Stein, R. M., Vonnahme, G., Byrne, M. and Wallach, D., 2008. Voting technology, election administration and voter performance. *Election Law Journal*, 7, pp. 123–135.

Street, J. (2001) *Mass media, politics, and democracy*. London: Palgrave.

Stromback, J., 2010. Democracy and the media: A social contract dissolved? In S. Dosenrode, ed., *Freedom of the press: On censorship, self-censorship, and press ethics*. Baden-Baden: Nomos, pp. 173–191.

Szasz, T. S., 1970. *The manufacture of madness*. New York: Dell.

Tajfel, H., 1981. *Human groups and social categories: Studies in social psychology*. Cambridge: Cambridge University Press.

Taylor, C., 1989. *Sources of the self: The making of the modern identity*. Cambridge: Cambridge University Press.

The Electoral Commission, 2007. *Handbook for polling station staff*. London: The Electoral Commission.

The Plowden Report, 1967. *Children and their primary schools: A report of the central advisory council for education*. London: HMSO.

Thompson, E. P., 1977. *William Morris: From Romantic to Revolutionary*, 2nd ed. London: Merlin Press.

Thompson, J. B., 1995. *The media and modernity: A social theory of the media*. Cambridge: Polity.

Thrift, N., 2008. *Non-representational theory: Space, politics, affect*. London: Routledge.

Tilly, C., 2002. *Stories, identities, and political change*. Lanham, MD: Rowman and Littlefield.

2008. *Contentious performances*. Cambridge: Cambridge University Press.

Tishman, S., Jay, E. and Perkins, D. N., 1993. Teaching thinking dispositions: From transmission to enculturation. *Theory into Practice*, 32(3), pp. 147–153.

Tomkins, S. S., 1963. *Affect imagery consciousness: The negative affects*, vol. 2. New York: Springer.

Torney-Purta, J., 2002 The school's role in developing civic engagement: A study of adolescents in twenty-eight countries. *Applied Developmental Science*, 6(4), pp. 203–212.

Torney-Purta, J., Lehmann, R., Oswald, H. and Schulz, W., 2001. *Citizenship and education in twenty-eight countries: Civic knowledge and engagement at age fourteen.* Amsterdam: IEA.

Torpey, J., 2000. *The invention of the passport: Surveillance, citizenship and the state.* Cambridge: Cambridge University Press.

Troman, G., Jeffrey, B. and Raggl, A., 2007. Creativity and performativity policies in primary school cultures. *Journal of Education Policy*, 22(2), pp. 549–572.

Tucker Jr., K. H., 2005. From the imaginary to subjectivation: Castoriadis and Touraine on the performative public sphere. *Thesis Eleven*, 83, pp. 42–60.

Turner, V., 1969. *The ritual process: Structure and anti-structure.* Chicago: Aldine.

1974. *Dramas, fields and metaphors: Symbolic action in human society.* Ithaca, NY: Cornell University Press.

Tversky, A. and Kahneman, D., 1983. Extension versus intuitive reasoning: The conjunction fallacy in probability judgment. *Psychological Review*, 90(4), pp. 293–315.

Tzanelli, R., 2008. The nation has two voices: Diforia and performativity in Athens 2004. *European Journal of Cultural Studies*, 11(4), pp. 489–508.

van Zoonen, L., 2005. *Entertaining the citizen: When politics and popular culture converge.* Lanham, MD: Rowman & Littlefield.

Wakefield, J., 1992. The concept of mental disorder. *American Psychologist*, 47, pp. 373–388.

Walton, D., 1997. *Appeal to pity: Argumentum ad misericordiam.* Albany: State University of New York Press.

Walzer, M., 1983. *Spheres of justice: A defence of pluralism and equality.* Oxford: Blackwell.

Warner, M., 2002. *Publics and counterpublics.* New York: Zone Books.

Weakliem, D., Andersen, R. and Heath, A., 2005. By popular demand: The effects of public opinion on income inequality. *Comparative Sociology*, 4, pp. 261–284.

Weinshall, M., 2003. Means, ends, and public Ignorance in Habermas's theory of democracy. *Critical Review*, 15(1–2), pp. 23–58.

Welshman, J., 2008. The cycle of deprivation: Myths and misconceptions, *Children & Society*, 22, pp. 75–85.

Wengraf, T., 2006. Interviewing for life-histories, lived situations and personal experience: The Biographic-Narrative Interpretative Method (BNIM) on its own and as part of a multi-method full

spectrum psycho-societal methodology. Available at http://www/
uel.ac.uk/cnr/Wengraf06.rtf (accessed 18 June 2012).

Westheimer, J. and Kahne, J., 2004. What kind of citizen? The politics of
educating for democracy. *American Educational Research Journal*,
41(2), pp. 237–269.

Williams, R., 1977. *Hegel's ethics of recognition*. Berkeley: University
of California Press.

Winn, M., 1987. *Unplugging the plug-in drug*. New York: Penguin.

Winnicott, D. W., 1974. Fear of breakdown. *International Review of
Psychoanalysis*, 1, pp. 103–107.

Wolin, S., 1997. What time is it? *Theory and Event*, 1(1), pp. 1–10.

Young, J., 1999. *The exclusive society: Social exclusion, crime and difference in late modernity*. London: Sage.

Zechmeister, E. J. and Luna, J. P., 2005. Representation in Latin America:
A study of elite-mass congruence in 9 countries. *Comparative
Political Studies*, 38(4), pp. 388–416.

Zembylas, M. 2007. Emotional capital and education: theoretical
insights from Bourdieu. *British Journal of Educational Studies*,
55(4), pp. 443–463.

2009. Global economies of fear: Affect, politics and pedagogical
implications. *Critical Studies in Education*, 50(2), pp. 1–13.

Zembylas, M. and Michaelides, P., 2004. The sound of silence in peda-
gogy. *Educational Theory*, 54, pp. 193–210.

Zigler, E. and Styfco, S. J., 2000. Pioneering steps (and fumbles) in developing a federal preschool intervention. *Topics in Early Childhood
Special Education*, 20, pp. 67–70.

Index

Abstention, 10, 33, 70, 132, 143
Aesthetic, 15, 89, 90, 100, 112,
    122, 126, 174, 178, 179, 187,
    188, 189, 191, 193, 208, 210,
    234, 245
Affirmation, 10, 76, 88, 126
Age, 9, 19, 52, 73, 113, 114, 116,
    120, 124, 125, 130, 142, 163,
    193, 204, 217, 221, 241, 244,
    248, 256, 257, 258, 260
Agency, 18, 124, 127, 166, 172, 183,
    184, 193, 238
Aggregate, 14, 27, 63, 65, 119, 146,
    225
Aggregation, 12, 15, 17, 28, 29, 37,
    51, 57, 72, 99, 128, 162, 167,
    180, 229
Agonistic, 41, 51, 127
agora, 36, 37, 142, 208
Alexander, J.C, 5, 49, 178, 211, 237
Ankersmit, F, 126, 161, 174, 188,
    234, 238
Anonymity, 36, 62, 73
Appearance, 3, 6, 16, 38, 103, 151,
    162, 165, 166, 172, 183, 184
Archer, M, 159, 160, 162, 238
Architecture, 62, 63, 209, 210
Arendt, H, 144, 151, 164, 179, 235,
    238, 249

Athenian, 36, 37, 38, 39, 41, 42,
    44, 248
Audience, 15, 32, 53, 182, 183, 184,
    187, 202, 214, 216, 217, 218,
    219, 221, 233

Back, L, 105
Bakhtin, M, 1, 9, 10, 93, 100, 103,
    239
Ballot, 3, 5, 6, 7, 8, 16, 19, 26, 27, 36,
    37, 51, 56, 59, 60, 61, 71, 83,
    109, 117, 118, 121, 126, 135,
    137, 156, 179, 180, 194, 195,
    226, 243, 254, 255
Ballot box, 6, 27, 59, 121
Ballot paper, 59
Barthes, R, 35, 239
Bauman, Z, 36, 37, 239
Berlant, L, 15, 179, 240
Blumler, J.G, i, 38, 181, 182, 216,
    217, 221, 227, 241, 243, 247
Body, 10, 11, 12, 13, 16, 23, 26, 27, 37,
    63, 77, 88, 126, 131, 132, 134,
    167, 168, 172, 178, 179, 182,
    189, 191, 202, 207, 240, 256
    Body politic, 12, 16, 27, 88,
        167, 172
Bottoms, S, 95, 241
Bush, G.W, 54, 55

The Chiltern Hundreds, 68, 69

Citizenship, 2, 16, 20, 21, 25, 26, 27, 29, 38, 39, 41, 42, 49, 54, 77, 79, 85, 87, 88, 96, 98, 100, 109, 112, 114, 115, 116, 118, 119, 191, 192, 193, 198, 199, 200, 201, 202, 204, 205, 208, 212, 216, 243, 244, 245, 247, 248, 250, 260

Civic, 2, 6, 15, 17, 23, 25, 27, 33, 35, 36, 39, 40, 46, 49, 52, 56, 58, 59, 60, 65, 76, 79, 82, 87, 88, 96, 97, 98, 99, 100, 101, 108, 114, 115, 124, 132, 135, 136, 137, 140, 157, 166, 173, 174, 179, 186, 191, 192, 193, 194, 195, 197, 198, 199, 200, 201, 202, 203, 205, 206, 207, 208, 214, 217, 223, 228, 240, 241, 247, 248, 256, 260

Civic education, 199, 204

Civic knowledge, 198

Civil death, 25, 26, 28, 165

Cognition, 196, 206, 246, 252

Cognitive, 4, 22, 24, 78, 81, 84, 85, 196, 197, 198, 200, 201, 213, 246

Communication, i, 1, 11, 12, 38, 86, 92, 103, 136, 141, 163, 183, 184, 211, 215, 216, 217, 221, 222, 235, 240, 241, 242, 244, 247, 249, 253, 254

Communicative, 2, 5, 12, 17, 104, 126, 213, 216, 222, 233, 246

Compromise, 11, 39

Congress, iv, 5

Connolly, W, 154, 171, 244

Couldry, N, 204, 231, 232

Count, i, 2, 8, 14, 22, 24, 28, 30, 39, 71, 88, 124, 138, 144, 215, 219, 220, 222, 229

Counted, i, 8, 10, 12, 14, 15, 19, 23, 26, 27, 28, 29, 30, 32, 36, 39, 54, 59, 71, 78, 82, 87, 88, 89, 113, 125, 126, 128, 134, 135, 145, 149, 160, 164, 165, 167, 179, 195, 214, 219, 229

Counterfactual, 89, 105, 156, 173, 178, 179

Crick, B, 206, 244

Cynical chic, 100, 139, 229

Dahl, R, 19, 227, 244

Deliberation, 36, 38, 44, 52, 73, 161, 162, 167, 182, 187, 220, 232, 246, 247

Democracy, i, 4, 8, 13, 17, 19, 33, 36, 37, 38, 39, 41, 42, 43, 52, 53, 56, 57, 59, 63, 64, 67, 70, 71, 73, 74, 79, 84, 87, 102, 109, 113, 117, 118, 121, 128, 135, 142, 151, 152, 156, 157, 164, 168, 173, 174, 175, 177, 179, 180, 181, 183, 184, 187, 190, 191, 192, 193, 194, 195, 199, 205, 206, 208, 217, 221, 227, 230, 233, 235, 237, 239, 240, 242, 244, 245, 247, 248, 250, 251, 252, 253, 254, 255, 256, 257, 258, 259, 260, 261

Democratic, i, 3, 4, 5, 6, 7, 8, 13, 15, 16, 19, 21, 24, 27, 28, 29, 36, 37, 39, 40, 41, 42, 44, 46, 49, 55, 57, 58, 60, 62, 63, 64, 67, 69, 70, 72, 74, 76, 79, 87, 88, 96, 108, 109, 112, 113, 115, 116, 120, 121, 126, 130, 140, 147, 148, 162, 173, 175, 177, 178, 179, 183, 184, 191, 192, 193, 194, 195, 197, 199, 200, 201, 203, 205, 206, 208, 210, 216, 217, 218, 219, 220, 221, 222, 223, 228, 231, 233, 234, 235, 238, 243, 245, 246, 247, 253, 255, 258, 259

Disappointment, 2, 99, 193, 205, 230

Disenfranchisement, 19, 20, 21, 25, 26, 117, 165, 167, 168, 246, 258

Disrespect, 28, 88, 128, 132, 137, 146, 229, 249

Drama, 3, 18, 19, 32, 33, 35, 36, 43, 52, 102, 118, 163, 171, 204, 214, 216, 217, 220, 222

Durkheim, E, 49, 245

Duty, 2, 6, 55, 77, 113, 132, 133, 134, 135, 136, 148, 180, 251

Eagleton, T, 191, 245
Edgar, D, 95, 245
Efficacy, 39, 64, 88, 97, 128, 134, 184, 199, 206, 208, 228, 231, 233, 239, 243, 245, 254
Embarrassed, 43, 82, 205
Embarrassment, 16, 140, 204
Event, 3, 13, 43, 45, 55, 79, 81, 82, 92, 95, 103, 105, 113, 160, 171, 176, 180, 184, 253

Forgetfulness, 79

Gallup, G, 63, 247
Game, 5, 9, 23, 28, 56, 100, 116, 122, 141, 161, 181, 183, 198, 202, 214, 239
Garfinkel, H, 57, 65, 247
General Will, 41, 70, 71
Goffman, E, 157, 159, 247
Goodin, R, 161, 247
Gore, A, 54, 55

Habermas, J, 73, 119, 184, 216, 248, 260
habitus, 87, 124, 202, 206, 208
Hacjing, I, 17, 30, 96, 248
Handbook for Polling Station Staff, 58, 59
Hidden transcripts, 41
Honneth, A, 137, 249
Hope, 2, 6, 19, 36, 81, 87, 101, 105, 125, 128, 143, 144, 145, 179, 205, 206, 207, 208, 229, 258
Hustings, 47, 58, 163, 187

Improvisation, 18, 170, 194, 235
Inequality, 39, 60, 107, 205, 229, 230, 239, 250, 251, 256, 258, 260
Information, i, 16, 24, 30, 50, 54, 80, 84, 86, 116, 150, 160, 181, 185, 211, 213, 249, 253
Information-processing, 84
International Institute for Democracy and Electoral Assistance, 64, 65, 66
Internet, i, iv, 213, 217
Interruption, 194, 195, 222, 235

Interview, i, 4, 81, 89, 90, 91, 92, 93, 94, 95, 96, 97, 99, 100, 101, 102, 103, 104, 105, 109, 110, 112, 123, 132, 173, 182, 194, 207, 219, 222, 245, 251
Ironist, 9, 172
Irony
  Ironic, 69, 172, 200, 216, 257
Isin, E, 27, 124, 250

Jameson, F, 35, 250
Jokes, 10, 172
Jury, 22, 43, 44, 45

Kristeva, J, 168, 251

Lazarsfeld, P, 185, 240, 252
Le Bon, G, 73
Lefort, C, 17, 50, 56, 72, 252
Legitimacy, 30, 49, 55, 63, 141, 172, 180, 192, 214, 227, 232, 234, 238
Levinas, E, 103, 252
Life in the UK Test, 76, 78, 88, 97, 197
Listening, 40, 92, 102, 123, 131, 171, 211, 239
Lot, 37, 41

Manin, B, 184, 216, 253
Media, 38, 53, 54, 55, 81, 83, 84, 94, 181, 183, 184, 185, 186, 188, 189, 211, 212, 213, 214, 215, 217, 218, 220, 221, 222, 240, 243, 244, 247, 250, 252, 254, 256, 258, 259
Media events, 83
Mediation, 17, 37, 53, 94, 179, 184, 213, 215, 217, 221, 235, 246
Memory
  Collective memory, 77, 78, 248
  Memories, i, 1, 33, 35, 76, 77, 78, 79, 83, 84, 87, 89, 90, 91, 92, 95, 96, 97, 98, 99, 100, 101, 102, 105, 119, 120, 171, 173, 187, 242, 246
Metaphor, 10, 13, 104, 174, 175, 182, 193, 204, 251

Metaphorical, *See* metaphor
Mouffe, C, 74, 254

Narrative, i, 10, 15, 33, 35, 36, 37, 38, 39, 40, 41, 42, 43, 44, 49, 50, 51, 52, 53, 54, 55, 57, 60, 65, 68, 69, 70, 75, 78, 93, 95, 96, 101, 103, 104, 114, 154, 186, 211, 212, 217, 220, 231, 245
National Socialists, 72
Nazi, 72, 242, 243, 255
Neoliberalism, 231, 232, 244, 248
New England Town Meeting, 42, 44, 63
Norms, 11, 18, 23, 27, 28, 34, 38, 49, 63, 64, 68, 113, 161, 166, 200, 212, 216, 245, 248, 251
Numbers, 8, 28, 30, 31, 47, 56, 60, 63, 80

The Observer, 65, 243

Panagia, D, 210, 220, 221, 255, 256
parents, 86, 108, 109, 110, 111, 114, 115, 117, 127, 147, 155
Parliament, 31, 60, 73, 74, 77, 208, 209, 249
Performance, 5, 6, 9, 15, 16, 18, 19, 22, 23, 27, 30, 35, 39, 46, 47, 48, 51, 52, 53, 55, 59, 63, 65, 68, 71, 72, 78, 79, 81, 82, 83, 87, 88, 91, 95, 96, 99, 102, 103, 104, 112, 114, 116, 160, 170, 171, 174, 175, 178, 179, 180, 181, 184, 189, 191, 193, 194, 195, 200, 202, 208, 210, 213, 216, 217, 221, 222, 223, 233, 235, 237, 246, 248, 250, 251, 259
performative, 4, 5, 15, 16, 17, 18, 19, 46, 70, 90, 91, 103, 114, 124, 127, 179, 200, 233, 234, 238, 242, 245, 250, 260
The Pickwick Papers, 44, 46
Pinter, H, 105
Pitkin, H, 49, 223, 233, 255
Pleasure, 6, 132, 179, 189, 193
Plebiscite, 3, 29, 36

Political parties, 76, 183, 189, 232, 257
Political science, 8
Political scientist, 9, 89
Pope, A, 10
Power, 5, 7, 14, 16, 17, 18, 31, 39, 49, 50, 56, 59, 61, 64, 67, 69, 74, 87, 91, 94, 95, 97, 98, 102, 103, 113, 114, 118, 124, 125, 127, 130, 132, 134, 135, 144, 152, 153, 154, 155, 157, 159, 165, 189, 193, 194, 207, 210, 217, 220, 229, 231, 234, 235, 237, 242, 244, 255
Prison, 25, 138, 140, 166, 167, 168
Prisoner, 26, 117, 165, 166, 167, 168
Projection, 11, 55, 113, 114, 147, 160
Psephology, 8
Public sphere, 118, 119, 184, 187, 217
Publicness, 49

Quantification, 10, 28, 29, 30, 31
Question Time (BBC), 182, 183, 187, 238

Rancière, J, 210, 211, 217, 219, 220, 235, 256
Realism, 91, 94
Recognition, i, 7, 30, 74, 87, 88, 96, 103, 105, 127, 132, 134, 136, 137, 139, 141, 152, 159, 160, 165, 193, 195, 203, 222, 223, 235, 261
Representation, 5, 15, 17, 28, 35, 37, 38, 39, 41, 46, 49, 52, 54, 63, 70, 91, 94, 97, 104, 113, 124, 126, 127, 128, 130, 132, 134, 136, 137, 140, 141, 143, 144, 145, 147, 148, 165, 172, 180, 186, 187, 188, 189, 208, 209, 223, 230, 233, 234, 239, 246, 255
Representative, 17, 33, 36, 37, 49, 56, 92, 98, 126, 127, 128, 133, 134, 137, 143, 144, 147, 189, 223, 233, 234, 235, 242, 247, 253
Represented, 17, 18, 21, 71, 72, 99, 131, 132, 147, 164, 171, 181, 186, 209, 221, 223, 233, 237

Respect, 19, 127, 139, 141, 143, 147, 168, 171, 193, 195
Returning officer, 47
Rhetoric, 7, 30, 50, 58, 95, 108
Ricoeur, P, 79, 256
Rite of passage, 116, 118, 124
Ritual, 2, 5, 27, 28, 35, 45, 46, 48, 49, 50, 51, 52, 53, 54, 56, 57, 61, 62, 64, 88, 97, 171, 177, 178, 183, 194, 199, 211, 235, 237, 255, 257, 260
The Road to Voting, 89, 90, 94
Rorty, R, 9, 96, 257
Routine, 2, 15, 23, 48, 52, 55, 57, 64, 68, 76, 103, 114, 116, 175, 176, 193, 208, 247

Sark, 7
Saward, M, 126, 188, 233, 234, 257
Sayer, A, 4, 257
Schechner, R, 15, 18, 91, 257
Schmitt, C, 73, 74, 254, 258
School, 23, 62, 68, 77, 99, 111, 114, 116, 117, 121, 122, 125, 130, 136, 140, 145, 147, 149, 180, 196, 199, 200, 203, 204, 205, 206, 241, 242, 244, 247, 259, 260
Scrutiny, 63
Secrecy, 59, 64, 155, 156, 157, 164
Secret ballot, 60, 156
Seeing (Jose Saramago), 56
Sennett, R, 208, 210, 258
Sensibility, 41, 43, 79, 184, 189, 191, 192, 193, 196, 199, 206, 208, 210, 215, 218, 219, 220, 221, 222, 235
Shame, 2, 4, 16, 32, 57, 60, 63, 81, 136, 137, 151, 154, 158, 160, 163, 244
Silence, 3, 19, 41, 56, 99, 101, 114, 155, 157, 205, 255, 261
Social choice, 70, 243, 257
Social scientist, 36
Socialisation, 87, 113, 166, 196, 198, 200, 201, 207

Socialist Party of Catalonia, 6
Sortition, 41
Speaker, 1, 40, 93, 103, 205, 219
Speaking, 11, 19, 40, 50, 64, 98, 100, 118, 124, 132, 144, 148, 151, 156, 157, 179, 187, 194, 202, 204, 205, 207, 219, 220, 221, 233, 234, 235
Spectacle, 45, 46, 48, 171, 180, 183, 187, 255
Spiral of silence, 157
Stories, 7, 10, 31, 36, 57, 99, 104, 131, 138, 139, 150, 181
Sure Start, 107, 108, 110, 111, 112, 125, 254, 255
Survey, 24, 79, 80, 82, 232

Technology, i, 12, 16, 38, 63, 68, 141, 217, 234, 253, 259
Television, 19, 23, 32, 37, 53, 54, 55, 56, 83, 96, 97, 100, 122, 154, 179, 180, 181, 182, 183, 187, 188, 213, 218, 238, 239, 253
Election-night results programme, 53
Theatre, 50, 65, 91, 94, 95, 103, 245, 248
Thrift, N, 171, 259
Tilly, C, 34, 48, 171, 259
Trust, 5, 54, 60, 95, 136, 178, 197, 216, 228, 230, 238, 243
Turner, V, 172, 212, 260
Twelve Angry Men, 43, 44

Ventriloquism, 209, 233
Verbatim theatre, 94, 95
Virtual representation, 49, 148
Voice, i, 8, 10, 11, 12, 13, 14, 15, 17, 19, 28, 30, 38, 40, 53, 109, 118, 124, 127, 132, 133, 137, 142, 148, 178, 193, 204, 206, 207, 208, 215, 223, 231, 244, 256, 258

Winnicott, D, 114, 261

CPSIA information can be obtained at www.ICGtesting.com
Printed in the USA
LVOW11*0424070314

376370LV00003B/4/P